AUSTRALIAN
PEOPLE

AUSTRALIAN
TALES

AUSTRALIAN PEOPLE
AUSTRALIAN TALES

NEIL MARKS

HarperCollinsPublishers

HarperCollins_Publishers_

First published in Australia in 1999
by HarperCollins_Publishers_ Pty Limited
ACN 009 913 517
A member of the HarperCollins_Publishers_ (Australia) Pty Limited Group
http://www.harpercollins.com.au

Copyright © Neil Marks 1999

HarperCollins_Publishers_
25 Ryde Road, Pymble, Sydney, NSW 2073, Australia
31 View Road, Glenfield, Auckland 10, New Zealand
77-85 Fulham Palace Road, London W6 8JB, United Kingdom
Hazelton Lanes, 55 Avenue Road, Suite 2900, Toronto, Ontario M5R 3L2
and 1995 Markham Road, Scarborough, Ontario M1B 5M8, Canada
10 East 53rd Street, New York NY 10022, USA

National Library of Australia Cataloguing-in-Publication data:

Marks, Neil. 1938- .
   Australian People, Australian Tales.
   ISBN 0 7322 5969 X.
   1. Australia - Biography. I.Title.
920.094

Printed in Australian by Griffin Press Pty Ltd on 79gsm Bulky Paperback

9 8 7 6 5 4 3 2 1
02 01 00 99

To two new Australians – my Grandsons,
Alec and Hamish

ACKNOWLEDGEMENTS

Thanks to Geoff Armstrong for coming up with the idea for this project and as always for his help and friendship. My appreciation to Alison Urquhart for her kindness and for assisting me to complete the book.

Also thanks to Ian Heads for being available at an inconvenient time and editing the manuscript. Good blokes are not always hard to find.

To all the Australians who are part of the book, I offer my heartfelt thanks for the time you gave me, your stories and for being wonderful people.

Finally, thanks to Sue for her invaluable help, Sandy and Vicki for their encouragement and, of course, to Herself who is still on the baseline and still hitting them back.

ABOUT THE AUTHOR

Neil Marks is an Australian. His childhood and teenage years were dominated by sport, particularly cricket and rugby, pastimes encouraged by his father, Alec, who represented New South Wales at both sports. Neil played first-grade cricket at the age of 15 and Sheffield Shield at 20. He scored 180 not out in his first game for New South Wales and is the Shield record holder for the sixth wicket partnership with Grahame Thomas.

At the age of 22 Marks was diagnosed as having a serious heart condition and after two operations in Australia was required to travel to the Mayo Clinic in the USA where an operation was performed that saved his life. He returned to normal life but he never played first-class cricket again, though for many years he continued to play club cricket.

From the time he left school Marks worked in the insurance industry — the last quarter of a century as a director of an insurance brokerage company with his cricketing friend, Warren Saunders. As a businessman and sportsman, Marks has come to know the personalities, idiosyncrasies and foibles of many Australian characters.

After retiring from the insurance brokerage business, Marks began to write about sport; the people he had known and the stories he had heard. He has since had two books published, *Tales from the Locker Room* and *Tales for All Seasons*. The critics commented favourably on these books and about the author's ability to write with both humour and pathos. Neil Marks's third book is not about sport (though some sporting stories are included), it is about Australia and Australians; a subject that Neil Marks knows and loves.

Known as 'Marksy' to his school and business friends and 'Harpo' to those in the cricket fraternity, he has three daughters and two grandchildren and lives in Sydney with his wife, Kay, whom he refers to as 'Herself'.

CONTENTS

INTRODUCTION

People keep telling me that Australia is changing and maybe it is. It is said that we have become a multicultural society and in many aspects of our day-to-day living it's true. 'Change', though, is a word that can have an emotive ring to it, a connotation of loss. Perhaps 'developing' is a better word. For, despite our problems, we are a decent and clever nation, far more tolerant than many would have us believe, with interesting traditions and folklore and a future which is challenging in its potential.

Notwithstanding the changes the past few decades have brought, I hold to the belief that many of our once acclaimed characteristics remain with us. Qualities such as strength, versatility, persistence and the old Australian stand-by — 'mateship' — are still very much part of our make-up. And always in the background dwells the ever-present Aussie sense of humour that, over the years, has allowed us to make fun of situations, authority, others and ourselves. These are not characteristics that are restricted to the Australian people alone — although our early isolation from the rest of the world, has stamped a typical 'Australianness' upon them. Australians are a confident lot who meet those of other nations as friends and equals. If we sometimes seem brash, it has more to do with our lack of conformity than our lack of discrimination. We remain an egalitarian society, a group of proud but passive patriots, a country of characters who keep saying 'she'll be right, mate' and then go out and make sure that it is.

In this book, I set out to write about Australians who were or are richly endowed with at least one of the characteristics typical of our people. Yet as each story unfolded, I found that these men and women possessed many attributes and to specify one did not really do justice to the 'whole' human. Hopefully, the reader will see each of these modest, special people for who they are and what they have achieved. For me, to write about Australians is a labour of love, although to capture — on paper — their personalities and spirit is a little more difficult. I can only hope that I have done them justice.

Please excuse my small personal indulgence in these pages — in the inclusion of a few stories in which I reflect on my own experiences: growing up in Sydney, my time in the insurance industry and my whereabouts during 'The Dismissal'. My aim throughout is to capture the flavour of an era and to bring briefly into the spotlight some other interesting Australian characters. I admit to succumbing to nostalgia when I wrote of the greatest marble player in history, the machinations of the Reinsurance Department and of that day in November 1975 when a group of 80 Australians split

AUSTRALIAN PEOPLE
AUSTRALIAN TALES

into two and faced each other across a putting green. I confess, too, that a tear was not far from my eye when I wrote of an afternoon spent with three grand old ladies at The Prince Edward Theatre, where I savoured a journey into the past and witnessed the dying gasp of vaudeville.

It may seem strange that in this collection of tales about Australians there is one about an American. However, Max's story is one with which people of his era may empathise — for many young Aussies also went through the inner agonies and the pressure that Max suffered. In the end, it was Australia which showed America's Max all was not lost, that there was another way. Max studied the people Down Under and he listened. What he heard was compassionate and positive ... and it probably saved his life.

All of us are different. So I cannot say that the people in this book are typical. There is though, a similarity between them, a common thread which links one to the other. 'Speed' followed the example of Pat and looked his foe 'straight in the eye'. Doug and Jimmy mixed with the high and mighty of the world but found no basic differences between 'the heads that wear the crowns' and 'the faces in the street'. In the lives of these characters the common thread of humour also emerges, despite the difficulties and setbacks. In the end they all did their best — each climbed their own mountain ... as Wendy climbed hers.

A poignant memory that will forever stay with me occurred when I was nearing the completion of the book. One Saturday morning, I rang my brother, Lynn, about a matter of no great importance and in the course of the conversation I mentioned that I was writing the story on 'A Bush Favourite'. We both laughed as we recalled funny incidents about the great little character involved. During the conversation, Lynn said, 'I don't believe I ever told you about Fave's journey to Green Mountain?' Then he recounted the story of Johnny Martin and Bernard O'Reilly. It was a lovely tale, so typically Australian and I knew that I must include it in the book. When Lynn completed his story, I thanked him, said goodbye and hung up. It was the last time I spoke to my brother. Lynn died the next morning.

It has been my pleasure (and honour) to tell tales of Australia and a few of its people. As I move around, seeing some of the world and learning more about my own land, I realise that all in this wide and lovely continent are blessed. Most of us will probably look back on our lives and accept the reality that there are no trophies on the wall and little money in the bank. Yet we know too that we have lived in a land of peace, opportunity and laughter. The riches and rewards of others may have passed us by ... but who cares? Just to be an Aussie is enough.

ONE

A BUSH FAVOURITE

No matter where he went, you'd have picked him for what he was. It wouldn't matter if he was eating a hot dog while dodging traffic on Madison Avenue, drinking coffee at a sidewalk cafe on the Champs Elysées or gliding along a Venetian canal in a gondola, singing *Santa Lucia*, you'd have picked him.

'I'll bet you're an Australian and you live in the bush!' 'That's right mate,' he would have answered, grinning, his hand shooting out to greet you. 'Johnny Martin's the name.'

A son of old Methodist stock, he was christened John Wesley Martin and grew up in a bush hamlet called Burrell Creek — a few miles 'as the cockatoo flies' from the town of Taree. The Martins were a prolific breed, known throughout the district and beyond. Johnny was the youngest of the ten children of Sam and Elsie Martin and, as with the last child in all large families, he was always the one bringing up the rear. He later claimed that it wasn't until he reached the age of four, that he realised his name was Johnny and not 'Hurry up'. The family were salt of the earth churchgoing folk, who owned farms, delivered the mail, influenced community affairs and helped others. They were also greatly esteemed for their ability at cricket and in the Manning River area of New South Wales men named Martin dominated with leather and willow for many decades. Indeed, they were so good at the game that the Martins would regularly challenge the town of Taree to cricket matches. These games are now part of the district's folklore.

The Martins versus Taree matches were played with immense gusto and great fun was had by all yet they were no less intense for all that. The scores and statistics from these encounters have now been erased by the tides of time but those still around who remember the contests have no hesitation in declaring that the Martins were too strong for their opposition and the 'Bush Ashes' never left Burrell Creek. The only time the Martins ever looked like being beaten was on a forfeit and it happened this way: Taree won the toss, batted, and were dismissed about half an hour before tea for 130. Cyril and Tom Martin opened the batting for the Martin XI and in the seven overs due before the break had amassed 43 runs, with Cyril making a 'slather and whack' 39 not out. The players were a little late back after tea but that was normal. The 'arvo tea' was delicious and, anyway, nothing starts on time in the bush. However, when the bowler was set to run in for the first ball on the resumption of play there was no batsman up the other end. The captain of the Taree team walked over to the non-striker and posed the question, 'Tom, where's Cyril?'.

'Not here,' answered Tom.

'I can see that! When will he be back?'

'Be a while yet.'

The fielding skipper scratched his head. 'Well, we might 'ave to claim a forfeit if Cyril don't come back. Where is he?'

'Over there, bringing them in for milking.' The captain turned, looked towards a nearby property and saw in the distance a group of cows lumbering towards the bales, while jogging behind them, waving a cricket bat, was a man dressed in flannels, batting gloves and pads.

'We can't wait till 'e finishes the bloody milkin',' said the captain.

Tom Martin shrugged his shoulders, 'Doesn't matter. Put him down as "retired hurt" — we'll still beat you anyway.'

I can't remember when I first met Johnny Martin, though more than likely it was at the nets on the Sydney Cricket Ground Number 2 when we had both been chosen for the New South Wales Sheffield Shield squad. It was here that he first received his nickname. There was a state selector at the time named Albert Vincent, who was getting on in years and a little inclined to live back in the days of Victor Trumper and Tibby Cotter. Nonetheless, Albert was a kindly man with more understanding of a budding young cricketer's feelings than one or two other members of the panel who talked only to 'the stars', puffed on cigarettes and treated the young colts with a mixture of aloofness and disdain. One afternoon, Johnny had gone through his paces and was heading towards the showers when Albert Vincent walked over to him, put his arm around the young man's shoulders and remarked, 'Johnny, Johnny, you're a great little player and, though I shouldn't tell you this, you've always been a little favourite of mine'. Standing nearby was Johnny's Petersham teammate, Kevin 'Crazy' Cantwell, who was a fine cricketer and All-Australian baseball catcher. 'Sucking up to selectors, eh, you cunning little bugger?' commented Crazy, laughing. 'A little favourite of Albert's, eh? Wait till I tell the boys.' Johnny Martin achieved fame in his beloved sport and though he was always known to his fans as 'Johnny', to his teammates he was ever after, 'The Little Favourite' (later, mostly shortened to 'Fave').

Fave was a nuggety little man, only five feet five inches in height, who had the perfect build for a rugby league scrum-half, which he was in his youth — good enough to be made an offer by the Newtown Club in Sydney. (We were talking football once and Fave said to me, 'There seems to be a lot of controversy about the scrum-half putting the ball under the feet of the second-row and I really can't understand why — it comes out a lot quicker from there.') Whereas the rest of us walked to where we wanted to go, Fave bounced. His thick little legs bounced him around the cricket grounds of the world and they took him from his bowling mark to the crease in an easy flowing action which brought his left arm over his shoulder, beside his ear, while his wrist revolved and his fingers made a fizzing sound as the ball left them. He bowled left arm wrist spinners (known in cricket parlance as 'chinamen') and spin he did — not always accurately but on occasions with such spitting venom that the 'keeper was often just as mystified as the batsman. Byes sometimes scored very well when Fave was on song. In spending a lifetime watching cricket, I would say that only Dave Sincock and today's Shane Warne, on the fifth day of a match, spun the ball more.

His batting was much the same as his bowling — a case of take a risk and have a go. He was one of those cricketers who eventually and inevitably die by the sword, yet, while they are living by it, they have an enormous amount of fun! With his wonderful natural skills, Fave had a lot of fun in all aspects of his cricket, though the thing he loved most in the game was hitting sixes. My favourite Fave memory is seeing him drop to one knee and, with the combination of his muscular little arms and perfect timing, 'hoiking' the ball long, hard and high over the midwicket fence, often into the houses beyond.

Fave counted every six he ever hit, though I'm not sure when he started this habit — the counting, not the sixes (he started hitting sixes before he was weaned). I remember playing against him at the Adelaide Oval when he smashed Richie Benaud into the Creswell Gardens and the ball bounced so far after it hit the ground that for a moment I thought it might interrupt Evensong in St Peter's Cathedral 400 metres away. As the ball was being retrieved from near the pulpit I walked over and said, 'You got a good piece of that one, mate'.

Fave nodded and replied, 'Number 768, Harpo'.

The following season, when Fave had returned from Adelaide and was back representing New South Wales, I played against him in a club game at Petersham Oval. The ex-international, Jimmy Burke, was bowling to him and once again, down on his knee went Fave and away flew the ball, so high that it looked as if it would sail over Fort Street Boys' High School and land in the brewery on top of Taverner's Hill. Cathedrals or breweries — when Fave hit sixes he didn't discriminate. 'How many is that, Fave?' I asked.

'That's 801.'

'You're slowing down, mate,' I replied.

He nodded, 'Yeah, Harpo, I've tightened up my defence'.

Fave remembered one six in particular. He was playing against Queensland at the Gabba, facing Test all-rounder Tom Veivers, and true to form Fave went down on his knee and swatted one over the fence. As the ball was sailing towards the back of the stand, a man sitting in the front seat jumped up and caught it in a manner that would have made any outfielder proud. Fave told me later, 'I thought to myself at the time, gee, I'm glad that bloke's not playing for Queensland. Then I looked again and saw that it was my own cousin who'd caught the ball. Still, with a name like his, you'd expect him to catch every one that came to him.'

'What was his name?' I asked

Fave replied laconically, 'He was christened Don Bradman Martin.'

To name the great cricketers who came from the bush would take too many pages by far; suffice to say here that Johnny Martin was one of those from cricket's 'Bush Hall of Fame'. (Fave played in eight Tests for Australia, made a tour of England, played 10 games for South Australia and 77 games for New South Wales, during which he made 2701 runs and took 273 wickets.) To make a name for themselves, these bush greats had to move from their quiet rural surroundings and take up lodgings in the city, where the opposition was more competitive, and players were under the eyes of the State selectors. Yet, apart from the one season in Adelaide, Fave never left the bush, rejecting the siren call of bright lights and the hedonistic ways of the city and opting for a home among the gum trees. To have his cake and eat it, too, Fave had to travel twice a week to Sydney and back again.

Nowadays, to travel by car from Sydney to Taree takes about three and a half hours along a well-constructed freeway, during which time the only problem drivers have is deciding at what speed they should set the cruise-control button and what type of music they should play. In the late 1950s and early 1960s, the trip by car along the curving single lane Pacific Highway was one which even Burke and Wills would surely have been too cowardly to embark upon. And even if Saint Christopher smiled and you were fortunate enough to arrive safely, you undoubtedly stepped out of the vehicle suffering from travel sickness, nervous exhaustion or a mysterious malady which these days would be diagnosed as 'creeping jet lag'.

This is the reason that Fave chose to travel and return by train (the 'Kempsey Mail') to play his cricket. The Kempsey Mail took a long while to reach its destination because it stopped at most stations en route to drop the mail and the papers. It was a tedious trip if you didn't have a sleeper and in his early days when trying to make a name for himself, Fave couldn't afford such luxuries. After ten years of travelling up and down, Fave came to know the regular passengers and those who worked on the Kempsey Mail like he knew his own family and he told some interesting stories of his time on the rails.

One regular was a commercial traveller working for a large wholesale grocery firm, who frequently made the journey up and down the coast calling upon customers. With other salesmen pals, he would wile away the hours playing poker. Of all the groups in the community, commercial travellers are recognised as the best poker players and those who journeyed on the Kempsey Mail were no exception. The card games were known to be tough and the money that changed hands amounted to very much more than the players made in salaries plus commissions — with the aforementioned grocery traveller being the recipient of most of it. One particular evening, there was a large pot in the middle of the table and only two players were left in the game — the 'grocery man' and a representative from a soap company. As the grocer was about to draw two cards, one player who was not participating in this particular hand leaned over and grabbed his arm, prising open the fingers and from them fell an ace which had been cleverly palmed. Pandemonium became the order of the day as it dawned on the card school that they had been conned, not only that evening, but for the last couple of years as well. The grocer asked weakly, 'Oh, how did that get there?', while the others grabbed him and pinned him to his seat.

'Throw him out the door,' shouted the soap salesman, a plan with which the others agreed and they began to drag the cheat towards the door. George, the guard, who had been working on the train since the Kempsey Mail had let out its first 'toot', heard the commotion and raced along to investigate. Confronted with the scene he yelled at the top of his voice, 'What the hell are you doing?'.

One of the card players explained. 'We caught this bastard cheating, so we're throwing him out the door.'

George shouted, 'Don't do that, you idiots; there's a tunnel coming up and when he hits the wall he will splatter everywhere and go all over the passengers in the carriages behind. Some of them are eating their dinner. Wait till we go across the Manning River and you can throw him out then. Not only will it get rid of the bugger, it will give the sharks a feed as well!'

Eventually George quietened things down, but the grocery salesman was never seen on the Kempsey Mail again.

Actually, Johnny Martin became such mates with the staff of the train that on Saturday evenings in the summer the Mail would not depart until Fave arrived. 'We'll be leaving shortly,' the guard would tell enquiring passengers, 'Johnny's playing at Manly today and he has a fair way to come. But he'll be here in a few minutes and we'll be off as soon as he arrives.'

George, the guard, became a great mate of Fave's and as the miles rattled by they would sit and yarn about railway days, cricket and growing up in the bush. George had a fund of tales, though Fave was never quite sure which of them were factual and which were legends handed down from the old days of steam. Nonetheless, they were told with such enthusiasm and humour that Fave retold them time and time again and always laughed heartily as if telling them for the first time.

The old guard was steeped in old-time values and believed in working an honest day and going above and beyond what was required. Fave once remarked to him that despite travelling in the wee small hours he had never seen George nod off. George grinned and answered, 'I learned me lesson once, mate, and I'll not be caught again. The Railways sent down a young lad named Rodney and they instructed me to look after him and show him the ropes. He seemed keen and I taught him a lot of things but he weren't too bright. Anyway, after a few weeks I thought it was time for him to have a go on his own. So I went over everything he had to do three times and when I was sure he had taken it all in, I decided to go off for some shut-eye. But before I left, I went to the lad a fourth time and I said, "Now Rodney, remember about Mr Harris in that sleeping compartment over there and don't forget that he wants to be put out at Dungog. I'll tell you once again, Mr Harris is a regular on this train and he is the heaviest sleeper I've ever known, so I don't care if you have to *throw* him out, just make sure that when the train stops, Harris is put out at Dungog Station." Rodney repeated that he understood what he had to do and promised not to let me down. Well that night I went out like a light, and I was only waked up because someone was shakin' me. It was Mr Harris beltin' me on the chest, calling me a bloody idiot and saying he was goin' to sue the Department of Railways. I looked out the window and saw we were well passed Dungog. So I race down to the guard's van to find Rodney and there he is sittin' on the guard's seat, as large as life. I grabbed him by the collar and I swore at him for half a minute.

'"What's wrong?" he asked, when I ran out of dirty words. "What's wrong?" I yelled. "I'll tell you what's bloody wrong — you are! If brains were dynamite you wouldn't blow yer cap off, you stupid bloody imbecile. I've just been abused by Mr Harris for not doing my duty, and in all my time working with the Railway I've never seen a passenger more angry."

'Rodney just looked at me, shrugged his shoulders and said, "Aw, I don't know about that. I bet he wasn't as angry as the bloke I threw out at Dungog."'

Fave was a great team man and although he loved to succeed personally he was just as happy when his teammates were the centre of attention. Brian Booth was a very fine Australian cricketer of the time, an Olympic representative in hockey and one of the most respected men in Australian sport. Booth too hailed from the bush — coming from Perthville, a little town in rural New South Wales ten kilometres from Bathurst. One day the New South Wales team was playing South Australia in a Sheffield Shield game at the Sydney Cricket Ground, when one of the South Australian batsmen called his partner for a quick single. From the covers Brian Booth swooped and in one action picked up the ball, threw, and knocked the middle stump out of the ground with the batter two yards out of his ground. As the 'Blues' team gathered around Booth to congratulate him, Fave bounced in from the outfield and proclaimed loudly, 'And now you all know why there are no rabbits left in Perthville!'.

I toured a few times with Fave on interstate cricket trips and he was always great fun to be with. Fave had a pleasant voice and loved to sing, leading the community singing in the team bus and in the showers, after even the most tiring of days. No matter how he or the team performed he never became despondent, nor did he look to cast blame on umpires, teammates or the crowd. Fave played the game of cricket because he loved it and because he enjoyed the comradeship of fellow cricketers. He was also a positive influence when his team was flagging, quick with a quip in the darkest hours, realising that the world didn't stop revolving if the result of a cricket match turned out the wrong way. I recall New South Wales playing Western Australia at the WACA once. We were bowling and being belted to all points of the compass, while the temperature hovered around 40 degrees Celsius. Fave and I were fielding in the covers and I must admit, it was not the happiest cricketing day of my life. 'Chin up, Harpo,' called Fave.

I snarled, 'How do I keep my chin up when my bum's dragging along the bloody ground?'.

'I'll sing you a song, then,' said Fave, smiling his impish grin, and from eight metres away he began warbling. 'It happened on the beach at Bali Bali.' [Misson moves in to bowl to Ken Meuleman], 'I saw her strolling on the golden sands.' [Meuleman leans back and cleverly steers it down to backward point. Flockton moves around the boundary and cuts off the four, but the batsmen run two.] 'I met her on the beach at Bali Bali.' [Misson moves in again — oh, a lovely shot by Meuleman, between Marks and Martin in the covers and Martin is off after it like a little greyhound.] 'Puff, puff, And it wasn't long till we were holding hands.' [Misson comes in with that aggressive action, head bobbing. Good length ball and it's another cover drive by Meuleman. Oh, my goodness, it goes straight between the legs of Marks at cover point. He turns around and chases it.] 'And then we strolled along the sand together.'

'Puff puff. What was that Fave?'

'And then we strolled along the sands together,' — 'She kissed me and she promised she'd be mine,' — 'You could have knocked me over with a feather.' [Meuleman is 48, as the now angry bowler again charges in. It's a rearing bouncer, which Meuleman ducks under.] 'When she told me that she came from Caroline.'

When I returned home from that trip, my father, who was an important member of the New South Wales team in the days of Bradman, O'Reilly and Jackson, asked me a question. 'Mate, I was listening to the radio and heard that you misfielded in the covers from a drive by Meuleman. What happened?'

'I wasn't concentrating, Dad.'

'Why?'

'Fave was teaching me a song.'

Dad arched his eyebrows and observed, 'Things are a bit different from when I played!'.

After we finished that game in Perth, we moved on to Adelaide to play South Australia. I was looking forward to Adelaide, because not only is it the best cricket ground in the world, it was also the town where Kay, my girlfriend, lived and I hadn't seen her for six months. Naturally, I had mentioned this fact to my teammates and when we arrived at the airport, sure enough, there was my future wife to meet me. As we were waiting for the luggage, holding hands and gazing into each others' eyes, Fave walked over to us, put out his hand and said to Herself, 'I'm Johnny Martin, you're Betty aren't you?'.

A little taken aback, Herself responded, 'No, sorry, I'm Kay'.

Fave looked mystified for a moment, then said, 'Oh, of course, this is Adelaide. It's Kay in Adelaide — Betty is in Brisbane.' Then he turned to me and murmured, 'I'm always getting this wrong aren't I, Harpo? Now let's see! Betty is Brisbane, Pauline is Perth, Kay is Adelaide, Myrtle is Melbourne, and, of course, Sally is Sydney.' He smiled again, put two hands above his head, like a winning boxer and exclaimed, 'You little beauty, I've got it right at last'. I took Herself out to dinner that evening — it was not a good night.

From the 1950s on into the 1960s Fave continued to be a force in the game he loved. I was no longer playing first-class cricket although my brother, Lynn, was now the regular opening batsman for the New South Wales team. One morning in October 1967, the Blues were on a flight to Brisbane for a Shield game and Fave and Lynn were sitting next to each other on the plane. As they flew over the border, Fave pointed into the distance and said to Lynn, 'Over there is Mount Warning, the McPherson Range and a place called Green Mountain. That's where I'm going on Sunday [then a rest day in Shield cricket], to speak to the bloke who has always been my hero.'

Lynn was mystified and asked, 'Who are you talking about and why is he a hero?'. Then Fave told him the story of Bernard O'Reilly and the Stinson.

In 1937 a Stinson Airliner, VH-UHH, owned by Airlines of Australia, left Brisbane with five passengers and two crew aboard to fly to Sydney. The plane failed to arrive. Within hours a search was organised, though it was not certain in what area the plane had gone down. There were reports that it had been sighted along the coast just off Newcastle and some people even said that they had spotted it in the vicinity of Broken Bay where the Hawkesbury River meets the sea — just a few 'flying' minutes from Sydney Airport. Though authorities were in a quandary, it was taken for granted that the plane had been flying for some hours before it had crashed. So the search continued in areas along the coast and on the northern perimeter of Sydney itself. There was, however, one man who believed that the authorities were wrong. The night the plane had disappeared, there had been a violent storm over Bernard O'Reilly's property at Green Mountain, the mountainous area just north of the Queensland–New South Wales border. While the storm was raging, a couple of O'Reilly's neighbours had heard the sound of a low flying plane. Later, O'Reilly read of the missing Stinson and of the search that was continuing further down into New South Wales. O'Reilly thought long and hard about the mystery and especially about one imponderable; if the plane had been sighted at various times along the coast, then why had it not been seen near Lismore, where passengers were waiting to be picked up?

Those in charge of the search blamed the storm and suggested that it had probably been too difficult to land and thus the pilot had ignored Lismore and journeyed on to Sydney. O'Reilly took out his map and drew a line from Green Mountain to Lismore and concluded that the Stinson had crashed on one of the northern ridges of the McPherson Range. A dogged character, he packed some provisions and set off into the rugged mountains to search for a crippled plane, which his 'bushie's' instinct told him was there, even though 'the experts' believed it to be beneath the Hawkesbury River or the Pacific Ocean — 500 miles away. Nine days after the crash and long after the 'official' search had wound down, O'Reilly was still exploring the uninhabited range, when he climbed a mountain and saw a burnt tree on the next ridge.

The McPherson Range is a rain-forest jungle in which there has not been a bushfire since the Dreamtime. Nothing burns in the McPhersons — unless it has petrol poured on it. O'Reilly shouted out a 'Coo-ee' and to his amazement a 'Coo-ee' was returned. He found his way to the burnt tree and close by was the wreck of the Stinson and two badly injured, emaciated survivors. O'Reilly realised that neither could last more than another 24 hours so, despite the fact that he had had no sleep for three days, he set off over the other side of the mountains to bring help.

The story of the next 24 hours is a story of pioneer Australia. The logistics involved, the improvisation, the courage and mateship in the day that followed as rescuers beat a path back to the wreck has now become part of our folklore. Both the men from the Stinson survived and went on to become influential members of the community, while the amazing Bernard O'Reilly became an Australian icon.

As a lad, Johnny Martin had read this wonderful saga (later made into a movie) and Bernard O'Reilly became his hero. O'Reilly's tenacity and courage appealed to the little bush boy from Burrell Creek, yet it was more than that. There was also an underlying Aussie individuality in O'Reilly's personality, a determination to prove a point and an inherent instinct and confidence to back himself and thumb his nose at those 'experts' in control. Johnny Martin admired these traits, for he possessed many of them himself. Now in his 30's, Fave set out to meet the hero of the days of his youth. In 1967, Bernard O'Reilly still owned a guesthouse at Green Mountain. Before he left for the game in Brisbane, Fave had rung the guesthouse to arrange a meeting with him for the following Sunday. He was told that O'Reilly was away for a few days but would definitely be back by Sunday.

Lynn was fascinated by the story. 'What are you going to say when you first meet him Fave?' Lynn asked.

'I've been thinking about that,' Fave replied. 'I'm going to stick out my hand and say, "G'day, Mr O'Reilly, I'm Johnny Martin and I'm here to tell you that you are my hero".'

Then Fave grinned and said, 'Hey, Full (Lynn's nickname), why don't you come with me?' Lynn, smitten by the tale, agreed that he would.

When Sunday arrived Lynn found that the previous two days of cricket had been exceptionally tiring (not to mention the impromptu locker-room party on the Saturday night). He felt that it would be more relaxing and productive to go to the beach that day, so he begged off. So early on Sunday morning Fave set out to meet his hero alone.

That evening, Lynn had returned from the surf and was sitting in his room when there was a knock at the door. Fave had returned. All day Lynn had been thinking of the meeting between Fave and Bernard O'Reilly and regretting that he had decided to sleep late and surf. So it was with an element of excitement that Lynn exclaimed, 'How did it go Fave?'.

The good-looking, open face beamed, 'Mate, it was one of the best days of my life! We had a wonderful yarn and we have become mates but let me tell you about the first part'.

'What happened?'

'I stuck out my hand and said, "G'day, Mr O'Reilly, my name is Johnny Martin and I'm here to tell you that ...", then Bernard O'Reilly interrupted.

'"Not Johnny Martin, the cricketer?"

'"That's right," I told him.

'"The spin bowler and the batsman who's always hitting sixes?"

'I said, "That's me!"

'Then he stuck out his hand, grabbed me by the shoulder and said, "Johnny Martin, gee, I've always wanted to meet you. You're my hero."'

In 1964 I was working for an insurance company and my job required me to make a tour of to the North Coast of New South Wales a couple of times a year. One of the towns I visited was Taree and when my business was completed, I would sometimes drive out to Burrell Creek to see Fave.

Fave's father ran the telephone exchange from the front of the house, with a small post office attached, and in the winter months, if not overseas playing cricket, Fave would help his Dad run the business. I was there one afternoon and Fave suggested that I clamber into the jeep and join him on the mail run. I must admit that as the vehicle took off I was a little concerned as to where we were going on our mission to 'run the mail'. As we sped down a bush track I could see nothing but eucalyptus trees, scrubby bush and the tail of a fox disappearing into undergrowth; the only sounds I heard were the intermittent chortling of a kookaburra and the ethereal sound of silence that is the *real* sound of the Australian bush. I could not see a sign of human habitation anywhere, though from the open cabin of the jeep the bush smells were wonderful. We turned off the bush track onto another track and about half a mile along Fave stopped, grabbed some letters and placed them in an old kerosene tin which, if my memory serves me correctly, was marked 'R.M.B. 26'. 'Who is that for,' I asked, 'Mr and Mrs Koala?'. There was not a building within the radius of an atom bomb explosion, let alone one anywhere near the letterbox. Then as Fave was getting back into the jeep, to my surprise, an old bus came up and stopped behind us. It was laden with a group of lady bowlers, dressed in their formal white uniforms, who appeared thoroughly out of place in the bush that surrounded us, where, it seemed to me, no human had walked for a thousand years. Where had they come from? Where were they going?

Heads and arms popped out of windows, and voices called, 'G'day Johnny.' ... 'I haven't seen you since you scored the century, Johnny, congratulations.' ... 'How many sixes Johnny?' ... 'I bought a bat for my grandson's birthday, Johnny, can I drop it in for you to autograph it?'.

Fave walked up and down the bus, waving to the ladies and touching their hands as if he was a politician on the campaign trail. 'How you going, Ruthie, how's Sid?' 'Thanks, Daph.' 'Two sixes, Mavis. Big ones, too!' 'Yeah, drop it in Joannie'.

Watching him speaking to these happy people, whom he had probably known all his life, I felt envious of little Johnny Martin, for he had succeeded in having the best of both worlds. Fave had climbed to the top of the mountain, worn the green and gold, toured the world, yet, although he loved every minute of it, he hadn't changed. He was just as happy in the bush, driving along the dirt track, delivering the mail, talking to his own. Later, he took me to the B.C.C.G. (the Burrell Creek Cricket Ground), with its matting wicket and brown outfield, where the only shade to be had for the spectator was inside an old tin dunny, leaning so precariously that it would most certainly tumble over the next time it was struck by a stray six-stitcher. Yet as Fave showed me his bare old bush ground, I doubted that Denis Compton, in extolling the glories of Lord's, would have shown any greater pride.

When he retired from first-class cricket, Fave did not stop playing the game. That would have been like asking Fred Astaire to give away dancing just because he stopped making movies. So he kept bowling his chinamen and hitting sixes, playing for Burrell Creek in the local Taree competition. The last story he ever told me concerned a game that was played on his home ground, when he was in his late 50s. He came on to bowl and facing him was a young Aboriginal boy, whose family had been friends of the Martins through the years and who always referred to Fave as 'Jack'. The first ball beat the bat, finishing in the keeper's gloves and as Fave followed through, he called to the batsman, 'G'day, Alby, how you going?'.

'Not too good, Jack, I'm always nervous when I'm facin' you,' the lad answered.

The next ball was thrown in the air, with the spin causing it to drift away. Alby stood his ground, hit across the line and landed it into the scrub for six. The fieldsman hopped over the fence and after searching in clumps of mulga and under dozing blue-tongue lizards, eventually found the ball and returned it to the bowler. The next ball was swept for four, the fourth smacked over the dunny for six and the last two balls of the over were driven for four. And there was no respite for the Australian all-rounder, for in the following over the batsman continued the slaughter, hitting two fours and two sixes. Next ball there would have been another four, but for a brilliant piece of fielding on the mid-on boundary which restricted the scoring to a single. The batsman reached the other end, mopped his brow and said to his opponent, 'I've done it at last, Jack'.

'Done what, Alby?' Fave asked.

With an obvious tone of relief in his voice, Alby answered, 'I've got away from the strike. Gee, I have terrible trouble pickin' your "wrong un", Jack'.

That was the great thing about Fave; he played the game because he loved it. Alby may have given him a 'terrible' thrashing on the matting wicket in the middle of the bush, yet in his halcyon days Fave played against the mighty West Indians at the Melbourne Cricket Ground in front of 70 000 fans, with millions watching on television, and he dismissed Kanhai, Sobers and Worrell in four deliveries. He played for New South Wales in a golden era when the 'Blues' were the greatest provincial team in the world and he was an integral part of that great side. When he retired from the big time, Fave returned to his roots and gave his all for Burrell Creek, at a time when the club sometimes couldn't find eleven players to make up the team.

Over the last decade of his life, Fave was afflicted with heart problems and was forced to have surgery on two occasions. Despite modern science, which kept Fave with us for a few more years than would once have been the case, he died of a heart attack in July 1991. He will be always remembered by those who knew him and by the many cricketers who were his friends. The old selector, Albert Vincent, wasn't on his own — Johnny Martin was everybody's 'Little Favourite'.

Taree's premier cricket ground is now called 'Johnny Martin Oval'. It is an excellent country ground set in pleasant surrounds, though it lacks the real bush atmosphere of the B.C.C.G., with its leaning dunny, situated as it was, next to the farm where Cyril Martin rounded up the cows with his pads on. Those days have gone now and Fave has gone too. Nevertheless, I reckon he is now residing in that 'better place' where all good cricketers go when their innings are over. One thing is for sure: Fave will still be playing the game — still hitting sixes.

I reckon the total would be well over a thousand by now!

Two

Pharmacist Cure Thyself

For a period of 28 years my father, Alec Marks, was Secretary-Manager of Pennant Hills Golf Club in north-west Sydney and though he was good friends with almost every member, Dad was particularly attracted to those individuals who were slightly offbeat, those blokes who possessed the typical Aussie characteristics of manliness and mateship, who loved a drink and a joke and who were never averse to calling a spade 'a bloody shovel'.

A couple of these characters were residents of the Balmain district of Sydney, Wally Pinerua and Mark

Deveridge. Wally owned a pharmacy in Darling Street and Mark was the licensee of a pub on Victoria Road.

One cold day in the middle of winter, Wally had left his pharmacy for a while and was walking down Darling Street when he met his friend Mark Deveridge coming from the opposite direction.

'Where are you off to, Mark?' asked Wally

The publican, looking the worse for wear, blew into his handkerchief and replied, 'Well actually, mate, I was on my way to see you. I've got this terrible flu and my missus said, "Go down and see Wally, he'll give you some tablets which will fix you up". Where are you going?'.

Wally Pinerua smiled, and answered, 'You wouldn't believe it but I've got this terrible flu and my missus said, "Go down and see Mark, he'll give you a stiff rum which will fix you up".'

The two men stared at each other for a moment, then Wally placed his hand on Mark's shoulder and they turned and walked towards the pub on Victoria Road ...

'Let's try your remedy first,' said the pharmacist.

THREE

UPPER HOUSES AND PLEASANT PALACES

Alf McClelland was an Australian steeped in the beliefs and lore of Labor politics. Between the years 1920 and 1932, he was elected a member of the New South Wales Parliament and served with distinction in a career dedicated to the goodwill of others. During his time in parliament, Alf's wife kept a scrapbook that bulged with clippings telling of her husband's deeds and the deeds of those who were part of that era. On the inside page of the scrapbook is a photograph of Alf looking out, determined and strong. Underneath is a quotation from Henry Lawson, 'My country, her very name is music to me'. In his time, Alf made 'music' for Australia; music of selfless dedication, without the accompaniment of blaring trumpets, played in unison with others in the orchestra pit of Australian history. Forty years later, his son topped the bill and strode the stage.

Alf's son, Doug, born in the outer Sydney suburb of Wentworthville, had a happy boyhood, due to a mother who made sacrifices for her family and a father who provided not only the income, but also the teachings and benevolent discipline of an old-fashioned Dad. Alf was a shining example for Doug's childhood, the mentor of his adolescent years and a role model for the rest of his life. Through the McClelland house walked a 'who's who' of Australian politics (former NSW Premier Jack Lang was a constant visitor) and at night young Doug would listen fascinated as Alf talked of the people he had known and of the problems of the times.

When Alf's soul needed awakening, he read the poetry of Henry Lawson. As a young man and a member of the Australian Workers' Union, Alf had known fellow member Lawson slightly. Once, when Alf was walking up the stairs to the A.W.U. offices, he passed Lawson coming down. Lawson recognised Alf as a tyro of the party and commented as they passed, 'The young man climbs the steps of success while the old man descends from the heights'. Lawson was an inspiration to Alf and his admiration for the poet's words and aspirations was passed down to his son.

> 'Tis the hope of something better than the present or the past —
> 'Tis the wish for something better — strong within us to the last.
> 'Tis the longing for redemption as our ruined souls descend;
> 'Tis the hope for something better that will save us in the end.

After leaving Arthur Phillip High School, Doug joined the Army in the last stages of World War II. However, the Germans were being forced back towards Berlin and the Japanese pushed out of islands and atolls in the Pacific, when Doug was trained and ready to fight. Suddenly the war was over and without firing a shot in anger he was back in civilian life. Doug had a natural ability as a shorthand writer and after a short time as a freelance reporter for a local Parramatta paper, he joined the public service as a court reporter. At the time, Doug was working his way up through the local branch of the Labor Party and playing rugby union for the Parramatta Club. In 1950 he married Lorna McNeill, the love of his life who was to be the mother of his children, his political partner and adviser and later his right arm in his diplomatic career. After the marriage, Lorna persuaded Doug to give up playing football and to set up home in Sydney's St George district, where she had lived most of her life. To this day Doug has not found cause to regret either decision and he now looks out at the world with one white eye and the other red — once a St George Dragon, always a Dragon!

During the 1950s the young man steadily 'climbed the stairs' to success and, after being elected to the Executive of the New South Wales Labor Party, was offered the Number 3 position on Labor's Senate ticket for the 1961 election. He received the required number of votes to become a senator but was forced to face a High Court challenge on the validity of his election. Eventually, the court found in Doug McClelland's favour and his life took a new direction. He would now be following in the footsteps of his father and influencing the affairs of the nation that they both loved so dearly.

The fate of families can take strange twists and turns as the generations come and go. If told by some crystal ball-gazing gypsy that his great-great-grandson would one day be a member of parliament, the first of the Australian McClellands would no doubt have assumed that his future offspring would be sitting in such a forum representing the landed gentry. For Granpop McClelland was what was known as a 'selector' — a man of property and influence who owned Wambramurra Station near Nundle in north-west New South Wales. But depression takes no account of individuals and in the 1890s the infant Australian economy was hit by what present-day economists would probably call 'a rural downturn', and not only the squattocracy were hit hard. Farmers left their properties, bush labourers could find no work and were forced to hump their swags, the shearers went on strike and a prevailing wind of disharmony swept across the dry land. The McClelland family had borrowed money from the banks to improve their property and, with the onset of the depression, found difficulty in making the repayments. And the banks, which in the 1890s made Ebenezer Scrooge seem philanthropic, responded by foreclosing on their home and land. Along with many of their neighbours, the McClellands were forced to leave — victims and witnesses of society's injustice. In less than a generation this family of the land had become part of a radical army.

My army, O my army! The time I dreamed of comes!
I want to see your colours; I long to hear your drums!
I heard them in my boyhood when all men's hearts seemed cold;
I heard them through the years of life — and now I'm growing old!
My army, O my army! The signs are manifold!

In city boy Doug lay a love of the bush and in the school holidays he would catch a train up to Nundle where some of his relatives still resided. School holidays for Doug were golden and through his life he would never forget the bush and its people. When he came to the Senate he well knew the bush's problems (his father had represented the country seats of Northern Tablelands and later Dubbo); Doug quickly made it clear that the well-being of bushfolk would be a top priority.

A position as a senator in either the Labor or Liberal/National parties is akin to working for your father-in-law — there is job security for life, providing you don't run off with the local barmaid. A senator's term lasts for six years and if, in a political context, he doesn't 'shoot through' with the barmaid, the senator can stand for the next six years and the next. Because of the vagaries of the Australian voting system, there is danger for a senator listed only third on the electoral ballot paper. In his first term, Doug was just that — third name on Labor's New South Wales Senate team and he decided he wasn't going to take the risk of missing out next term if Labor's popularity slipped. The young McClelland toured the state, getting to know the 'powers that be' and making sure that come the next election he would be higher up the pecking order.

To describe an Australian as 'a good bloke' (whatever the gender) is close to the ultimate compliment. To describe a member of parliament as 'a clever politician' is seen as, at best, damning with faint praise and, at worst, an oxymoron. The Aussie in the street is inherently suspicious of politicians — equally distrustful of both sides

> Now on his own dominions
> Works with his overseers;
> Hasn't any opinions,
> Hasn't any 'idears'.

With some politicians Lawson's view is undoubtedly correct; fortunately, there are others who enter parliament and work hard for cause and country, driven by motives that are genuinely noble. Doug McClelland, a 'good bloke', came into that category. In his second Senate election the Labor Party hierarchy placed him Number 1 on the ballot paper, recognition of hard work, dedication and 'his fair dinkumness'. Doug has never changed. When he speaks to people it is not with an ulterior motive; there is no hidden agenda behind his firm handshake and laughing eyes, Doug genuinely likes those he meets and shows that he is more than happy to be where he is at the moment. Yet with all his generosity and genuineness, he remains the consummate politician and recognises that popularity is a pollie's greatest asset. Even today, long-retired, the old habits live on.

Earlier in the year I was present at a sporting luncheon and after a couple of hours, as is the way of things at such get-togethers, many of the guests headed to the gentleman's bathroom. In swept Doug and suddenly there were greetings and conversation where previously there had been little else than the sound of flushing pipes. 'G'day, George, how's the missus?' — 'Tom, good to see you, great function isn't it?' — 'Marksy, when is the Sheffield Shield coming back where it belongs?' — 'Saw you at the footy on Saturday, er, mate, wonderful try by Coyne.' — 'Bluey, great function isn't it?'

They reckon that Bob Hawke could work a room better than anyone but he'd have to be darn good to surpass Doug McClelland — and I've got money to bet that Hawke couldn't work a urinal the way Doug can!

When Doug entered parliament in 1962 an era was coming to an end. It was the last term for the tough old characters who had fought in the trenches in World War I. Men such as Les Haylen, Reg Pollard and Theo Nicholls fought for their country on the bloody battlefields of the Somme and Gallipoli and had come home to fight different bloody conflicts in draughty halls at Labor branch meetings and in the more salubrious, but just as vicious, parliament in Canberra. Doug once asked wily old veteran Nicholls why he had never volunteered for any overseas fact-finding tours (junkets). Nicholls answered seriously, 'You've got to be joking, son, there is no way I'm leaving this wonderful land again. I volunteered to go on a trip back in 1914 and it took me five fuckin' years to get home.'

> They'll tell the tales of the nights before and the tales of ship and fort
> Till the sons of Australia take to war as their fathers took to sport,
> Till their breath comes deep and their eyes grow bright
> at the tales of our chivalry
> And every boy will want to fight, nor care what the cause may be.

Doug learned from the old-timers and also from his first leader, Arthur Calwell, who helped him in every possible way. Calwell was a kind man, still grieving for his son who died at a very young age; every day Calwell wore a black tie in the boy's memory. Doug believes that Calwell saw in him and one or two of the newer members a vision of what his lad would have been like had he lived, and this vision drew Arthur Calwell to them. Calwell, a devout Catholic, was torn and damaged by the sectarian/factional split which ravaged the Labor Party in the 1950s and 1960s and which kept it from power for 23 years. Dr H.V. 'Bert' Evatt, whom Calwell succeeded, was embroiled in the split and had the added burden of being unable to compete with the Prime Minister, Robert Menzies, on the floor of the House or from the rostrums of the nation. Calwell, being both a Catholic and left-winger, believed he could reconcile the warring factions in the split but it was not to be (though Labor came within just a few dozen votes of claiming power in 1961). Despite his love of Calwell, McClelland has little doubt that had Reg Pollard taken over from Evatt, Labor would have won Government in 1961.

There is a story of the time which sums up Labor's travails. The member for West Sydney then was a crusty Irishman named Dan Minogue, who was having a difficult time endeavouring to straddle a split in his branch which was turning into a chasm, with one section dominated by pro-Catholic Action (Groupers) and the other adamantly supporting the left wing. The Groupers were violently anti Evatt (the former Labor Party leader) while the others were with him. During a caucus meeting, Minogue asked a question. 'Dr Evatt, did you get a telegram recently from the Glebe North branch of my electorate, congratulating you on your brilliant and courageous leadership?'

'I did,' replied Evatt, 'and I was most gratified to receive it.'

Minogue nodded and replied, 'That's good, because it was never sent.'

When Alf McClelland entered parliament, World War I had been over little more than a year and the nation was attending to the task of finding jobs for the returned soldiers. When Alf left parliament in 1932, Australia was in the midst of the worst depression that it had ever known, with unemployment hounding the nation and its people into poverty. How different it was when Doug first walked through King's Hall as a senator. Australia then was an affluent, trading nation with inflation down and unemployment at a minimum.

McClelland jnr was far more aligned towards the political centre than his Dad had been, reflecting a direction in which the voting public was moving although it was many years before the Labor Party as a whole recognised the trend and moved along that path itself. In his 25 years in parliament, Doug was in Government for only seven years, yet they were years of immense drama. Along the way he was destined to play a starring role in the most dramatic piece of theatre in the history of the Australian parliament and to rub shoulders with some legendary figures.

Even today, many years on, it is to that time and place that Doug McClelland's memory so often returns and if you are fortunate enough to be with him, when he is discussing this era, then you are fortunate indeed — for political giants and wonderful characters are paraded before you and history takes on a new meaning as the stories flow.

Robert Gordon Menzies was a giant among politicians, a man who became Prime Minister at the age of 44. However, soon after World War II began, he was thrown out and reviled. Gone forever they said. But Menzies was made of sterner stuff, achieved a remarkable comeback and was elected again — then continually re-elected, serving 17 years as Liberal Prime Minister. Menzies was not noted for dramatic initiatives or flair in bringing about change, preferring a 'steady as she goes attitude', but his oratory was Churchillian and his wit cutting. His verbal rallies with Labor's staunch socialist, and colourful orator, Eddie Ward, were epics in their content and style and to this day those who witnessed them marvel at the substance of their arguments and the performances of the participants. It was commonly supposed that 'Ming', as Menzies was known, was loathed by all Labor parliamentarians. Yet soon after his entry to the Senate, Doug McClelland was surprised to find that beneath the criticism and the expletives, there was an abiding respect on the Labor side for the establishment man with the bushy eyebrows. Though Doug disagreed with many of Menzies's principles, he acknowledges him as a great Australian.

There was much give and take in the parliamentary exchanges of the time. Once at Question Time, while endeavouring to explain a bill which the Opposition insisted was anti-worker, Menzies made the statement, 'Honourable members on the other side must begin to realise that your worker friends are now voting for us. Why, only the other day when my car had stopped at a light, a truck driver leaned from his window and called out, "You're doing a great job, Bob".' From the Opposition benches came the voice of Jim Cope, 'He should have been arrested for drunken driving'.

Despite the greatness of Menzies at the rostrum, Doug still regards Eddie Ward as the best speaker he ever heard. Doug once asked Ward what was the secret of being a great public speaker. Eddie didn't hesitate. 'Never move your feet son, never move your feet! You can swing your head around, gravitate your torso, wave your arms and shout your head off and they'll say you're inspired, but the minute you take one step they reckon you're shifty.'

The story brings back memories for me. As a kid, I recall my grandfather taking my brother and me down to the Sydney Domain where the spruikers stood on their soapboxes, waxing lyrical on every topic known to humankind, from the constitution to prostitution, from body odour to bodyline bowling, from the army to Armageddon. There they stood, on bits of wood, the people speaking their minds; 'the King is an imbecile' — 'the Pope is a profligate' — 'Stalin is the saviour of the world' — 'Ginger Meggs for Prime Minister'. Thousands milled around, moving from soapbox to soapbox and in the centre, on an average-looking box, stood Eddie Ward, the Bradman of the Domain.

The crowd cheered and the crowd booed. I was eight, my brother was four and though we didn't realise it at the time, we were living in a wonderful democracy, where streets were safe and speech was free and there was no censorship in the form of political correctness, or any other correctness. It was a case of just, 'let 'er rip'. 'Say what ya want mate, then I'll tell ya what a goose ya are.' The Domain is still there, but it is now just a place for touch footy and for strolling — a green area between the Art Gallery and State Parliament. Yet I knew the Domain when, in front of thousands, Australia's first world boxing champion Jimmy Carruthers fought an illegal bare-knuckle fight against 'Mustard' Coleman and knocked him down dozens of times before Mustard eventually quit. And I knew the Domain when Australians used to say what they wanted to and never hedged their words and people booed and laughed and listened. Wonderful days!

Soon after his arrival in Canberra, Doug's daughter, Jan, mentioned that her Sunday school teacher would be in Canberra the following week and would it be possible for her to have a tour around Parliament House? Doug checked his diary and suggested that if the teacher arrived at a certain time towards late afternoon, he would be able to show her around the building himself and, if she so wished, she could have dinner in the Parliamentary dining room later. Like most fathers, Doug was pleased to do anything for his daughter, but secretly he was not looking forward to spending a few hours with his vision of a 'Sunday school teacher' who might look down her nose when he ordered a beer.

A week later Doug was paged to King's Hall to meet a Miss Jenkins. When he walked down the only person there was a particularly attractive young lady who was standing by herself gazing at the portraits. Passing press hounds from the gallery had noticed her too. Yep, you guessed it. It was Jan's Sunday school teacher, a most vivacious young lady, fashionably dressed who, when offered, declared that she was, 'really looking forward to a drink'.

Over dinner, Doug was in full flight, waxing lyrical on the Machiavellian machinations of party politics, when Miss Jenkins interrupted and said, 'Excuse me, Senator, but isn't that Eddie Ward over there?'.

'That's right,' agreed Doug, 'I'll call him over and introduce you' — an offer that obviously thrilled the young lady.

Doug caught Ward's eye and he wandered over, appraising the senator's companion as he did so. 'Eddie, I'd like you to meet Miss Jenkins.' Noticing that Ward was grinning at him, Doug realised that further explanation was required. 'Er, Miss Jenkins happens to be my young daughter's Sunday school teacher.' There was dead silence for a few seconds, then Eddie Ward threw back his head and laughed; a laugh that echoed all around the quiet dining room. Miss Jenkins turned bright red but the laugh continued until eventually Ward placed his hand on Doug's shoulder and roared, 'Son, I've been here a long while and in that time I thought I'd met 'em all. I've met so-called constituents, cousins and the branch secretary's sister. I've met neighbours, job applicants and "the wife's best friend". But up until this moment nobody ever had the gall to call his companion, "my young daughter's Sunday school teacher".' He lifted his hand and slammed it on Doug's shoulder. 'You'll go far son. You've got flair!' Eddie Ward bade them both goodbye and walked away chortling loudly.

The first Prime Minister to make an impression on Doug McClelland was John Curtin. Curtin was speaking one day at the Sydney Town Hall, and teenager Doug can clearly remember the broad Australian accent, the talk of 'our gallant lads fighting in Tobruk' (which Curtin pronounced as 'Toe/bruck'). Curtin is regarded by some as Australia's greatest Prime Minister, an alcoholic who never touched a drop while he was the country's leader. It is an indictment of our present society that Curtin, because of his unattractive appearance, would almost certainly be overlooked as Prime Minister in this age of television.

The Prime Minister who television *made* was Edward Gough Whitlam — although Gough would no doubt argue the reverse — that he made television. There were many similarities between Whitlam and Menzies. Like Bob Menzies, Gough Whitlam was a charismatic politician with a patrician demeanour, and a seemingly inherent knowledge that at birth the gods had stamped 'born to lead' on his forehead. Though egalitarian in outlook, Whitlam strode the halls of power as if he had designed them. If the plebs wanted to bend the knee and touch the forelock as he walked his preordained way, then so be it. What saved Whitlam from being proved guilty of the sins of arrogance and pride (of which he was accused many times), was a brilliant mind, a slick tongue and a sense of humour which was very sharp, very clever and often self-deprecating. Doug regards Whitlam as an 'amazing man' who was always in control and always ahead of the pack. Yet according to Doug, he was more than that; Gough Whitlam was also one of the world's great thespians. Wherever he went he commanded centre stage. The crowd could cheer, the crowd could hiss and fruit could be hurled from the cheap seats, but at centre stage Gough remained, knowing his lines and playing his part, always confident of his right to be there.

In 1972, after 23 years of conservative rule, Gough Whitlam became the first Labor Prime Minister since Ben Chifley. In the end, it wasn't that tough, with the Liberals losing confidence and becoming increasingly stale after so long in power while the leader, Billy McMahon, was not trusted by many in his own party. ('I guess I'm my own worst enemy,' McMahon once stated in parliament. From the Government backbench came the familiar voice of Jim Killen, 'You're not while I'm alive'.) In parliament and on the hustings, Whitlam dominated his smaller insecure rival like a heavyweight champion fighting a featherweight contender. 'Tiberius on a telephone,' was just one of the many verbal punches that the big man threw at McMahon. They all seemed to land.

Doug McClelland was named Minister for the Media in the first Whitlam Cabinet and was also Manager of Government Business in the Senate. He remembers the time with excitement and nostalgia, particularly the 'nothing asked and nothing given' debates with his tough rival (and friend) on the Opposition benches, Reg 'Toecutter' Withers. At last he felt that he could do something constructive for his country. Later, he was appointed Special Minister for State, his duties including responsibility for the Tariff Board, Commonwealth Grants Commission (distribution of Federal monies to the states) and the Electoral Commission. Doug is proud of his record and achievements as a minister but leaves any judgement to history, far preferring to reminisce about the wonderful characters that he met and the funny incidents that occurred. It should be stated, though, that he did introduce FM broadcasting and established the Australian Film Commission.

The Minister for Transport in the Whitlam Government was a tough up-from-the-ranks union man named Charles Jones. Charlie Jones had joined the party in the Newcastle area of New South Wales and among other things worked as a boilermaker before moving on to Federal Parliament. There was some surprise on both sides of the House when the Prime Minister made Jones Minister for Transport, but he handled the job with great skill and the Opposition found far less to criticise in Charlie Jones' handling of his portfolio, than they did with a few of his higher profile and personally ambitious colleagues. For some time after the Whitlam Government came to power, Jones and his department worked on a far-sighted plan to reorganise the entire transport system of the Commonwealth. New systems were initiated to streamline the continent's highways, byways and skyways. The best brains in the land were consulted and much midnight oil burnt in the offices of the Department of Transport in Canberra. At the forefront throughout was Charlie Jones. At last came the day when the document was to be presented to Cabinet.

The fact that all ministers believe that their portfolio is the most important, ensures that one of the unenviable tasks of the Prime Minister is to prioritise the immense amount of government business and endeavour to keep business flowing on a 'first things first' basis. Whitlam could see big problems emerging from Charlie Jones' document and, as it was, his Government was receiving criticism enough from Opposition, press and polls at that time. So, as brilliant a scheme as Charlie's was, perhaps the new transport system should remain on the back-burner for a while longer. The Prime Minister sat up the front and waited for Jones to begin.

Charlie eyed his fellow Cabinet ministers. 'Have youse all got a copy of the document?' Whitlam interrupted, 'Please, Charlie, "you", not "youse"'.

'Okay, okay. Have you all got your copy of the document?' Everybody nodded. 'Are there any questions before I begin taking you through it?'

Whitlam again, 'Yes Charlie, page eight, line five, the sentence ends with a preposition'.

Jones rolled his eyes, 'So what?'

'Bad grammar, Charlie.'

'Shit!'

'Also, Charlie, on page 19, there's a split infinitive in the third line.'

'What about it?'

'Inelegant writing.'

'God help us!'

Whitlam flicked the pages. 'On page 32, second paragraph, the syntax is all wrong, Charlie.'

'Bloody hell!'

'Which member of your staff wrote this document, Charlie?'

'I did.'

'Well I think you should take it back and re-write it, Charlie, making sure that your grammar and syntax are perfectly correct this time.'

Charlie Jones said nothing for a moment, then he picked up his document and hurled it to the floor, sending papers flying everywhere. He stood up, looked round the room and called loudly to all assembled, 'Youse can all get stuffed'.

In the 1972 election, the seat of Kingston in South Australia was won for the Labor Party, against the odds, by a local anaesthetist, Dr Richie Gunn. Gunn was a conscientious member who worked hard, but he was regarded as somewhat abrasive and pedantic by his leader. At caucus meetings Gunn was continually interrupting and asking questions. 'Before we hear from the Treasurer, may I ask the Prime Minister a question?' ... 'Thank you for your answer, Prime Minister, but that is not the question I asked.' ... 'Could the Prime Minister be a little more explicit?' ... etc, etc.

Gunn's quest for answers annoyed and exasperated his leader and Whitlam would either make his frustration obvious or come out with some cutting remark which belittled the Member for Kingston. This didn't seem to perturb Richie Gunn in the least; he just kept on interrupting, using an especially thick skin as a shield.

During the 1975 election campaign, Whitlam was scheduled to speak in the electorate of Kingston in support of Gunn. While sitting on the stage waiting to be called to the rostrum, Gough was flicking through Gunn's campaign brochures and found in one a statement which read: 'The Prime Minister has stated publicly that, in his opinion, Dr Gunn is the best and most knowledgeable person ever to enter Federal Parliament.' After the rally had ended Whitlam drew Gunn aside, pointed to the literature and asked in his most distinctive voice (a combination of a whisper and a purr), 'What rubbish is this?'.

Gunn looked at it and answered, 'Well isn't that what you said?'

Whitlam was angry. 'Of course not. I've never said such a thing and never will.'

'Then I'm sorry to say, Gough, that your memory must be failing you,' answered Gunn.

Gough Whitlam was not a man who believed he had any weaknesses and if he did, a failing memory certainly wasn't one of them. 'My memory is not failing me! I have never said that you were the best and most knowledgeable man ever to enter parliament. When am I supposed to have uttered this unbelievable untruth?'

Gunn answered quietly. 'Well it was last year, actually. You were walking down a corridor in Parliament House with some of your staff and I came up and corrected you on an answer you'd given me in caucus that day. Then you turned to me and said, "Gunn, you are the greatest fucking know-all ever to enter this place!".'

Lionel Bowen, Deputy Prime Minister, and a close friend of Doug McClelland's, tells of the time he and Whitlam descended from the Prime Ministerial plane in Athens to be met by an entourage of VIPs. It was early in the morning, the temperature was at the lower end of the thermometer and a freezing wind was blowing across the tarmac. Whitlam was rugged up in a long warm coat and gloves, while Bowen was in a smartly cut business suit. When they reached the bottom of the stairs, the band struck up the first of the national anthems. While everybody was standing to attention, Whitlam whispered out of the side of his mouth, 'Lionel, put your coat on'.

From the opposite corner of his mouth, Bowen replied, 'I haven't got a coat'.

Another whisper, 'Well go out and buy one.'

'I don't need one.'

'Yes you do. Get one immediately.'

'I hate bloody coats.'

The bandmaster continued waving the baton, the music blared and the whispers continued. 'Bowen, I am telling you to get a coat.'

'And I am telling you, I won't.'

'Bowen, I am ordering you to get a coat. I refuse to stand beside you on these State occasions and have you make me look a wimp.'

Towards the end of 1975, the Whitlam Government was increasingly unpopular with the Australian electorate and the polls were showing that if an election was held, the Government would be annihilated. The Opposition, now led by Malcolm Fraser, had been in office for a long period of time and after three years on the 'boring benches' were impatient to get their hands back on the tiller. And there was a way to do it — they had the numbers in the Upper House. In normal circumstances, this would be a minor advantage only. The Senate could prolong legislation or amend it but it could not initiate anything. More importantly, nor was it anywhere near the 'tiller' of power. However, there was one ploy, unused before and fraught with danger — the Opposition could block the Supply Bill and stop the flow of money going through to the Public Service. This would eventually bring the wheels of the system to a grinding halt and the Government would be forced to call an election and ask the people to decide the outcome. In 1975 it was what the Opposition wanted ... and the Government wished to avoid.

Eventually such a strategy was put into place and, over the next couple of weeks, the country held its breath. The advantage seemed to swing from one side then to the other and parliamentary broadcasts, which had previously rated on radio about as highly as pre-dawn recitals of chamber music, were now almost compulsory listening. Both sides tore into each other waiting for the first sign of weakness, the media barked and brayed, consultants and advisers roamed the draughty halls of power, gave lofty opinions and pontificated, people stood on the footpaths holding up placards. Meanwhile, in the bearpit that is parliament, the fight went on. It was a stoush that would not have been recognised by Hoyle and one the Marquis of Queensberry would have refused to attend.

The Senate, which had always been the less glamorous of the Houses, became the centre of attention. In the vortex of this political whirlwind stood the Manager of Government Business, Doug McClelland. Doug handled it brilliantly, matched against his rival in the Upper House, 'Toecutter' Withers, as the battle ebbed and flowed. On Tuesday morning, 11 November 1975, Whitlam called his generals together and told them that he had decided to ask the Governor-General to approve a half-Senate Election which would give the Opposition a piece of what they wanted, yet still allow the Supply Bill to be passed and thus give the Government breathing space. Whitlam explained that he, and senior Labor men Frank Crean and Fred Daly, had met the Opposition hierarchy, Fraser, Doug Anthony and Ian Sinclair, earlier that morning. The evening before, Doug had had a drink in the bar with fellow minister James 'Diamond Jim' McClelland (no relation). For a long time Diamond Jim had been a mate of the Governor-General, Sir John Kerr. 'You don't think that the G-G could do something silly, do you Jim?' Doug asked.

Jim McClelland shook his head, 'Doug, I've known John Kerr all of our professional lives and there is no way in the world he would ever let us down'. That night Doug slept easy.

After the meeting between the two groups, Doug spoke to Frank Crean. 'How did it go, mate?' he enquired.

Crean shrugged his shoulders, 'All right, I guess. Gough told them about the half-Senate Election and they didn't say much — but I don't like it, Doug'.

'What do you mean?'

Crean, who never swore, shook his head saying, 'Too bally cocky. They are just too bally cocky! I reckon they've got something up their sleeve. Could it be the Governor-General?'.

In the Senate that afternoon, Doug was prepared for another tough session on the floor of the House. Yet when the Government moved that the Supply Bill be passed, the Opposition acquiesced without a whimper, to the amazement of all Government senators. Doug immediately rang one of his aides, Bill Rigby, and exclaimed, 'Mate they've caved in. It's passed.' Rigby answered, with news of a rumour sweeping the corridors of parliament — that the Government had been sacked!

In the turmoil of the dismissal, those in the Upper House were the last to know. Yet Doug McClelland is adamant today that the passing of the Supply Bill was invalid because although the Governor-General had signed a document which threw the Government out of office and although Malcolm Fraser was sworn in as Prime Minister, there were no other ministers sworn in. Therefore the Senate had no Minister in authority to propose passage of the Supply Bill. Only a Minister in Parliament, or a person delegated by him, can represent the Government of the day. There was, in fact, no Minister.

The public at large have many images of those dramatic hours, though Doug remembers only the feeling of being shell-shocked — a feeling shared by his colleagues. There is a story that in the middle of the controversy, Gough Whitlam drove home to The Lodge at lunchtime and devoured a large steak. Doug is not sure if this story is true and he has never verified it with Whitlam, but he believes it is probably a fact. Doug grinned as he explained, 'Come hell or high water, nothing could turn the Big Fella off his tucker'.

The general election was held a few weeks later and, true to predictions, the Labor Party was beaten comprehensively. It was to be another eight years in the wilderness before Doug McClelland and his mates came back to Government.

Gough Whitlam resigned in 1977 and the leadership was taken on by Bill Hayden. Hayden had come into parliament in 1961, in the same batch as Doug McClelland. For a time the two were close but gradually they drifted apart and as the years passed they had very little in common. McClelland in the end had little faith in Hayden's leadership and, though he is the first to admit that there are two sides to every tale, he has not changed his opinion to this day. So when Bob Hawke entered parliament, Doug was especially pleased. He knew Hawke to be a charismatic man with great potential as a political leader. In assessing the leaders of his time McClelland reckoned that apart from Chifley, Menzies and possibly Gorton (though never really given a chance), he could not come up with any who really understood 'average Australia'. Whitlam was brilliant, but failed to grasp the thoughts and feelings of the 'Averages'. Fraser was ruthless, but with a squatter's mentality, driven by the polls. In Hawke, Doug figured he could see a leader who could show the way to the 'Promised Land'. When Hawke asked him if he had his support in the Hawke push for leadership, Doug answered, 'Mate, I'll not only support you, I'll lead the whole bloody parade and wave a flag if you want'. Hawke became leader, ambushed Fraser in the 1983 election and was Prime Minister for eight years. Bill Hayden picked up his drover's dog and eventually moved on to loftier heights.

Hawke may have lacked the grandeur of Whitlam and the 'light on the hill' vision of Chifley, but like Menzies, he calmed the insecurities of Middle Australia. Bob Hawke led a Government of stability and less controversy than any of Labor's past leaders — and did it by metaphorically strolling down and having a beer with the 'Averages'. The ordinary people then got on with their own lives and forgot that the Government was there — which is exactly the way that Australians seem to like it.

During the Hawke days, Doug was made President of the Senate, the equivalent to Speaker of the House of Representatives, and presided over the Upper House with a firm and understanding hand. They were days of fulfilment for Doug and at the end he looked back on them with a sense of satisfaction. As no doubt would have his Dad, Alf, who had shown him the way.

Twenty-five years is a long time in parliament. One evening Doug was sitting in his room in Canberra, having just hung up from a long phone conversation with his wife Lorna at home. For a long time he gazed at the four walls and wrestled with the thought, *What am I doing here?* A few days later he called on the Prime Minister. 'Bob, I've had enough, I want to get out.'

Hawke was surprised at first and then he posed a question, 'Doug, have you ever given any thought to London?'.

'London? Not much, it's a bit cold. London? I like it but I don't think about it much.'

'Think about becoming High Commissioner,' said the PM.

In six months, Australia's new High Commissioner to London and Mrs McClelland were aboard a Qantas 747 en route to London.

Hold up your head in England,
Tread firm the London streets;
We come from where the strong heart
Of all Australia beats!
From where the glorious sunset
On sweeps of mulga glows
Ah! we know more than England,
And more than Europe knows!

The designation 'High Commissioner' means nothing more or less than the term 'ambassador'. It is no more than a throwback to the days of the Empire when those who still belonged to the exclusive Empirical Club wished to be treated slightly differently in London to, say, those Americans who, for reasons known only to them, had long ago resigned from the club and gone their own way.

No matter where Doug or Lorna had travelled over the years, they seemed to fit in naturally with the people and the environment and the word 'naturally' is chosen carefully. Yet in the first couple of months on the diplomatic circuit, Doug found the going more difficult than ever before and after one tiring evening of observing protocol and speaking 'diplomatese', Doug found himself confiding to a British friend that he felt like a fish out of water. The friend smiled and said, 'Doug, it is very easy if you'll only be yourself. After all, you are an Aussie and that's what we British expect and that's what we British want. Forget all the claptrap, just act normally.' Those words of advice were the best Doug ever received and from then on for him it was just like being in the bar at the St George League's Club, where everybody was greeted normally and everybody was a friend. At a Lord Mayor's reception, one day, a functionary of the Mayor's came over to Doug and said, 'Excuse me, High Commissioner, but there may be a few of us close by this evening when you greet the United States Ambassador. I hope you don't mind but we love to listen to you both'.

At the end of the evening, Doug walked over to the man and asked, 'Did I say the right thing?'.

The man beamed and replied, 'Oh, indeed you both did. It's so different from what we are used to over here'.

'What did we say?'

The man could hardly contain his enthusiasm as he explained. 'The Ambassador came up, put out his hand and said, "Well, hi, Doug". And you shook his hand and answered, "Yeah g'day, Charles, great to see ya mate". It was absolutely wonderful!'.

The only thing Doug never really came to terms with were the modes of dress that were expected of the High Commissioner and his lady. It was here he depended on Lorna, who quickly came to understand what was required. Early on, they were invited to a private residence for Sunday lunch, for which the host insisted that the dress was 'entirely casual'. Doug dressed in slacks, casual shoes and open-neck shirt, but Lorna had reservations. 'Put on a tie and coat Doug,' she insisted.

'No need to, love, this is an entirely casual affair,' replied the High Commissioner.

Lorna walked up to Doug's wardrobe, pulled out a smart sportscoat and a tie and repeated her advice that he put them on.

On arrival, Doug was quick to realise that he was by far the most casually dressed in the place. Not only was he under-dressed but if his wife had not insisted that he wear a coat and tie, he would have been regarded as 'diplomatically naked'. Doug still puzzles over the difference between the British terms 'casual' and 'informal', yet if forced to give a definition he would opt for the following: Informal = Your best and heaviest Sunday suit with well-pressed white shirt and regimental tie: Casual = Your *second*-best and heaviest Sunday suit with well-pressed white shirt and regimental tie.

With a touch of soft cynicism and sadness, Doug noted that those most lavishly dressed and arrayed in the more expensive and opulent accessories on such days, were inevitably the representatives of the nations where millions of people were struggling to exist from day-to-day.

After four years as High Commissioner, Doug McClelland wore out two dinner suits and a set of tails — and his shorts were never taken out of the suitcase.

> *The King is robed in royal state, with medals on his breast,*
> *And like the mother Queen she is Her Majesty is dressed.*
> *The Lady's dressed in simple black and sports no precious stones,*
> *And I in simple reach-me-downs I bought from Davey Jones.*

The McClellands time in London were productive years for them and for their country. The friends they made and the contacts acquired are beyond price and when they return now, it's like going home. Though Doug has always been a republican, he speaks with open admiration of the Queen, whom he found to be a delightful, intelligent person, fun to be with and who trod the line perfectly between treating him with the deference the British believed his official position demanded and the easiness and comfort of a friend. He found in the many times he was in her company that she was always ready with good advice and never short of a joke or a quip. Doug hesitates to say that they became friends, yet in the end he found that both he and Lorna used to look forward to their times with the Queen. On one occasion Doug was at Ascot races, in his top hat and tails, and received a message that 'Her Majesty would be pleased to see the High Commissioner in the Royal Box'.

'Would you like a cup of tea, High Commissioner, and did you back my horse in the last race?' the Queen asked when Doug arrived.

'I'd love a cuppa, your Majesty and, yes, I did have some money on your horse in the last,' Doug replied.

As an aide poured the tea for Doug, the Queen explained, 'Well, the trainer told me that the horse wasn't quite ready and wouldn't win but that it would benefit from the outing. So after some thought, I decided to let it have the run.'

Doug looked over the rim of his cup and said, 'With all due respect, your Majesty, I wish we had had this cup of tea before the race'. She threw back her head and laughed heartily.

The Queen was invited to Canberra in 1988 to open the new 'state of the art' Parliament House — that billion-dollar eyesore, with its towering phallic symbol which our politicians keep insisting is 'worth every cent'. As she was being shown around, the Queen noticed a small pond which was situated in the foyer of the building. She pointed out to her host that this pond was not enclosed and suggested that it might be wise to fence it as it had been her experience that little children and those with a taste for the stronger stimulants were inclined to be drawn to such crystal pools, which shimmered in the moonlight. The host thanked the monarch, made the appropriate comments and then forgot all about it. During his term as High Commissioner, Doug was talking to a political pal from Australia and asked him how a particular function at Parliament House had gone. 'Great,' replied his friend, 'but a few of the boys slipped on the floor and fell into that pond'.

The next day, Doug was required to call upon the Queen in regard to some matter and repeated to her the story he had been told the day before. The Queen called to her husband, 'Phillip, come and listen to this story the High Commissioner is telling'. Doug repeated the story. The Queen grinned and remarked, 'High Commissioner, it would be wrong of me to say I told you so'. Then she roared with laughter, clapped her hands and remarked, 'So instead I'll just say, "Goody, goody". Perhaps they will now do something about it, before a serious accident occurs'.

To represent Australia at the highest level in London is to feel proud and humble. White settlement in this land began a little over 200 years ago but it is less than 100 years since Australia became a federation. In that small time span we have seen a 360 degree change in attitude by the British towards Australians. In the early days of this century Aussies touched the forelock and the Poms were suitably condescending. Then came the wars in which the tiny population of Australia sacrificed tens of thousands of their sons in conflicts that were not really ours. Through the years our sportsmen and women performed great deeds, our musicians and artists became famous on the Continent, and soon after World War II Australians began to travel and be seen. Today, we are, per head of population, the most travelled people in the world. We may not be regarded as being as sophisticated as some of the 'older' nations but we are worldly wise and our dealings with others are polite and understanding, without us ever losing our openness and friendly attitude. For four years Doug McClelland was the most important Australian in the United Kingdom, a friend of many (and all wanted to be his friend) yet he was no different from the bush girl just out of her teens, tramping Europe, carrying her backpack. She, like the High Commissioner, would come to realise that just being an Aussie is a passport to friendship and respect. There is no need to be sophisticated or to have the benefit of a background of wealth, or to come from a family whose ancestors landed with William the Conqueror. The world is a smaller place and we are no longer a backwater.

The flaunting flag of progress
Is in the West unfurled,
The mighty Bush with iron rails
Is tethered to the world.

It was the attitude of affection and respect that existed towards his country that most touched Doug's heart as he travelled around the United Kingdom and Europe. It did not change his attitude towards his country but it made him see it in a different light. The Japanese Ambassador once observed to him that 'Australians are the hardest workers in the world' — a statement that would come as a great shock to most Aussies. 'You people are our truest friends,' stated a high-level American. The declaration, 'I wish we could be as open and confident as you Aussies,' was one Doug heard many times from British friends. Once he was attending an Anzac Day ceremony in the little French town of Villers-Bretonneux, so well known to Diggers who fought on the Western Front. After the ceremony, the Mayor asked Doug back to his home for a drink. On the wall, in a frame above the mantelpiece, were the Tricolour and the Australian flags crossed together. During the course of the conversation, Doug thanked the Mayor for going to the trouble of having the flags placed on the wall, presuming it was done to impress the guest from Australia. 'That was a most kindly gesture, Monsieur Mayor. It makes an old Australian, twelve thousand miles away from his shores, feel at home.'

The Mayor shook his head and replied, 'Oh, but you are wrong High Commissioner. These flags were not brought in to impress you. They are always here. They belonged to my grandfather, who passed them on to my father, who passed them on to me. I will pass them on to my children and they to theirs. You see, during the Great War, your Australian soldiers saved our town twice from German occupation and our townspeople will be forever indebted to them. They are the greatest fighting men who ever lived. Villers-Bretonneux is part of Australia and Australia is part of Villers-Bretonneux. You are not twelve thousand miles from home, High Commissioner, you are home.'

As I write these words, it has been seven years since Doug and Lorna McClelland returned from London. Doug believes that his time in the United Kingdom was marked by a number of achievements that were of benefit to his country and to the world at large. There is no ego in such a statement — just a touch of pride that he did his job to the best of his ability. While High Commissioner, Doug met and spoke to the famous; men such as François Mitterrand and Ronald Reagan. Two of the people who impressed him most were Mikhail Gorbachev and Pope John Paul II. Gorbachev seemed to be a clever man, genuinely wanting peace, while the Pontiff had a certain strength in his face the like of which Doug had never seen before in any other person. Though most of her political opinions are anathema to Doug, Margaret Thatcher is a person whom he admires greatly and he became particularly friendly with her and her husband Denis, in London and later when he accompanied them on their tour of Australia.

It was not so unusual that Denis Thatcher and the Australian High Commissioner hit it off pretty well, Thatcher being a former rugby referee and a fanatic about the game, and a bloke who loved a beer.

The McClellands say they were pleased to return to the 'world's greatest country' and Doug admits that he now enjoys sitting back and looking at the political scene — without having to worry about the votes. He was sorry to see Labor lose Government but he puts it down to an 'it's time' factor and the possible overconfidence of Paul Keating. Keating has a brilliant mind, 'up there with Gough's, and a passion' — according to McClelland — 'which is genuinely felt and acted upon'. However, Keating was a man who could not see anything good in his opposition and he was a hater. Doug doesn't believe that John Howard is the man to lead Australia, though he knows him as a hard worker and a decent bloke. His warning to Howard is that he should keep his eye on the Melbourne Liberal Establishment. If not, Howard will go the way he went before ... and the way of Gorton.

Doug is no longer influencing world events but he is back home in Sydney influencing interesting events, nevertheless. He is now the president of the St George Rugby League Club and was in the thick of the rugby league civil war of 1995–97 which tore the code apart. In his so-called retirement he doubts he needs this sort of confrontation but he loves the club and wants to do what he can for the game to make it right again and was deeply involved recently in the merger between St. George and Illawarra. Doug believes that rugby league is too good a game not to survive, although he admits to having given up hope of ever seeing champions of the calibre of Reg Gasnier and Johnny Raper again. As I stated, once a Dragon, always a Dragon.

It is a pity that Doug McClelland has decided not to write a book. He thought about it but reckons he was on the horns of a dilemma. To tell the full story, he would be forced to criticise people with whom he worked and with whom he shared a common cause. If he ignored such people, the book would not be factual and he would be taking money under false pretences. So Doug is content with his memories and when the opportunity arises he has a drink with his mates and yarns of the things he has seen and the people he has known ... and he laughs a lot. Sometimes, too, he gets together with his old political colleagues and great days are relived. Doug McClelland has thousands of friends and even more acquaintances, the kids and grandkids are never far away and there is always Lorna, his best mate and the number one diplomat of the family, ever on hand to make sure her husband wears a tie when appropriate. And if it happens by some chance that Doug McClelland is on his own for a while, he'll never be lonely — because close by there is always Henry to keep him company.

The light of passion in dreamy eyes and a page of truth well read,
The glorious thrill in heart grown cold of the spirit I thought was dead,
A song that goes to a comrade's heart and a tear of a pride let fall —
And my soul is strong! And the world to me is a grand world after all!

[The quoted passages in this chapter are from the various works of Henry Lawson.]

Four

Putts on Remembrance Day

If an American is asked, 'Where were you when you first heard the news?' he or she will probably answer along the lines, 'I was having a cup of coffee with my accountant when his secretary ran in shouting, "the President has been shot!".'

If an Australian is asked the same question, he or she will think for a moment and answer (something like), 'Oh, I was stopped at a red light and the bloke in the car next to me wound down his window and called, 'It's just come over the radio that the Governor-General has sacked Whitlam, and Fraser is now prime minister!'.

I certainly know where I was on the 11th of November 1975, because I happened to be in close contact with a group of about 80 Australians (mainly men) and was able to witness at close hand the actions, reactions and interactions of these people to this extraordinary event. I hesitate to classify those assembled as a cross-section of Australian society, but they were a reasonably intelligent group of people who had made, or were making, their way in the world. I wrote no notes at the time and many of my memories have faded, but these are some of the things I remember from that remarkable Remembrance Day.

In 1966, I joined my friend, Warren Saunders, in an insurance brokerage business and we worked together for 24 years before I sold my shares in 1989. When I started out with Warren, the brokerage was only a two-person business but by 1975 it had grown to around a dozen people. Insurance is a 'people business' and as important as the product is, it is tactical to sell yourself first before you discuss the product. An insurance brokers' most important task is to give service to the clients. Nevertheless, it is also worthwhile to be different, to try something which is noted and appreciated by your clients and about which they talk to others. That is exactly the reason that, each November, our company held a golf day for our bigger clients, instead of throwing a Christmas party — since Christmas parties abound ad nauseam in the CBDs of our capital cities in the month of December. The venue for the golf day was Pennant Hills Golf Club in the north-western suburbs of Sydney, and in the year of 1975 the event was held on the 11th of November.

Warren and I never played in these golf days, preferring to be on hand as hosts to assist and mix with our clients. On the early afternoon of 11 November 1975, the frantic rush and bustle of getting the field off was over and after having a cup of tea and a sandwich, the two of us strolled down the path from the clubhouse, out over the rustic bridge which spans the creek at the 9th hole. We wandered up to the 6th green nearby to greet the four players who were duffing their way up the fairway. When they eventually reached the green, we listened as they told us of their shocking luck on the previous five holes, watched them putt out and walked with them up to the 7th tee. As the man holding the 'honour' placed his tee in the ground, I noticed an electric golf cart roaring through the trees. At the wheel, driving with the dedicated ferocity of a Formula One racer, was our office manager, John 'Chalky' McLaughlin. He jumped out while the cart was still moving and called loudly, 'The Governor-General has sacked the Government and he's made Fraser prime minister!'.

The first reaction of all of us was bewilderment. Then the questions began. 'Can he do that?' — 'Did you say *Fraser* is the P.M.?' — 'Have you been on the turps again, Chalky?'

McLaughlin tried to explain though, like the rest of his countrymen, the 'Richter scale' of his emotions was varying between bemusement and astonishment. Explanations from legal experts which we were to later hear sounded like a load of 'gobbledygook', so what chance had a layman in such circumstances? 'That's what I just heard,' said Chalky. 'The television stations have cancelled all other programs and there is nothing else on.' He shrugged his shoulders, hopped back into the cart and headed over to the 5th fairway to let another group know of the events. As he drove away, Chalky reminded me of an old-time town crier ... in an electric golf cart.

Warren and I walked back to the clubhouse to catch up with the story and as we strolled, I looked down to where another group of four was coming from the 5th green. I watched Chalky announcing the news to them. From about 150 metres away, I saw a man in a blue pullover clench his fist in the air and heard him cry, 'You bloody little beauty!'. Beside him his playing partner hurled the club he was holding into the bush.

'This could be a tough afternoon,' I said to my colleague.

Warren nodded, grinned and replied, 'Yes, whatever we do, let's keep the conversation light'.

As we walked across the bridge somebody shouted, 'What's all the commotion about?'.

I called loudly, 'Apparently Kerr has sacked Labor from office and Malcolm Fraser is prime minister.' From the green came a number of excited comments, though Bob, who was crouched over a putt, said nothing. I continued in my 'town crier' role, 'I can't tell you much but Chalky McLaughlin just informed us that ...'

Bob pulled away from the ball, stood up and called, 'Would you bloody well shut up, Marksy, I've got this 10-footer downhill for a birdie'. Suitably chastened, I closed my mouth immediately and watched silently as he stroked the putt. 'Stroked' is probably the wrong word because although Bob managed to connect the club with the ball, it was a shot which would best be described as 'half a shank'/'half a top' and it missed the hole by the length of a shovel. We all watched as it gathered pace down the slope and finished on the edge of the green, just short of the bunker. Bob let out an expletive, then turned around to where I was standing and vehemently suggested that Malcolm Fraser and myself go away and engage in a peculiar act that was once deemed illegal but which now seems to be acceptable, provided it is performed by consenting adults. (I was later told that this was as close as Bob got to a birdie all day and he didn't make any pars either.)

In past golf days, at the end of the round, the tradition had been for players to grab a beer and sit with their fellow players to discuss the events of the day and their horrid luck on the putting surfaces. The only non-golf questions normally asked are, 'You don't know what won the Flying at Gosford do you?' or 'Have you heard the Shield score?'.

This particular day, thoughts of horseracing and cricket were well and truly in the back of people's minds and once clubs were placed in boots of cars, all headed for the television set. There, the arguments began.

To give even the most passionate of them their due on that day, each realised that they were guests and that our organisation was footing the bill for golf and dinner, so for most of the evening the arguments were only *slightly* less than polite and when they occasionally did head towards belligerence, somebody would step in and turn the conversation back to Ted's bet in the Gosford Flying. There were, however, a couple of verbal incidents in which accusations reverberated loudly around the large clubhouse and when Warren Saunders and I were called upon to act as referees. 'The trouble with your mob,' called a distinguished man in his late 50s, a valued client who owned a large manufacturing business, 'is that they believe they have been born to rule. They have sat on their fat bums for over 20 years, coasted along doing bugger-all for the country and then when at last the Australian people said "Enough", and kicked them out, they go and use some devious legal ploy to get rid of the rightful Government. It is shameful. We may as well be living in Nazi Germany'.

The object of the manufacturer's rage was his playing partner, a young man in his very early 30s who, with a touch of entrepreneurial enterprise and the help of a large bank loan, had started a trucking business. 'Whaddya mean, Nazi Germany?' he said. 'For the last three years Labor 'as been tryin' to turn Australia into Soviet Russia. They want to kill little businesses and 'ave everything owned by the fuckin' Government.'

The man sitting beside the two looked on quizzically at the confrontation. He grinned and interrupted, 'That's correct, Commissar Cairns is soon to be placed in charge of the five-year plan to increase egg production'.

Most of the arguments were muted, yet as I walked around the clubhouse it was like being in the middle of the bush in the heat of summer where, when one fire is extinguished, another breaks out a few seconds later. There was one incident which would have no doubt led to fisticuffs but for the intervention of 'referee' Saunders. A successful engineer, whose best days were well and truly behind him, had a sub-contract drainer pinned to a wall and was banging his finger against the drainer's chest. One finger turned into two and then two began turning into a fist. The engineer was in a state of red-hot anger, shouting that Gough Whitlam was the greatest statesman that the country had ever known. The drainer, a very strong young man who was showing great patience by not using a fist of his own, answered rather laconically, considering the situation, 'I reckon Whitlam should not only have been sacked but thrown into bloody Lake Burley Griffin as well'. Saunders stepped in between the two, led them to the bar and after buying three large beers (by this stage of the evening, Warren badly needed a drink himself), managed to settle things down.

As I sit here, over 24 years later, thinking about those hours, I am still confused. Obviously, we did not take a poll on how each person felt about the Dismissal, so I am relying on anecdotal evidence and a memory which, in the intervening years, has become a shade too selective and ravaged by an over-indulgence in alcohol. However, given the fact that our guests were people who mostly ran their own businesses, or who were employees influential in such businesses, I would make so bold as to guess that if a poll had been taken that night, the result would have been 60/40 pro the Fraser-led conservatives — or maybe 60/40 'anti-Labor' would be a better way to put it. Yet no matter what their political colour, everyone remained bewildered by Kerr's action in sacking the Government and appointing Fraser as prime minister.

At our gathering, the supporters of each side did not fall into the pattern that had, over the years, been so stereotyped by the press and the cartoonists. Those in favour of the Dismissal included many who worked with their hands, albeit in their own (small) businesses. Among those who stood against Kerr's action, there were quite a few who controlled large firms, two who were on the boards of listed public companies. It seemed the blue-collared 'tradesman' was tilting to the Right, while others, who in days past would be depicted as 'bloated capitalists', were marching more with Henry Lawson's army of the Left.

When Warren Saunders first went into the insurance business he was given some very sound advice by his father, Frank (Fatty) Saunders, a great old St George Rugby League footballer and a man who had sold insurance all his life. 'Son,' said the father, 'insurance is all about talking to people but there are three subjects that you must never discuss: religion, politics and gambling. If you mention the first two you can lose a prospect in a matter of seconds and if you talk about gambling, your client will begin to think that you're off to punt his premium at Randwick races.' Later, Frank Saunders counselled me in the same vein. Fatty was a wise old man!

I must have instinctively taken heed of Fatty's advice because on the 11th of November 1975, I was accosted by people from both sides — all of whom believed that I agreed with them. 'Mate, this is the best thing that could happen for the country. That arrogant Whitlam and his mob are out and now there's nobody to interfere with us little businesspeople. I can get on with business. I can now stand or fall on my own.' I nodded my head wisely, and then went to the bar and bought us both a beer.

'What is our country coming to, Marksy? We used to be proud that we were a democracy and then some bastard who nobody's ever heard of goes and sacks the people's elected representatives. I feel I want to leave the country.' I nodded my head wisely and then went to the bar and bought us both a beer. There were a lot of people who got drunk that night at Pennant Hills Golf Club.

At the end of the night, the mood was mellow and although politics lingered at the forefront of many minds, the heat had gone from the arguments. There was to be an election in a month, it would all be sorted out then. Bob laughed and spoke about the diversion which prevented him sinking the 'gimme' putt on the 9th and Ted eventually found out who won the Gosford Flying, though the bad news was, it wasn't the horse he'd backed. The stars had glowed bright for some hours and it was time to go. Tomorrow was another day and next year there would be another golf day. We had also received a request from the engineer and the drainer that they be paired together in 12-months time, because now they were good mates again. Gradually, the inebriated guests wended their weary paths home.

Yet, to the end the old Aussie sense of humour was alive and kicking. As the last few of the guests walked through the door and we began to lock up, I heard one of them say, 'Gough is lucky — he can sleep-in tomorrow. I've got to get up early and go to bloody work.'

FIVE

THE 'ALL-AMERICAN' BOY

This is not an Australian story, although Australia plays an important part in it. It is a story of *our* times, nevertheless. It is the story of Max, an All-American boy, who was torn between two eras and who did not understand either of them. And it is a story of his country, America, with all its power and influence, which, like Max, lost its way. It is a tale of a time still too close to those involved to produce a verdict; a time that history will eventually judge. Yet even then care will be needed, for history's judgements are too often made by those with ulterior motives, by those who wish to prove a point about today ... by giving their own biased interpretation of yesterday. The background of the story goes back to the days when I was a small boy, when life was an adventure and the world was wide.

+ + +

One of the clearest memories of my childhood is of sitting in my uncle's bedroom reading the *Saturday Evening Post. The Post* (as it was known) was a glossy American news magazine, popular because of its excellent short stories and its syrupy, slightly jingoistic articles on politicians, businessmen and entertainers. It was also noted for its high-class full-page colour advertisements showing luxuries of the American way of life. In ration-plagued Sydney these were the cause of much drooling and envy. Yet, as a little boy at the end of World War II, the two things I most remember about *The Post* were its covers and its cartoons. The latter consisted of single panel drawings which poked fun at the very way of life that the articles and ads glorified. For example: a large man smoking a cigar, standing with his hand on the shoulder of a pimply faced teenager. Nearby, looking on, was a rather nervous looking group of employees whom the large man addressed with these encouraging words: 'My son here is joining the firm today and after thinking long and hard, I have decided to start him at the bottom — so I'm putting him in charge of this department.'

The covers of *The Post* were an art form in themselves — classics in their style, creating a genre later emulated by others. Norman Rockwell was the greatest of *The Post's* artists and though his paintings could not be compared to Van Dyke, Monet or Turner, they captured, in a homespun way, the beauty of the New England landscapes which he knew and loved and the idiosyncratic and very parochial lifestyle of its inhabitants. When a Rockwell painting was on the cover of *The Post*, weekly sales rose by 50 per cent. Norman Rockwell became an American icon and it was because of him that as a little boy 10 000 miles away in Sydney, I fell in love with the New England area of the United States of America.

The little boy grew up and married — and after the kids left home, began to travel. One day the childhood fantasies of the little boy became real — and he visited New England. That little boy was me. Herself and I had decided to book a coach tour, basically because I refuse to drive a car on the wrong side of the road, and our trip combined a historical tour around the battlefields of the north-east with a tour of New England in the fall (autumn). It was an experience that fully lived up to our expectations. The autumn colours were breathtaking, the weather was kind and in a land populated by almost 300 million people I often felt at peace and at home.

We strolled through the villages and small towns I had once seen on the covers of *The Post* and when we visited the Norman Rockwell Museum and then sauntered around the painter's home town of Stockbridge, Massachusetts, a feeling of wistfulness overcame me; a sense of journey's end. Yet, notwithstanding all the nostalgia and beauty, the time that touched me most was our few hours in Gettysburg.

It was late in the day when we arrived at our olde-worlde hotel in Gettysburg and after dumping the luggage in our room, I ripped the bottle of 12-year-old malt whisky out of the carry bag and headed for the ice machine. Soon after the blessed liquid crashed against the rocks, I was renewed in spirit and debilitating torpor was no longer my constant companion. On the bus that day, somebody had announced that there was to be a full moon during the night, along with a partial eclipse — although another disputed the statement, saying it was next month that the eclipse was due. An argument ensued but most of us were too tired to care. Gettysburg is a small town which has an English look about it and although it is a little 'touristy' I felt a certain spooky ambience of dramatic days long gone and the eerie sensation of hair rising up the back of my neck. Let me tell you, imagination can run wild when one has spent the day in close association with torpor, has just 'skolled' a stiff malt scotch and suspects that, at the witching hour, there is to be an eclipse of the full moon.

Our group met that evening, for a candlelight dinner in a 'duck your head as you walk up the stairs' pre-Civil War building which had been transformed into a restaurant. The food was excellent and we sat in a curtained alcove with two of our travelling companions, Linda and Bob. We tucked into the four courses and drank the booze — and while the candlelight flickered we reminisced about our youth. Linda spoke of her high school formal, her dress of many petticoats and her football hero-boyfriend with the yellow Corvette sports car. Eventually, Linda married the football hero but after a couple of years both realised the marriage was wrong and they agreed to a divorce. Later she married Bob, a man dealing in machines that fly and who could best be described as an aerial entrepreneur. Bob owns his own plane and spends most of his days jetting around the world, with Linda sitting up the blunt end. They move to and from the continents of the globe, dealing regularly with the movers and shakers of the world. Yet as the candle burnt low that evening, Linda spoke with a faraway look in her eye, drank a little more than her limit and swung in her mood from nostalgia to melancholy. Ahead, she could see only more of the same; and what others would regard as an exciting and stimulating lifestyle, to Linda, was becoming tiring and mundane. So, when the mood takes her these days, she yearns for times that have gone; days when she struggled to rearrange her cluster of petticoats within the tiny cabin of a Corvette; when life was like a short story in *The Post* and the future was perfect. Gettysburg has that effect on people — it makes them remember!

After dinner we walked back through the old town under a yellow moon and my hair and my neck kept reminding me that they were still there.

I don't know whether there was an eclipse or not but my head throbbed all night — not, I suspect, from what I had drunk but rather from the large yellow globe beaming down on a little town so deeply engrained in the psyche of all Americans. After returning from dinner, I crawled into bed quickly but, as I tossed and turned, my imagination took control.

The moon shone over Gettysburg that night as ghostly soldiers rose from their graves and re-fought the battle of long ago; a battle of carnage and suffering. Shadows moved across the moon; shadows of figures that changed the world forever, yet the suffering continued. Tomorrow, I thought, I will witness the battle in daylight when, in the chill of a magnificent morn, I stand on top of a hill and look down on a vista of fields with a grove of trees in the background. But that is tomorrow when the moon is gone!

At 7.30 am, the local guide met us on top of a tiny hill known as 'Little Round Top'. He was a small man with smiling eyes, who talked with the knowledge of quiz king Barry Jones, and at the pace of racecaller Johnny Tapp describing a Flying Handicap. However, he had a Southern accent. 'And them little old boys from Alabamy, came a-chargin' up that thar hill, a-wavin' Confederate flags and a-screaming Rebel yells,' he told us.

Our guide brought the battle alive in all its goriness and all its glory. He told the story of twin boys born a moment apart, who died a moment apart. He told of a low ranking engineer who, against all protocol, called for reinforcements to protect Little Round Top and by so doing saved the North from defeat. His commentary affected us all — in different ways. Some regarded it as just another coach tour lecture, while others saw it as an on-the-spot history lesson, then there was a small minority of us who were *there*. We saw the Battle of Gettysburg happening; the bravery and the futility.

We moved down from Little Round Top and stood where the Northern troops had waited behind a small brick wall, on the third and final day of the battle. The South's general, Robert E. Lee, desperate for victory, made the most monumental military blunder since some idiot at Balaclava called to the assembled Light Brigade, 'Let's ride this way, chaps!'.

After an artillery bombardment, Lee ordered his troops to charge the Yankee guns across an open field, once an orchard, and what followed was slaughter in its most cataclysmic form, as precision rifle fire and cannon with the cruellest of ammunition — (nails, bits of steel, parts of bricks, pieces of sharp wire and worse) — ripped the Rebels to pieces. A daring Southern swashbuckler, long blond hair streaming down his back, Pickett by name, led the charge across the field with foolhardiness and egotistical bravado but, undeniably, with immense courage. Upon a magnificent white stallion rode Pickett, waving his sword in the air and challenging the Yankees to shoot him down. The Northeners didn't shoot Pickett, but they won the battle and they won the war.

Our guide did not tell us what happened to Pickett, for which I am sorry. Before the Civil War Pickett probably owned a cotton plantation where he ran slaves in business hours and at night made love to beautiful Southern belles. That day at Gettysburg, though, was the end of the era; Robert E. Lee, Scarlett O'Hara, slavery and the Confederacy were finished. Yet for a few magnificent moments, blond hair flying, sword sparkling in the sun, his white stallion rearing high, Pickett made sure that the Old South went down in a blaze of heroic glory. Perhaps the progeny of Pickett are influencing the affairs of the South to this day, with deeds of derring-do. Perhaps, in the heat of the afternoons, on many a weathered old porch in Kentucky and Alabama men and women with the blood of rebel ancestors still coursing through their veins, are raising a mint julep to the memory of the South's greatest cavalier. Meanwhile, Pickett's statue stands, stark and splendid in a place of honour in Richmond, Virginia, waiting for the Old South to rise again.

Despite the brave efforts of Pickett and his cohorts, the Rebels were forced to retreat to the safety of their lines, behind the grove of trees. It was far too late! More than 6000 Southern troops lay dead on the killing field of Gettysburg and, after the battle, it was possible for observers to walk across the field from body to body without their feet ever touching the ground.

Before we stepped back onto the bus, some of us strolled over and tipped our guide for his fascinating 'call' of the Battle of Gettysburg.

'Any more of these today?' I asked.

'Seven,' he replied.

'Same stories?'

'More or less.' He smiled. 'Same guys keep winning.'

The old bore who sat in front of us on the coach and who lived so far north of the Mason-Dixon Line that he was domiciled almost in Canada, heard the conversation and remarked, 'And a damn good thing they did!' Maybe. But tell that to the bride of the dead Irishman who had volunteered to fight for the South a few days after they had married and emigrated from

Dublin. Tell it to the mother of the twin boys or to the fiancée of the 19 year old who had his balls blown off. Tell it to the horses who had to be put down, after lying for agonising hours in pools of blood with shrapnel and bayonets lodged in their hides. Tell it to the man from South Carolina who lived till he was 83 with one arm, one leg and no eyes. Or to the bloke who owned the orchard and to the little drummer boy. Tell it to those who inflicted fatal wounds on their fellow Americans and had to live with the guilt of it for the rest of their lives. Tell it to Max, who was born 90 years later but who knows and understands and who came back onto the bus crying.

+ + +

I didn't like Max when I first saw him. To be precise, I heard his voice before I actually looked at him and I immediately placed him away in the filing system of my brain under the category of 'Smart-arses'. It was the first evening of our American coach tour and the group had met at the Vista Hotel, Washington, DC, for what is known in the trade as a 'welcome drink'. Our guide for the coming two weeks had given us the required spiel about listening to instructions, being on time, loving thy neighbour, not peeing in the coach's toilet unless you were on medication of severe diuretics and a couple of other things which I have now forgotten. Then she asked a rhetorical question. 'I guess everybody's here?'

From the back of the room came a voice, 'Anyone who's not here, please put up their hand'. Herself raised her eyebrows and gave me one of her 'uh, oh, we've got one of *those*' looks.

I glanced back and spotted the culprit. Sitting next to an elderly woman and grinning, waiting, it seemed, for the chance to fire off another 'brilliant' one-liner, was a man who looked to be in his early forties, dressed in a casual collared shirt and jeans. He wore a larger than normal hearing aid, possessed kind eyes and a face which, though just a mite short of being handsome, would probably be described by most as good-looking in an All-American sort of way. His dark blond hair was swept back reaching the nape of his neck, from which point it was pulled tightly together and tied in a wispy ponytail that dropped down and rested along the line of his backbone. The effect of this ponytail was slightly incongruous considering his middle-class looks; it was akin to seeing a bishop wearing a Merv Hughes moustache. I noticed later that he walked with a pronounced limp.

Early in the tour, I spoke occasionally to Max and to the charming woman — who turned out to be his mother, but neither he nor I made any real endeavour to get close and the conversations were mostly flippant, though he did tell me he was 51, which surprised me, as he looked far younger. He mentioned that he had once journeyed to Australia and that both the country and its people had meant much to him. I didn't pursue this comment, as we were the only Aussies on the trip and, as a result, were the object of great curiosity among our fellow passengers. After all it's not every day that ordinary Americans can gaze with impunity on a peculiar species from another hemisphere! And, although we were always polite, we were becoming a little disgruntled answering questions about Crocodile Dundee or whether we fed our pet kangaroo dinners of 'those cute little coca-cola bears who live up trees and carry their joeys in their pouch!'. It was not until Gettysburg that Max began to fascinate me. 'You're interested in Max aren't you?' smiled Herself. I nodded . . . a man can be married too long.

A couple of days later, the coach stopped at a beautiful national park. We stepped from the vehicle into an attractive shop–coffee lounge, bought coffee in plastic cups and walked out onto a balcony overlooking a lovely lake. I beckoned to Herself, and headed to the table where Max and his mother were sitting.

He was drinking his coffee from one of those popular polypropylene cups with a pointed spout — a drinking utensil with a type of horizontal straw which the Yanks use frequently to transport their beloved coffee. Written on the outside of the black cup, in white lettering, were the words, 'Vietnam Helicopter Crew Members' Association'. I commented on the drink holder and he replied that it was one of his few souvenirs of the war. We sat on a wooden bench beside a long wooden table, drank our coffee, ate doughnuts and looked onto the beautiful little lake. The day was cloudless and warm, a weeping willow bent low and dipped into the water, autumn bestrode the landscape. Then, with some reluctance, Max began to tell his story.

+ + +

Max's father was of Polish extraction, brought up in the less-salubrious suburbs of Detroit, where a quick fist was far more effective than a thousand reasoned arguments and where a man could abuse the law but never the Flag. He was a proud veteran of the Korean War — serving as a flight mechanic, before returning home to his family and then moving to California and getting on with life. Max idolised his father and grew up in a happy home with his parents and younger brother.

In 1966, in the most powerful country in the world, life for the middle class was probably better than it had ever been. For Max it certainly was. By then he had completed college, had married his schoolgirl sweetheart and was looking forward to a career in commerce. Yet just beneath his calm and pleasant exterior there were stirrings inside Max — an ache for adventure. Max wanted to crank up his pulse and kick-start his adrenalin. He yearned to follow a star and conquer the world.

There were also stirrings in the most powerful country in the world but these were no longer below the surface; they were now bubbling away on top because thousands of miles from California, in a place called Vietnam, young Americans were dying. Young men had died in battle far from home in the past but they had, at least, been sure they were fighting for a just cause. In Vietnam, however, there were many who were not so sure. Some of those with doubts and many who believed that the Government was radically wrong, began shaking the foundations of the democratic system and even storming that impregnable citadel of patriotism. The foundations wobbled and gaps appeared in the walls. America became divided as it had not been since the days of Gettysburg.

Those who became known as the 'Silent Majority' would have no truck with those who questioned America's policy. 'My country right or wrong,' they declared, not always silently. Max believed unreservedly that his country was right. This is what he had been taught by his father; and, after all, hadn't President Johnson been elected by a huge majority and wasn't he not only the President but also Commander-In-Chief? Moreover, Max was a supporter of the 'Domino Theory' and believed that democracy would be gobbled up by communism if Uncle Sam didn't march out and protect the weak of the world. Max had read about the French being annihilated in Vietnam and knew of their message to the US — not to fight in the steamy jungles of South-East Asia. But, Max, like his Government, ignored the warning. When he thought of Vietnam, his adrenalin began pumping fiercely and in his bones he felt that the star he was destined to follow shone brightly over Hanoi. So Max enlisted.

As the pace of enlistment was quickening, the army was having difficulty recruiting men of sufficient calibre to lead the ever-increasing numbers that were required. As a result 'pressure cooker' programs were established to overcome the shortage. One of these was a scheme known as the 'Warrant Officer Program' which was, metaphorically, a 'McDonald's for officers'. A recruit entered the back door, was rushed through a few weeks of training, then walked out the front door with pips on his shoulder and buck privates saluting him. Max opted for such a course, was accepted, and in a few weeks walked through the front door, an officer in the United States army.

In the course of his training Max had been introduced to helicopters, which he instantly recognised as an adventurous and glamorous way to fight a war. The army had come to the realisation that choppers were best flown by those who had no fixed wing experience and were encouraging recruits to embark on flying courses. Again Max was sent to school and this time, when he emerged, he had his 'wings'.

His preparation ended, Max was sent to Vietnam. In his whole life he had never felt more vibrant and alive. Soon he was flying magnificent machines, making new friends and serving his country on the field of battle against the 'forces of evil'.

Max's job comprised flying into the combat zones, dropping his cargo and flying away as fast as he could before the enemy had time to blast him out of the sky. While the battles raged in the jungles, Max slept securely at night, in a well-protected compound, with all the comforts of home. This is not to say that there were not dangers associated with his duties — it was just that the dangers were mainly confined to business hours.

Before long Max had flown 195 hours without suffering a scratch. But the safety of a chopper pilot in Vietnam diminished the more hours he flew ... the law of averages came into play. There came a day, when he was flying to the combat zone to deliver troops and ammunition, that Max lost control of his machine — and it began to spin around like a feather in a gale. He fought with the controls, but could not stop the machine from its downward spiral. At the last moment, using every ounce of his strength, Max managed to steer the chopper into some sandbags, lessening the shock as the spinning machine came down.

Among the ammunition he was carrying was a box of C–4 plastic explosives capable of destroying half a city block if set off. As the helicopter hit the sandbags these explosives should have detonated, obliterating the machine, all those in it and anyone within a radius of 150 yards. It was the instant before the chopper hit the ground that Max remembered the C–4 explosives and thought in that moment he would die in an enormous burst of flame. They were his last thoughts as he lapsed into unconsciousness at impact.

Despite the cushioning effect of the sandbags, the helicopter was ripped apart as it hit the ground, and a young lieutenant died. When he eventually awoke, Max was lying in a field hospital in a place called Qin Noy. How did I not die? he thought. 'Thank you God, thank you, for the miracle of the non-explosion,' he prayed quietly. Within two days Max, encased in a plaster cast, was flown to the Philippines. His femur was crushed, there was internal damage and his hearing was severely impaired. From the Philippines he was flown to Hawaii for two difficult operations; post-operative complications set in, causing constant chest pains and back spasms. For a time Max's life was threatened but after a painful and traumatic period he pulled through. Even so, the war had ended for him and he knew he would never return to Vietnam. When he had recovered enough to be mobile again, Max was declared unfit for military service and flown back to California to recuperate. Though his star remained in the sky it was now only for looking at ... no longer for following.

Gradually, Max recovered, physically at least — but the body was only part of the problem. Now, the greatest pain that he faced was in his mind and his feeling of guilt became chronic. He was responsible for killing a stranger and injuring others through his own stupidity (through 'pilot error' as he had been told officially). How could he live with himself? His wife tried to understand but she struggled to comprehend when Max turned his guilt upon her. And what about his pals back in 'Nam? They still had to continue the job while he was sitting back in sunny California. His pals and other young Americans were out there fighting for their country while Max was 'unfit for military service' — a failure.

At night, sleep came with difficulty and when Max eventually did nod off, the nightmares began. He was once again in the spinning chopper, trying to steer it into the sandbags and knowing he was going to die. Then he would wake up ... and remember that it was somebody else who was dead. That was the worst part; knowing that he had been spared for a reason and not understanding why.

Max would carry the baggage of these physical and mental scars through many years, the baggage becoming heavier as the years passed by. Nevertheless, at 25 he persuaded himself that a new life lay ahead — such things as free university education (thanks to the GI Bill), a return to married life and, soon, children. He accepted lifetime medical benefits in lieu of a cash settlement (despite the fact that the army had pushed for the settlement) and attempted to start again. Max was soon to learn that what he had been through in the last 18 months was no more than a practice session compared with what was to come.

+ + +

In wars past, America's returned soldiers had been treated as heroes. The attitude of many Americans towards the Vietnam War and its men was, however, the antithesis of this attitude. Despite all the pain and the guilt he was suffering, Max believed that the one blessing which had emerged from his ordeal was that he had, at least, earned respect from his family, peers and society at large. It took a single night for this illusion to be shattered. Soon after he returned to California, in the time of his rehabilitation, Max's family took him out to a classy restaurant for dinner. Max arrived in his uniform, partly to enhance his self-esteem and partly to impress his father. The night turned out a tragedy. Unbeknown to Max, his brother had become an anti-war agitator and had joined a hippy community. While Max stood at the bar that night wearing his well-pressed uniform, on which were pinned a Purple Heart and other medals of service, his bearded brother slumped in a chair clothed in a crushed, garish ensemble from which hung dozens of strange looking beads. As the night progressed his brother began to abuse Max, accusing him of supporting 'the fascist policies' of the United States Government and suggesting he would be happy if he never saw Max again. What made matters worse was that the staff at the restaurant never seemed to look him in the eye when serving the meals and drinks and answered his questions only in monosyllabic grunts. Many of the patrons of the restaurant seemed to have the same attitude and although his parents were supportive, Max eventually left in a state of shock. From that night Max stopped wearing his uniform.

Worse was to come when Max went to university. He was mortified when some undergraduates yelled at him and called him 'a baby burner', clicking their heels together and giving him a Nazi salute. At least he could hit back at such people. What he couldn't respond to were those who turned away when he came into their space, those who uttered single word answers and whispered behind his back. There were other occasions, too, when Max was shoved and spat upon, leading to nasty confrontations, verbal and physical. Disenchanted, Max left the university and took a job.

His wife had no idea how to handle the situation and became upset and confused. She could see that Max was doing well in overcoming his physical infirmities — so why couldn't he stop worrying and live his life like the rest of their community? Yet, ticking away beneath the surface, was an enormous feeling of frustration and confusion and always the guilt. Max *did* stop talking about the war, mainly because he didn't know what to say and, anyway, nobody really wanted to listen. During the day Max went about his business and kept his fears bottled ... often by opening a bottle. But in the wee small hours the nightmares continued.

Through this period of his life, the only good thing to happen to Max was the birth of his son. Suddenly there was someone to love, and for a time Max felt as if life was good after all. With love, though, comes responsibility and in a short time, this, too, began to weigh heavily on Max as he saw the child progressing while he was regressing, too often finding solace in drink. He saw too a troubled wife who was doing the best she could, but saddled with a husband who wasn't. And always there was the guilt (I killed a man) and the question (Why did *he* die and not me?).

Eventually the dejected, volatile husband became too much for the naive, demoralised wife, and she filed for divorce and took the little boy with her. If previously Max's life had been a journey downhill, it now became a toboggan slide from the summit of a slippery mountain. He didn't see much of his son or his parents and ignored his old friends. He threw himself into his jobs, working long hours seven days a week — not for reasons of money or ambition — but because Max had discovered that work was the best place to hide. He continued to drink, rationalising it as self-medication, although he never became 'rolling down throwing up' drunk, just keeping the alcoholic intake at a level which partly assuaged the guilt and made him feel pleasantly sorry for himself. In the years after his divorce, Max had many jobs, around 40 in 23 years. These were mainly in the sales area but whenever work colleagues or clients became too friendly, he would move on. Max left some very highly paid positions because people had discovered his hiding place.

During this 'toboggan period' of his life the guilt manifested itself in rage. Max began to hate his fellows and his Government, after all were they not the reason that he wore hearing aids and the cause of his limp? Of course they were! They had made him suffer and now they hated him for doing the job that they asked him to do. Well fuck 'em all! So he began to carry a gun and run other cars off the road if they got in his way. He picked fights, mostly with blokes bigger than he was — and lost most of them. He raged at the world and shook his fist at God. It didn't make him feel any better but it made him forget for a while.

Occasionally, he would come in contact with other Vietnam veterans and at those times he found that talk was helpful because they had the same problems. They, too, felt alone, that nobody understood, and, worst of all, shared a sense of guilt. Like Max, though, these vets shied away from friendship and from talking of their deepest fears.

Despite all the bile that had built up inside him and his penchant for changing jobs, Max was still able to earn enough money to live reasonably. For despite everything, there still remained in Max the All-American boy, the clean-cut personality who could charm others with his eloquent speech and sparkling smile. But, as he drifted around the cities and towns of the land that he once loved deeply, Max was not quite sure himself what was real and what was facade. His good looks and eloquence sometimes charmed women back to his room for the night, but in the morning Max would buy breakfast, say a hurried goodbye and conveniently forget to leave any forwarding address. Then he met someone who was as mixed up as he was and after a short time they married.

The attraction was based on communication; each would take a turn at talking and each would take a turn at listening. Wife Number 2 had been through her own form of hell, with broken relationships and drug problems. She understood something of what Max was suffering and related well to him. Talking about Vietnam had a therapeutic effect on Max and he began to expose some of his fears and discuss the nightmares. Slowly, it dawned on him that by trying to forget he had actually heightened the problem. From this starting point, Max moved to the position of thinking about how the problem could be resolved. Meanwhile, his wife continued to talk of *her* problems, though she would change the subject when Max suggested that they both take genuine steps to overcome, or at least minimise, these problems. Before long the relationship fell apart as Max began to seek the remedy, while his wife wanted only to discuss the illness. The marriage ended in divorce. Again Max felt guilty; his wife had begun the process of cleansing and had started him thinking a little more clearly, even though this was not what she had intended. However, the guilt remained. Max felt he had let yet another person down.

Max was now seeing more of his son and communicating far more with his parents, who had done their best all along to understand and help with his problems. It had been particularly hard for the father to relate to the son's troubled state. Max's Dad had fought a war which had not been easy but the war experiences had never become part of his psyche, just a couple of years spent in another world with good comrades, fighting the enemy — fading snapshots in memory's album. As the father saw it, his son had also been through a war, but a war that was now well and truly over. Try as he did, the father could not understand why, nearly 20 years later, his boy was still so greatly affected by it. Discussing the problem over a drink one day, Max's Dad lost his temper and shouted, 'You guys are just a bunch of cry babies'. Max was hurt by the comment and tried to explain by equating the Vietnam War with World War II and Korea. His Dad shook his head and said quietly, 'Son, don't try to compare your war with ours. The difference is, you guys lost.'

That was the unkindest cut of all. Max considered he was hated by most of society but now he realised he was shunned by his own kind, the veterans of other wars — not because of what he had done but because he had been beaten.

Twice divorced, guilty and disillusioned, Max decided to take a break. He needed to leave the country that he no longer loved and that no longer loved him. His aim was to get as far away as possible, so he booked a flight to Australia.

+ + +

As the coach trip moved towards its last days I became more friendly with Max. Often we would have coffee together, me out of a plastic cup and he out of his Helicopter Association container. On the penultimate day of our journey we sat up the back of the coach and talked for a couple of hours. I also talked to Max's mother, in a gondola travelling up and down a mountain in the White Mountains of New Hampshire. She spoke proudly and touchingly of her son and of her now dead husband and, like most Mums, only wanted what was best for her children.

'You have helped Max by taking an interest in him and listening,' she remarked when we reached the top of the mountain.

'Well he has a very interesting story to tell,' I replied.

'Yes I guess you could say it's ... (she shrugged her shoulders) ... interesting.' Smiling, she continued. 'Anyway, he wants to give you a present.'

I was embarrassed. 'That's certainly not necessary. Please tell him not to bother.'

She smiled again. 'Oh well, that's Max. It may not seem so on the surface, but he's the most giving person I know.'

+ + +

Max had always wanted to go to Australia, though, if asked, he couldn't really explain why. He had certainly read about the country, been impressed by photographs and been inspired by the travel industry hyperbole that Australia was 'the last frontier'. Whatever the reason he made the trip, touching down in Darwin. On his second day of touring, Max was sweating as he had not done since Vietnam and was soon ready for a long cool drink. He asked directions from a passer-by. 'Yeah, by the looks of ya I reckon ya could wrap yaself around a large beer, mate,' came the grinning reply. 'Try the RSL just down the street.'

A trifle bemused, Max replied, 'Excuse me, what is an aresel?'.

'Yank, an RSL's an RSL. Ya drink beer there and meet ya mates. It's just down the street, ya won't miss it.'

When Max found the RSL, he was surprised to realise that it was a large club and even more surprised when the doorman revealed that lack of membership didn't mean that you couldn't have the same privileges as members. A little different from the country club back home, Max thought. 'What does RSL stand for?' Max asked the doorman.

'"Returned Services League". There are hundreds of these all round the country. They were formed and are run by ex-diggers — veterans you'd call 'em — but they are available for use by all Australians and visitors like yourself are always welcome.'

Leaning on the bar, his first Aussie beer tasted magnificent to Max. 'Like another one mate? My shout.' Max looked up to see a casually dressed man in his late 60s, smiling and clutching a large beer himself. Max answered the question in the affirmative.

'Frank at the door says yer over 'ere from the States.' He held out a large hand. 'Bloody glad to meetcha.'

Max took the hand and mutual introductions took place. Their thirst quenched, they exchanged pleasantries. Before long his new acquaintance asked the question. 'I don't mean to sound rude, Max, but I couldn't 'elp noticing ya limp. Were ya in an accident?'

Max was hesitant but he was thousands of miles away from home — they couldn't hurt him here. So he nodded his head and replied, 'Many years ago, while I was in the army.'

The man seemed surprised. 'Where did it happen?'

Instinctively Max lowered his eyes. 'Vietnam.'

'Vietnam,' the Aussie exclaimed, 'I'll be buggered. Vietnam! Hell of a war you boys fought over there and most of the time ya Government had ya hands tied behind ya bloody back.' He lifted his glass in the air, then took a sip, 'Vietnam, eh, good on ya son!'.

He sipped again, then grabbed Max's arm and said, 'Come over and meet the blokes. Don fought at Kokoda, Paddy flew bombers and I fought in the desert meself against Rommel. Hell of a bloody general, Rommel. And ya'll want to meet Muzza. He was in Vietnam, like you.'

They walked over to a table where some ageing, yet tough-looking characters were drinking large beers. Max's new mate did the honours. 'Fellas, the Darwin RSL is honoured today by a visit from a Yank what was shot up in Vietnam. This 'ere is Max.'

The men at the table all stood up and offered their hands. Max stared disbelievingly at the extended hands and the smiling faces and thought, 'My God, I'm a hero!'

By the time he was due to leave Darwin, Max had made many friends, gone home for dinner — 'to meet the missus' — and been presented with the badge of honorary membership of the club, which also entitled him to membership of every other RSL club in Australia ... not that Max couldn't have just walked in anyway.

As he toured Australia, Max found more of the same. The other cities were a far cry from Darwin, with their skyscrapers, tranquil gardens, golden beaches and fine harbours but none of the places Max visited could ever be mistaken for being anywhere *but* Australia. The people in the Eastern States seemed more hurried in their lifestyle than the Darwinians, but beneath the surface was the same basic friendliness and laid-back attitude. 'G'day mate, like a beer?' Max recognised in Australia a bounding vitality, a lack of conventions. Girls in bikinis walked down the main streets of bustling coastal towns — not to flaunt their wares, but just because it was natural to do so. Golf courses abounded, ferries took people to places of business where they worked hard, yet, somehow, leisure was a way of life.

And there was another thing that meant much to Max. Australia had also fought in Vietnam, its sons and daughters had died and the opposition to the war back home had been no less intense than it was in the US. Yet the anti-war attitude was never directed at the fighting men, only at the Government. Australia's pride in its achievements in past wars was palpable — its warriors had always been revered. In such an atmosphere, Max spoke with increasing openness about Vietnam, learning much about Australians, learning of an attitude different to that of his own country.

Sometimes Max would sit in an RSL club and ask questions of Vietnam vets. 'How do you feel now about Vietnam?'

'Nam was shit, my number was drawn out of a barrel, but I'm not angry anymore. I shot at them and they shot back and most of the time we both missed. Those bloody little 'Cong were great jungle fighters, though. Still, I reckon we matched 'em, except they had the advantage of fighting on their own dunghill. One of my group got taken prisoner. That wasn't easy. Another is crippled. He's pretty dirty. A few others didn't come back! Yeah, Nam was shit but I still keep in touch with a few mates and we march together.'

'You march. Where?'

'Anzac Day.'

'What's that?'

'Just a day when all the old diggers march again. The people line the streets in thousands and cheer us and then we go to the club and get pissed.'

'They cheer you?'

'Yeah, it's a tradition. My Grandpop, who's been dead 20 years, used to march. Dad did, too, but he's been crook lately and the doctor won't let him. They got pissed as well.'

It was not long after Max had returned to California that Australians at last became fully reconciled with those who had fought in Vietnam, when a special day was set aside for the vets to march together. The footpaths were packed with cheering onlookers and as the diggers strode along the streets that morning, the volume of tears shed would have ended the drought. In

Sydney, those who participated say that the most moving moment came at the end of the march when former Vietnam vet, pop singer and musical comedy star Normie Rowe appeared on the rostrum. Rowe, who that season was starring in the musical *Les Miserables*, stood in front of the microphone about to sing the show's rousing marching song and if someone had dropped a pin at that moment it would have sounded like a thousand jackhammers:

> *Do you hear the people call, singing a song of angry men,*
> *It is the music of a people who will not be slaves again,*
> *When the beating of your heart echoes the beating of the drums,*
> *A new world's about to start when tomorrow comes.*

Australia had not exorcised Max's demons but it had at least helped him to understand that he should face up to them. He also realised that, despite all the trials and tribulations, he had taken himself too seriously — he hadn't really laughed for years. In Australia he had laughed with and at Australians and they had done the same to him and nobody was hurt. Australians weren't fragile. They could say the rudest and cruellest things about each other and about themselves and everyone would laugh and somebody would fill up the glasses. Sadly, he realised that most Americans couldn't do this and, up until that point, neither could he.

Max was dispirited on the day he flew out of Sydney's Kingsford Smith Airport. He was sorry to leave the beaches and the sun, but sorrier still to leave the people. He was heading home to try and start again in the country he had served, but that had rejected him. Maybe things would change. Yet whatever happened, Max knew that there would be times in the future when he would walk down the street and wish he was somewhere else ... like an RSL club where he could call in and have a beer with his mates.

+ + +

On his return, Max noticed for the first time that attitudes in America were different from those that he had known over the last two decades. Perhaps it was just that he had been too self-absorbed to see the change that had been occurring gradually. The people seemed to be more inward-looking, and conservatism was the dominating doctrine in the halls of power. 'Vietnam' was now the name of a country rather than a cause and the veterans of the war were starting to come out of the closet. The furore of the war years had died down and a mood of 'let bygones be bygones' was prevalent through the land. This reconciliation was endorsed by the American people when they agreed, albeit belatedly, to recognise the contribution made by the hundreds of thousands of men and women who fought in the conflict. A day dawned when these forgotten warriors marched together again.

At first Max didn't even contemplate marching. He had carried too much baggage for too long and, besides, how could he march properly with his limp? Yet something was tugging at his heartstrings. He thought of the kid who died in the chopper, of a laughing people on golden beaches and of what their Anzac Day meant to them and Max thought of his father.

In the 1987 Fourth of July Parade at Huntington Beach, California, Max and thousands of other veterans of the Vietnam War marched in an extraordinary display of passion and pride. The day will never be forgotten by those who witnessed it and for those who took part it was a spiritual experience. The bands played stirring music, the medals glinted in the sunlight and the crowds cheered loudly enough to deafen the gods. The emotion that poured forth gained a power of its own. Old Glory fluttered straight from the tops of buildings, seemingly without the benefit of a breeze. Adults cried and babies laughed. Kids who had not been born at the time these soldiers were at war waved flags and jumped up and down as if Santa was about to come around the corner leading the next platoon. And through the immense throng moved patriotism, intangible yet living — risen again.

Max was swept away in the euphoria. He heard the cheers, saw the flags and accepted the tears. He felt no limp, no bile, no guilt. It was a sublime moment, the band played and the soldiers of Nam marched as one:

When the beating of your heart echoes the beating of the drums,
A new world's about to start — when tomorrow comes.

And above the drums and the cheering he heard America calling, 'Welcome home, Max! Welcome home!'

+ + +

His experiences in Australia and the Huntington Beach march had boosted Max's low esteem and alleviated some of his nightmares and he now became more positive about the future. First, he engaged in some entrepreneurial ventures which would allow him to work for himself, rather than remaining the transient employee he had become over the last two decades. Then after a long period of soul-searching, Max decided to embark on a journey into his past and learn the reason for the helicopter crash of so long ago — the real cause of his traumatic life. To face his tomorrow Max realised he would have to come to terms with yesterday. So with a good deal of courage and not inconsiderable trepidation, Max set out on the last leg of his Vietnam journey.

The marches held all around the land had been the turning point for many Vietnam vets and, like Max, these people began to find themselves after two decades. More importantly, they began to find others and soon branches of Vietnam Support Groups grew stronger all around the nation. New friendships were made and old friendships re-formed as veterans began at last to talk about the problems that had burnt away inside them for years, problems they once believed nobody could understand but which they now realised were shared by thousands of others. Seminars and workshops were organised and, later still, the Internet was alight with words of information, help and assistance. As middle-aged men became aware of their mortality, they also realised that they had no wish to spend the rest of their lives, or go to their deaths, with guilt and hatred in their souls.

Max decided he wanted to contact those he had known in Vietnam and especially those who were in the cabin of the ill-fated chopper at the time of the crash. However, first he wanted to read the official report on the crash which, like a million other reports, was locked away in a forgotten vault in the Pentagon, untouched, gathering dust and destined eventually to disintegrate in the misty millenniums of time. Max believed, as an American citizen, that he had the right to access this report under the Freedom of Information Act.

'Freedom' is one of the most misunderstood, complex words in the English language. You are free to walk in the park anytime you wish, yet you can't walk there if they put an electric fence around it and lock the gate. 'Information' is a little like freedom — dependent on the interpretation. It is easy to gather, providing you know where to look and what you're looking for and providing the documents are not controlled by the same people who built the electric fence around the park.

Herein lay Max's problem. As he tried to lay his hands on the official report, he found that every step he took was thwarted by some army bureaucrat. The 'powers that be' knew that the helicopter fell out of the sky, knew that the cause was 'pilot error' and knew there was a report but, for some unaccountable reason, they couldn't find it.

Every time Max seemed to be getting close to the report, another fence went up. As the weeks turned into months, he became more frustrated at what appeared to be, at best, bureaucratic bungling or, at worst, deliberate stalling by the army. Max was mystified and frustrated by the whole exercise. All that he wanted was a copy of a report; a document of concern only to himself, of no possible consequence to the rest of humanity. It wasn't as if he was trying to steal the secrets of the latest Stealth Bomber! Eventually, with assistance from the Vietnam Vets lobby and some political arm-twisting, he broke through and received a copy of the elusive report.

At about this time, one of Max's business ventures had failed, forcing him into bankruptcy, a situation which caused him more worry and stress. The report, when it surfaced, added to the trauma. If Max had been required to face these events ten or twelve years before, he would probably have tried to bomb the Pentagon in his rage. Now, inoculated by the experience of past suffering and strengthened by his recent dialogues with Vietnam peers, he was more mellow, a little more objective. The financial matters would be handled, he could overcome these; he had faith in his ability and had learnt by the experience. On the other hand though, the official report was like a grenade exploding in the centre of a life that was just beginning to come together again. Nevertheless, he sat down determined to read it dispassionately and then sit back and think about how to handle the situation. As he reached the report's final sentence, his brain was awash with turmoil. Objective as he tried to be, he could not avoid the mixed feelings of disgust, extreme rage and relief. Nor could Max prevent the sorrow that overcame him and the tears that welled up inside and poured down his cheeks, like the rivers rushing over the falls at Niagara.

+ + +

Max's search did not end with the report. His investigation continued and the more information that came to the surface, the more he became disillusioned and angry. For the reality of the situation was that Max had been deliberately deceived by his own Government, which had lied to him so that it would not be seen to be in the wrong. The report showed the Government to not only have been wrong but also calculating and cruel.

+ + +

Before the helicopter had left its base on the fateful morning, there were mechanical deficiencies that should have been rectified. In simple terms the chopper should not have flown that day. The fact that it was flown and soldiers (as passengers) were allowed to fly in it, was neglect of the highest order; allowing C–4 explosives to be placed aboard and then permitting it to fly over a well-populated base area, was little short of criminal. The report stated that the machine had been in the air for only a few minutes when the bolt came off the tail rotor which, subsequently, snapped the boom, causing the helicopter to spin wildly. The reason that there was not a huge explosion of the C–4 materials — which Max had put down to some inexplicable Heavenly intervention — came down to the young lieutenant who died when the helicopter hit the ground. Keeping cool, despite the wildly spinning machine, the lieutenant managed, somehow, to rip the blasting caps from the top of the explosives, rendering them inoperative just before the crash. Patently there was no 'pilot error' — indeed, the report inferred that if Max hadn't somehow directed the out-of-control machine into the sandbags, everybody on board would have been killed and some soldiers on the ground could possibly be dead as well. Max was not a killer — he was a very competent pilot — and quite possibly a hero. Max's superiors were the ones in error and the Government had compounded the felony by trying to hide the facts.

As Max dug deeper, more facts came to light — for example, the army's phobia about mass litigation and its calculating adroitness at passing the responsibility up and down the chain of command. Nothing, it seemed, was ever the fault of anyone. A bizarre fact unearthed by Max concerned the method of recruitment for the Warrant Officers Program. Researching the background of the recruits, Max was amazed to find that in nearly every case the young men selected for the course appeared to be clean-cut All-American boys and almost all of them were the eldest sons of close families. To Max this seemed more than a coincidence, though army spokespersons regarded it as completely irrelevant. After much pressured investigation, Max finally had it explained to him, off the record. Apparently, the army psychologists had come up with the theory that the eldest son is more inclined to be conscientious in his duties and to feel stronger responsibility for his family than his siblings. This feeling of conscientious responsibility was exactly the sort of attitude the army required from new recruits. The army wanted men who would regard their comrades as brothers and their superiors as a surrogate Mum and Dad. Soldiers who met this classification would obey orders without question, would die for a cause and when things went awry, would blame themselves and carry the guilt.

For a quarter of a century, Max had carried *his* guilt. The burden had been intolerable and it had almost ruined his life. Now at long last he knew that it was not his fault. He could go where he wanted, find his place in the sun and remain there without guilt for the rest of his life. 'We find the defendant not guilty, your Honour, and free to go,' announced the jury of his conscience. But the incident had occurred 25 years ago in a war not known to a new generation of Americans; a war only to be read about in books. It was too late. There was really no place for Max to go ... except where he was.

He discussed litigation with lawyers in the hope that he might gain some compensation for his injuries and for the mental problems which had dogged him, although Max would have settled for an apology, but eventually came to the realisation that litigation could cost him a lot of money with no certain outcome. Anyway, he was too tired. His rage had by now turned to resignation and his hate to cynicism. In the end, he just got on with life. Still, Max didn't want to forget. He wished to protest in some specific way, to show that he disagreed with the hypocritical ethics of those in power — if only to prove something to himself. So the clean-cut All-American boy grew a ponytail!

+ + +

After our last discussion in the back of the bus, we paused for the final comfort stop of the tour. We sat in yet another cafe and drank coffee near the up-market, horse-racing town of Saratoga Springs. Tomorrow the group was splitting up, each of us wending our different ways home. We would not be speaking again, other than to say goodbye.

'Thank you for listening to me,' Max said as the time came to board the bus again.

'Mate, it has been a pleasure,' I responded in words which bordered on cliché but were genuine.

'I'd like you to have this,' he murmured, pushing something into my hand. He put his arm round my shoulder, squeezed it and limped away. I felt a little sad as I slowly raised the black coffee holder and read the inscription again: 'Vietnam Helicopter Crew Members' Association.'

People milled around on this beautiful New England day; the sun was shining and in the background the autumn foliage was only just beginning to lose its colour, splendid still. I tried to take it all in for one exalted moment and wished that someone could capture the scene for me on canvas. Yet, deep down, I knew that could never be. There was only one who could capture this place, this moment ... and Norman Rockwell was long gone.

Six

Cheque Book Journalism

Jon Cleary is one of Australia's most prolific writers of fiction. His stories hold the reader's interest from the first line to the last, the plot stays solid and plausible and the characters, predominantly Australians, are typical but never stereotypes. Yet throughout the storyline runs a thread of humour which even in the most tense of plot situations can make the reader smile, and sometimes cause a belly laugh. It is the humour of our country — laconic, candid and often politically incorrect. In one story, Cleary's wonderful character, Detective Inspector Scobie Malone, and his partner are investigating a murder which takes them to a suburban coffee shop. There they come across four musicians from a well-known rock band who are sitting in a dimly lit booth. In the mode of their industry, all four are wearing dark sunglasses. As the detectives walk past the group, Malone's partner saunters across and sneers, 'Who's your lead singer? A seeing-eye dog?'

In the 1970s, Jon and his wife, Joy, lived in Missouri in the United States for six months, while Jon was writing his book, *Vortex*. Whilst researching his story, Jon came across an interesting fact regarding the music of the Deep South. The moving 'negro spiritual' is widely known to all lovers of music, yet there remain many spirituals and songs from the cotton fields which are still sung regularly though they are heard only in certain areas of the South. When Jon made enquiries about this music he was told that if he wanted to hear some of the original music he would be well advised to visit Mississippi, which could be described as the negro spiritual capital of the world. So when he had a couple of days to spare, Jon journeyed to Mississippi and found himself in a little town not far from Oxford.

'The best spiritual music this side of Heaven can be heard at the church two blocks down the road,' Jon was told by a local. So at 9.55 am the next day, Sunday, Jon arrived at a little white clapboard building and stood in front of the noticeboard. 'The Third Southern Baptist Pentecostal Church Of Born Again Believers — Preacher, Reverend W. R Phipps,' announced the noticeboard.

Jon waited until the large, all-black, congregation had gone inside, then slipped in and stood at the back. Not that his presence passed unnoticed, for he had been there just a few seconds when most of the congregation began turning and staring at him. It then dawned upon Jon that, quite possibly, he was the only white man ever to enter the little church and, what's more, he was probably the first Australian any of the congregation had ever set eyes on.

Then the organ played a note, the congregation stood and through a side door entered a portly man wearing a black robe over a well-cut suit. There was a murmur from the congregation and someone called, 'Yes, Frogmouth'.

The preacher walked up some stairs onto a dais, raised one arm and called to those below, 'Praise the Lord'.

'Hallejulah, praise the Lord,' the congregation called back in unison.

Near Jon an elderly lady shouted, 'God bless you, Frogmouth. God bless you'.

The preacher then raised his other arm, and grinned down on his flock. It was a grin like no other Jon had ever seen. The preacher's lips curled back over his teeth, showing the inside of his mouth, a cavernous aperture that would make the entrance to Luna Park pale into insignificance. Catching the rays of the morning sun, a magnificent set of teeth sparkled in the preacher's mouth. They were large and gleaming white, resembling a row of ivory piano keys upon which Liberace could quite comfortably have played 'Fantasy Impromptu' and then returned for an encore. 'I have spoken to the Lord,' shouted the preacher in a deep baritone voice.

'Tell us about it. Tell us about it, Frogmouth,' shouted the same elderly lady.

'Brothers and sisters, I will tell you everything, but first let us sing in praise of Jesus,' intoned the preacher. The grin spread, the aperture widened and the ivories sparkled. Then the music began. Within a few seconds, Jon realised that his informant hadn't been exaggerating.

It *was* the sweetest music this side of Heaven. If Mahalia Jackson and Paul Robeson had sung in the congregation that day, they would have been just 'one of the mob'. As the notes soared into the atmosphere, the sound lifted the spirits and the melancholy melody misted the eyes. It was the music of a people in bondage, whose bodies were enslaved but whose hearts and souls remained forever free.

The music continued in this vein and then followed the sermon from the Reverend W. R. Phipps. Reverend Phipps pulled no punches.

'Praise the Lord,' shouted a young man nursing a baby. 'Jesus bless you, Frogmouth,' cried the elderly lady.

At the end of the service Jon waited until the preacher was free from his adoring congregation, then walked over and introduced himself. 'I was most impressed with the service, Reverend Phipps,' said Jon.

'Call me Frogmouth,' replied the preacher.

Jon put on his most serious face and continued. 'Frogmouth, I'm an author from Australia researching a book and I was particularly impressed with the lovely spiritual music that I heard sung so beautifully in your church today.'

'That is nice of you to say so, Brother Cleary,' answered 'Frogmouth' Phipps.

Jon had come a long way to glean some information and he wasn't going to spend the rest of the day making small talk, so he got straight to the point. 'Frogmouth, I was hoping that I may be able to speak to you for a short while and ask you some questions about that wonderful music and about your religion.'

'Well I'd be glad to Brother Cleary, although in such cases the church usually receives an honorarium,' (Frogmouth pronounced the 'h' in 'honorarium'.)

Jon is not a fan of chequebook journalism but he wanted the information so he put principles aside for the moment. 'Will you take a cheque, Frogmouth.'

The grin flashed. 'Certainly, Brother Cleary.'

'Twenty dollars?' asked Jon. Frogmouth's grin disappeared and his eyes looked over the Aussie's shoulder.

'Fifty?' The eyes continued to look into the distance and the teeth remained hidden.

'One hundred?' The Reverend's eyes met Jon's and the teeth emerged from their hiding place.

Jon took out his chequebook and pen, saying as he did, 'What is the name of the church again, Frogmouth?'.

The portly preacher replied smoothly, 'The Third Southern Baptist Pentecostal Church Of Born Again Believers'.

Jon stopped writing, looked up at the big man and said, 'I'm sorry, Frogmouth, I won't be able to fit all that on the one cheque'.

The eyes of the preacher glowed happily as he looked at the cheque, the lips wound back and the teeth twinkled like the lights of Broadway. 'Make it out to cash, brother,' said Frogmouth Phipps.

SEVEN

ALL IN THE FAMILY

Fanatical football fans are the same the world over. They vary only in the degree of their fanaticism and their manner of expressing it. These people look at their game with one eye only — an eye which is jaundiced, reflecting vast emotional swings, beaming wildly in moments of exhilarating victory and weeping uncontrollable tears of frustration and humiliation when their team is vanquished. The fanatical fan's demeanour is a mixture of supreme confidence, a dash of naivety, a large helping of intolerance and a serving of gross stupidity. When this personality potion is mixed with envy and alcohol you have a lethal combination waiting to explode — quite capable of causing embarrassment and possibly even physical harm to those nearby.

Although fanatical fans have many similarities, they do not necessarily have physical characteristics in common, nor do occupation, gender, financial considerations, religion or political affiliation have much to do with it. When the weekend comes, they move instinctively to their battlegrounds and set about their fervent involvement in their own particular style. Let me introduce you to some members of the species 'Barrackus Stupidious'. (Although the styles don't vary much from code to code I will use Australia's most popular form of football, Australian Football, or 'Aussie Rules' as it is colloquially known, to make my point.)

Jekyll & Hyde: This species member is always male, though not necessarily one of the most masculine of the gender. Herself once had a relation in Adelaide who fitted perfectly into the category. He was a mild-mannered little man who worked in an office from nine to five every weekday, rearranging papers for a government department. In the evening he would return home and slip quietly beneath the thumb of his tall thin wife. But on Saturdays the world changed for Dr Jekyll! On Saturdays a door would open and he would enter a magic fantasyland of excitement and pseudo-masculinity where he gathered with other members of his tribe to watch his army do battle, an army of which he considered himself an important part. On match day, within moments the mild-mannered paper-shuffler would change into his secret identity and become Mr Hyde, a loathsome bully who, secure in the knowledge that his tribe was always close by, would attack any opposition barracker who happened by wretched chance to wander onto his territory.

'What's it like barracking for [*$!*!!] Torrens — the dirtiest team in the league?' Mr Hyde would sneeringly ask the intruder.

'Are you talking to me, mate?'

'Yeah, I'm talking to you, [*$!*!!]. You've got a long day ahead of you, [*$!*!!], 'cause we're going to thrash you today, even worse than you were thrashed by "The Bays" last [*$!*!!] week.'

Before the first ball had been bounced, people would be dragging the two apart, which was exactly what Mr Hyde always counted on, for if the physical confrontation continued he would have been thrashed in a manner far worse than The Bays had thrashed Torrens the previous week. Mr Hyde really came into his own when he had the opportunity to pick on someone smaller and younger than himself. His 'clever' one-liners were particularly effective in embarrassing ten-year-old fans of the opposition and always gave a good laugh to those around him.

'Do you do maths at school son?' Mr Hyde would smirk at a little boy.
'Yes, sir.'

'Well, if you're good at sums, be so kind as to tell me how many points your team is behind?' (Guffaws of laughter from those nearby.) If as the match progressed, however, Mr Hyde's team began to lose, he would get more personal. 'Why are you here today son? Did Mum send you out so she could be alone with the butcher?' (More laughter.)

As far as insults went Mr Hyde had a million of them. As the umpire came off at half-time he would yell, 'You'll be able to buy a new house with the bribes you've taken, you cheating [*$!*!!].' When the opposition team ran onto the field he would yell in a sing-song voice, 'You're all a bunch of poofters.' And there were others. 'Ya couldn't catch a cold'; 'Hit him where it hurts'; 'Get back to the mission station you [**!!$!!!].' Though, I believe, he would modestly claim that his most effective piece of barracking occurred when the opposition full-forward was moving in to kick for goal and at the vital moment, the effusive Mr Hyde would shout at the top of his lungs, 'Chewy on yer boot!'.

At the end of the game Dr Jekyll never stayed with the tribe for a drink. Precedent had taught him that after a few beers people sometimes become loud and make fools of themselves and besides, his tall thin wife often said that alcohol was only for the masses and was not necessary for 'decent' people. Yes, without doubt, Saturday was Dr Jekyll's favourite day of the week although he didn't mind Sunday and never missed church.

Name-dropper: This fan knows all the players intimately. 'Go get 'im, Shifty!' ... 'Great play, Ginger!' ... 'Macka's hammy is causing him trouble again.'

To Name-dropper no member of his team was ever given a christian name by his mother and none of them had a secret — at least not a secret that was hidden from Name-dropper.

Name-dropper will tell you (providing you promise not to tell anyone else) that: 'Doc', the captain, is having trouble with the committee who for years has been holding the club back; 'Sneezy' is injury prone; 'Happy' is a good team man but lacks the dedication and intensity to ever become a champion; the partner of 'Bashful' is having an affair with Sneezy, though she really has the hots for 'Prince Charming'; 'Grumpy' is causing dissension among the other players and wants Doc's job; 'Sleepy' is good on occasions but cannot be relied upon to play consistently for four quarters; 'Dopey' takes too long to make decisions on the field, always gets caught with the ball, kicks into the man on the mark, passes across the face of goal, leaves his opponent unmarked and is only in the team because his father is chairman of selectors.

It doesn't matter how dull the game may be, if you go to the footy and are lucky enough to sit next to Name-dropper, I promise that you will come away fulfilled and informed. However, you must promise not to tell anyone the closely kept secrets to which you are now privy.

Turncoat: This member of the species arrives at the game well dressed and holding the hand of a little boy who is wearing a team shirt and a beanie knitted in the team colours. The man has followed the team since *he* was a little boy and nowadays takes his small grandson with him to the game as he used to take his son and his own father used to take him. He is the team's most loyal fan, provided they win — but if they lose, watch out!

Unlike Mr Hyde, he doesn't look for a scapegoat in the opposition or among the brigade of umpires, but turns upon his own and when this situation occurs it is indeed a pathetic sight. 'Retire you old pensioner,' he screams at the captain — arguably the greatest player in the history of his club and former Brownlow Medal winner — as he fluffs a mark. 'We paid four hundred thousand for *you*?' he yells to the glamour player of the League. 'You're not worth a case of rotten apples and a packet of boiled lollies,' he continues.

Turncoat is not only quick with the one-liners he is also one of the world's greatest booers. As his team walks from the field defeated and disgraced, Turncoat stands near the race and begins to make his noise.

'Boo-ooo-oo.' In its own kind of way this is a wonderful sound. It is more than a registration of disgust, it is a musical note. The 'ooo' part is clear and melodic and merges with the next 'oo' without an intake of breath. I do not say that Turncoat would be mistaken for Pavarotti but there is no doubting the man's musicality as he holds the last 'ooo' until the players disappear into the bowels of the stand. Meanwhile, his small grandson pulls his beanie down a little lower and wishes he had gone to the movies with his sister.

Kath was the most fanatical footy fan I have ever known. She followed Essendon and had seen all this club's greatest players from John Coleman to James Hird. She missed only one match and that happened to be the day her daughter was born. For years afterwards, Kath insisted that the doctor was a Collingwood supporter and deliberately induced the babe so that Essendon would have one less barracker at the game.

Though she was a pretty person and most ladylike, there was a modicum of Mr Hyde lurking deep inside Kath. I'm not saying that she went looking for confrontations but if the opportunity arose she never took a backward step. Kath wielded her umbrella like D'Artagnan wielded the sword and there was many a Carlton and Collingwood supporter who retired from

Windy Hill, nursing the back of his skull and regretting the insult he had hurled at the men in red and black.

Kath lived in the suburb of Hughesdale which, in Melbourne terms, is about as far away as you can get from Essendon, unless you live in Geelong. Nevertheless, the 'Bombers' were Kath's team and she felt it an obligation and duty to convert all her neighbours, the people in the streets nearby and everybody she met in the Oakleigh shopping centre to the Bombers' cause. She was so successful that this little section of suburbia became an Essendon enclave and many of her converts are still there, wearing red and black and espousing the glories of the great club with the conviction of religious fanatics. So well did Kath's band of disciples understand her that when she returned home one fateful grand-final evening after the Bombers had been beaten, she found a huge black wreath hanging on the door and a brand new cutthroat razor standing on the step.

Although Kath took her footy very seriously, she had a great sense of humour and was never averse to telling a story against herself. Attending most of the social functions and often the players' training evenings, Kath believed that she was a good friend of a few of the players and knew all of them quite well. One day she turned up at the airport to see the team off on their end-of-season trip. Kath was then in her late 30s to early 40s, a pretty and vivacious woman. In her enthusiasm for her team, she kissed one of the players goodbye, not realising that his wife was standing near.

'Who was that?' the indignant wife asked her husband.

And Kath heard his reply. 'I don't know her name. She's just some old bag who hangs around the team.'

Kath died recently. The world lost an enthusiast and Essendon lost a great fan. Neither can afford it.

Tell It How It Is: About five years ago Number 3 daughter was moved to Melbourne by her company and it wasn't long before her new friends were taking her along to the Aussie Rules. After she had been living in the 'Garden State' for a few months, we travelled down to visit her and when the weekend arrived we accompanied Number 3 and two of her friends to the footy.

The game we watched was at Princes Park (now known as Optus Oval), Carlton v North Melbourne. Because our two hosts followed North Melbourne, we were seated in the outer where the North tribe congregated. (It is interesting to note that throughout Australia, whenever a football team has two names, people automatically shorten the title by dropping the last name. In the states where Aussie Rules is the preferred game, North Melbourne becomes 'North', South Adelaide is 'South' and so on. However, in the rugby-playing states the last name is not only dropped but an 's' is added as well. Thus, South Sydney is referred to as 'Souths' and Western Suburbs 'Wests' etc. I have no idea why this is so.)

Anyway, there we were at Princes Park this fine but cool autumn Saturday, sitting in front of the scoreboard among a group of blue-and-white supporters who were screaming for North. Sitting next to us was Pammy.

'Get back to ya kennel ya mongrel,' she yelled to a Carlton player who took a mark close to where we were sitting. 'Kick th' [*!!$*!!] in th' [tender part of his anatomy], Wayne,' she advised one of her North heroes, as she waved her blue-and-white scarf in the air. 'Ya got th' big 'eaded [*!!$*!!] in trouble, North, their bums is draggin' on th' ground.' I turned around to look at the scoreboard and noticed that although their posteriors were apparently rolling the grass, Carlton was leading quite comfortably.

Herself is one of those people who likes talking to people, whether she knows them or not and whether they wish to talk or not. 'How are you? My name is Kay and this is my husband, Marksy,' Herself said to the barracker next to her that day. 'Pleased to meet youse, me name's Pammy,' the woman replied, exhaling a puff of smoke in our direction. Then, seeing something that pleased her in the middle, she jumped from her seat, pointed her finger towards a Carlton player and shouted, 'Stick that up ya Dorotich'.

'You follow North do you, Pammy?' my wife asked. Herself is not only very good at striking up conversations but also excellent at stating the obvious.

'Yeah, North is a family club. Not like bloody Carlton which is run by Elliott and all them business tycoons who are up 'emselves. All us at North are part of th' family.' Once again she did the drawback and we passively received the outcome a moment later.

As the game continued, so did Pammy's commentary. She was a woman in her mid 60s, weather-beaten and showing her age. Her hair was blonde in clumps with other colours peeping through here and there. She smoked incessantly and inhaled so deeply that I gained the impression that she had not only impaired the health of her lungs but could have caused serious damage to the gaps between her toes as well.

I was quietly watching the ebb and flow of the game, when she turned to me and yelled, 'Johnny's done it again. 'E's killin' 'em'.

'Who's Johnny?' I asked.

'Johnny Longmire o'course.' Pammy gave me a look like I would get from the parish priest if I were to ask him the name of the last female pope. She turned her attention back to the game and screamed virulent abuse at one of the Carlton players, accusing him of a sexual act that is not only unprintable but probably physically impossible as well.

We were nearing half-time and as interval in any footy match causes people to realise that they have a terrible thirst, I offered to buy our group a beer. 'Would you like a beer, Pammy?' I asked our new mate as she lit another cigarette. 'Don't mind if I do,' she replied. 'I'll 'ave a can of VB' (What else!). Then as she blew the smoke in my direction, she continued, 'Two. It'll save youse goin' back when th' rush is on.' She held up the first two fingers of her right hand. 'Two VBs.'

When I returned laden with green cans and a watered-down G&T for Herself, Pammy was standing with a cigarette in one hand and a transistor radio in the other listening to the half-time scores from other games. She took the two cans from me and muttered, 'I 'ope they's cold. At this joint they give youse anything. Not like Arden Street; they look after th' family at Arden Street.'

The game eventually got going again. North was not travelling too well and Pammy wasn't happy. Her remarks were becoming more insulting and the VB hadn't helped her mood either. 'Yer a fairy, Kernahan' — 'Leave 'im alone, Madden, ya brainless lookin' ox.'

'Who does youse go for?' Pammy's spleen had been vented for the moment so, as she lit up yet again, she once more turned her attention towards us.

'No team in particular,' I replied.

'Where youse from?'

'Sydney.'

Pammy wrinkled her nose, nodded her head and remarked, 'I thought so ... I could smell youse.'

Those of us whose heritage is linked to European culture are really not much different from the first Australians whose past stretches back into the Dreamtime. We share a lingering village mentality and yearn for the security of the tribe. The Australian tribes in existence at the end of the 20th century are not found so much in the vast distances of the bush but in the sprawling suburbs of our coastal towns. They congregate at the weekend in vast stadia where they play out their dreams and fantasies as well as participating in the tribal ritual that has been handed down over the last six generations. Those who gather together are all different but bound as one by their love and loyalty for 'the team'. Some go further and say that footy is a religion and that fans attend the games as others worship at churches, temples and mosques.

Whatever the reason for its being, football will always be part of our culture and, despite its many faults, a force for good. For every Mr Hyde there are hundreds of other sports lovers who can accept the result and give credit to the talented players from the other team. I got the feeling that Pammy had lived a tough and sad life and maybe this was the reason for her 'hate the world', 'them and us' attitude. Obviously, Pammy did not have much of a formal education and was coarse and rough but I could not help noticing that when the game finished she left alone. Did she go home to a loved one or was she alone for the night? Did she have a close friend? Whatever her circumstances, every Saturday of the footy season, Pammy was at the game and for a short time was, in her personal way, fulfilled and even more importantly — in the company of other members of her 'family'.

Like most Aussies, I am disillusioned and disheartened by politics. Recently I was watching a television debate between two ambitious hacks of opposing parties. They were arguing about a particular piece of legislation which most of the electorate neither understood nor cared about. While the two participants became more emotional, I became more bored and disillusioned.

Where are you, Kath? I thought. If you were here now, you could belt them with your brolly.

I sat shaking my head watching the so-called 'future leaders' of our nation until I could take no more. I stood up, walked to the set and as I turned it off I said to both the figures on the screen, 'Chewy on yer boot'. And I went to bed.

EIGHT

PUNDITS, POTTS AND PASSING SHOTS

In early 1998 Jim Russell accepted a position as a liaison officer to SOCOG's media section for the Sydney 2000 Olympics, at which time he will be in the 92nd year of his life. Jim admits that there are a few who have registered doubts about him being able to perform this onerous task at such an age. However, Jim is quick to point out that though he may be too young for the duties required of him, he will give it his best shot. He says that though he is a little green, he will learn on the job and listen to what his elders have to say because, after all, the torch must eventually be passed to younger people like himself. As an afterthought, Jim mentions that he has been a liaison person, manager or press officer at seven Olympic Games, going back to 1956. In the sport of tennis he has been an administrator for even longer — so, despite his youth, he may just get by in Sydney. But, as much as I admire Jim, I believe he is wrong on this occasion. Compared to those around him, Jim is far too young; too young in mind, too young at heart.

In his short 90 years (so far!), many honours have been bestowed upon Jim Russell. He has been granted an Order of Australia (OA) and an MBE; in earlier times he would have been knighted. But Jim's life is more than honours, money or fame. For within this wonderful man exist most of the characteristics that people would see as typical of a regular Aussie bloke. He is the battler who made good, the character who makes others laugh, the convinced socialist who turned himself into a wealthy entrepreneur, the patriotic Australian who regards himself as a citizen of the world. Jim is old-fashioned and modern, a person who talks of the past, lives in the present and yearns for the future. He is an Australian icon, a part of the vanishing breed of all-rounders who will soon be gone forever.

To list Jim Russell's achievements would require a book of its own and to even briefly summarise them takes space enough: cartoonist, painter, journalist, travel agent, novelist, scriptwriter, film producer, radio star, television personality, boxer, tennis player, tennis administrator, athletics administrator, swimming administrator, press liaison officer, public relations consultant, guest speaker, charity worker, entrepreneur, raconteur, husband, brother, father, grandfather, great-grandfather, counsellor, teacher, friend — and I'm not yet anywhere *near* the partridge in the pear tree!

The youngest of four children, Jim was born in the western Sydney suburb of Campsie, where his early memories were of his parents' involvement in Labor politics. His father was president of the Plumbers' Union, and was due to stand for the safe seat of West Sydney in an up-coming Federal election. Fate took its turn and he fell from a ladder and was killed, when Jim was only six years of age. There was little money in the Russell kitty, so his mother turned the front bedroom of the house into a grocery shop. The venture could hardly be called a success but the family ate the tinned goods, drank the milk and survived. Soon after daylight broke and on cold wet winter afternoons, Jim sold papers on Belmore Railway Station for the sum of seven shillings and six pence a week. When he was a little boy, his sister and brother would sit in the lounge room doing their homework; Jim, still too young to write, would draw. This early pastime turned into a hobby, then became a passion and finally Jim realised that drawing was what he wished to do as his life's work.

The only unhappy part of Jim's youth was his schooling. His mother was a devout Catholic and wanted for her children the comfort she had found in the faith. So Jim attended a number of Catholic schools until he left to go into the workforce at 15. His schoolboy memories are bitter ones. A number of the brothers were cruel, bordering on sadistic. To enforce discipline they used an implement which was part strap, part whip, bringing it round from behind their backs like a javelin thrower, to gain maximum power. Their cruelty alienated Jim from the church forever and though he now sees humanity and understanding coming back into religious orders, the vivid memories remain. Years after he had left school, Jim was working down at the Sydney Stadium ticket office, fighting four-rounders to supplement his income, when, one evening, he saw one of his former teachers outside the 'reserve' window, waiting in heavy rain to pick up a ticket. This brother had been particularly brutal and had given Jim some dreadful thrashings in earlier days.

'I know Brother X, leave him to me,' Jim said to his offsider in the box office. There had never been any cover outside the 'Old Tin Shed' and on this night the rain pelted down and the wind whistled off Rushcutters Bay while Brother X stood at the mercy of the elements, shivering.

'Hey Jim what about the ticket for the brother?' the other man called.

'Getting it now,' answered Jim while Brother X continued standing there with teeth chattering, as those around him collected their tickets and rushed in out of the rain.

After another miserable 20 minutes, Brother X came to the window and demanded of Jim's offsider, 'Where's my ticket?'.

'Where's the brother's ticket, Jim?'

'I'm busy at the moment, you get it,' came the reply.

Mystified, the offsider found the ticket and handed it over to the now-soaked brother, who yelled, 'What is going on here? I could catch my death of cold'. From somewhere in the background the offsider heard a quiet voice remark, 'With a bit of luck!'.

Jim's mother kept the faith, in both the religious sense and in the political sense (in the years to come Mrs Russell who had by then remarried became the first female member of the Legislative Council — the upper house of the NSW Parliament). Jim's sister, Aileen, became a nun and lived a productive life devoted to her church and her God. Called Mother Bonaventure, she eventually rose to a high position in her order. Aileen was forever trying to bring her younger brother back to the church but Jim would have none of it. Still, as he found out, it is very difficult to overcome a determined, dedicated nun. One afternoon, many years later, after Jim had married, Aileen called in to her brother's place to visit her niece. 'What about I give you two a rest and take Judy out for the afternoon,' she said to Jim and his wife, Billie. Being normal parents, the Russells were relieved to get their daughter off their hands for a while. A few hours later, after Aileen had dropped Judy back home and returned to the convent, Jim asked, 'Did you have fun, love?'.

'Yes,' replied his daughter.

'What did you do?'

'I got baptised.'

Jim's first job in journalism was as a copyboy with the group that ran the *Daily Guardian* and *Smith's Weekly*. *Smith's Weekly* was known as 'The Digger's Paper', because it had been set up to look after the rights of the returned soldiers after World War I. Though *Smith's* folded five decades ago it is still spoken of fondly by those who remember it as a paper that searched for the truth and which employed some of Australia's greatest writers and cartoonists. In his 18 months there, Jim met many famous people, some of whom would later play an important part in his future. Kenneth Slessor, one of Australia's greatest writers, worked for *Smith's*, as did Stan Cross — arguably our greatest cartoonist. *Smith's* and *The Daily Guardian* were part-owned by Robert Clyde Packer, grandfather of Kerry, and founder of the Packer dynasty. Unlike some Packer biographers, Jim found 'Bob' Packer a tough but reasonable man; honest, loyal to his staff and a journalist who kept his pledge of standing up for the rights of the ex-diggers, no matter what the personal costs. 'Ruthless' was never a word that Jim would use in connection with Bob Packer.

Unfortunately, after a year and a half, the papers were forced to cut costs and Jim was sacked. (The terms 'made redundant' and 'downsized' were not used much in the 1920s.) Notwithstanding, young Russell had become so popular with the staff that they took the hat round and threw in enough to send him to Julian Ashton's Art School to study. There, Jim's drawing improved significantly and three-quarters of a century later, he remains grateful to the people at *Smith's Weekly* who gave him the opportunity. Jim's ambition was to be a cartoonist, however his dream was loftier than this and just as every boy who picks up a bat wants to be Bradman, so Jim believed that the day would come when the works of Rembrandt and Picasso would be stored down in the cellar while the Art Gallery was displaying 'The Russell Exhibition'. It did not take long for Jim to revert to his 'cartoon option', when he looked at the drawings by the young man who worked beside him at the art studio. Young as he was, Jim realised that here was a unique talent and that he was working next to a genius. The drawings next to Jim showed a beauty of line and accuracy of detail, yet with an ethereal quality that stamped the artisit with future greatness. The young painter's name was William Dobell. After art classes the two would go out for coffee and sometimes, if they could afford it, to the pub, where they talked of art and their hopes for the future. Jim Russell and Bill Dobell became firm friends; a friendship which remained rock solid until the great artist's death at 52.

After completing his course at the art school, Jim could still not get a job in journalism so he worked in a factory and at the Sydney Stadium where extra cash came from the fights he had in the preliminaries. Later he obtained a position at Fox Films as the commercial artist responsible for the drawings on the advertising billboards. These jobs were putting a bit of cash in Jim's pocket and giving him experience, though he yearned to get back into journalism. Jim Russell was never afraid of hard work, yet all his life Jim reckoned he walked side by side with a silent partner by the name of 'Good Luck'. In 1930, the partnership delivered again when Jim was offered a job with Gayne Dexter as an 'all-round artist' at the *Evening News*. Though the paper lasted only another nine months before closing, Jim was back, as he had hoped, in journalism. A few weeks later he was appointed as an artist/cartoonist with his beloved *Smith's Weekly* and since then, for a period of 68 years, Jim has continued to work in the print media. As at the time of writing, there is no talk of Jim being downsized.

On the day the *Evening News* closed Jim married Billie (Lillian). In the long years that followed they were blessed with a daughter, Judy, and 65 years of marriage in its happiest sense. Billie was a smiling, vibrant lady who sustained, encouraged and understood her gifted husband. Billie died in June 1995 after years of sickness which caused her to deteriorate physically but which never curbed her humour or blunted her courage. When Billie was lying in hospital, just before her death, Jim told her that the day was the 65th anniversary of their wedding, to which Billie nodded and smiled. 'Tell me, Sweetie, if you could go back 65 years and I proposed to you again, would you accept?' Jim asked.

Billie opened her eyes and said slowly and with great effort, 'Well, I'd consider it'.

While on *Smith's Weekly*, Jim became more prominent as a cartoonist and with the guidance of people such as his friend and mentor, Stan Cross, he began to be seen in the avant-garde haunts of Sydney, such as The Journalists' Club in Phillip Street. Here he got to know the movers and shakers of society at that time and many of the unusual characters of the cosmopolitan city — people like Ernie Thornton, Rupert Lockwood and Jim Healy, communist agitators waiting for, and hoping to ferment, the coming revolution which would hand the reins of government over to the proletariat. Jim was never a communist, he was far too Australian for that, but he was a socialist who had seen the evils of the Depression and he wanted to change society. (Nearly 70 years later he rates himself slightly left of centre.) The conservative media branded The Journalists' Club a hotbed of insurrection but it was really nothing more than a meeting place for intelligent writers, would-be activists, bohemians and journalists (most of whom could be placed in all, or any, of the other three categories). The stories and jokes told in that club would make the comics on the Tivoli Circuit sound like priests at Holy Communion. Jim knew The Journalists' Club in its halcyon days and he remembers with fondness the characters he met there, such as Arthur Mailey and Eric Baume.

Arthur Mailey is known primarily as a test cricketer, a man who claimed 99 Test wickets as a leg-spin bowler. Mailey, however, also worked as a journalist and cartoonist and had a sense of humour that was second to none. Jim was a good mate of Arthur's and speaks with great affection of the little man from Balmain with the wicked 'wrong un' and the cheeky grin. There is a story often told — that in a Shield game for New South Wales, Mailey finished with the horrendous figures of 4 for 362. When asked by the press to comment on the performance, Arthur stated blandly that it was all the fault of bad fielding. The pressmen looked surprised until Mailey explained, 'If that chap in a brown derby hat at the back of the grandstand had held his chances we'd have had them out days ago!'.

Mailey hated anything which smacked of pomposity or pretentiousness and was not averse to putting anyone who displayed those characteristics in their place. In 1958, as he stood watching the New South Wales cricket team practising in the nets before their early season game against Peter May's English team, Arthur was approached by a partisan English journalist named Crawford White, and asked, 'Is this Norman O'Neill, who everybody keeps telling me is going to rip our bowlers to shreds?'. His gaze was on the player batting in the nets, O'Neill, the new superstar of Australian cricket, whom none of the English contingent had seen.

'Yeah, that's him,' said Mailey.

After a few minutes watching O'Neill bat, Crawford White shook his head, turned to Mailey and remarked, 'I say, old chap, this fellow won't do very well. He has too much of a backlift'.

Mailey took a drag on his cigarette, and answered in his broad Aussie drawl, 'Yeah, you could be right but from what I've seen of O'Neill, I've noticed that he never makes many runs when his bat is moving back. It's when his bat's going front that he hits all his fours'.

Once on a ship travelling to Britain, a pukka Englishman came up to Arthur Mailey and asked a question: 'Mailey, my dear fellow, would you do me the great favour of introducing me to Don Bradman?'

The little spinner from Balmain shrugged his shoulders and replied, 'I don't see why I should — nobody did the great favour of introducing me to you'.

Eric Baume was a famous personality, firstly as a journalist and later as a radio and television commentator. Jim got to know Baume when Baume was subeditor on the *Daily Guardian* and then editor of the *Daily Mirror* and later worked with him in the other two media areas. Although Baume was a man who made interesting company, Jim also noticed that he was never averse to looking for a 'lurk' and there was generally a Baume story doing the rounds in Sydney. While working in an executive position for the *Mirror*, Baume had an argument with the publisher, the tough, cantankerous, and penny-pinching Ezra Norton. 'You're fired, Baume, and you can leave now,' shouted Norton.

'Certainly,' Baume replied, 'but give me my 18 months pay before I go.'

'What are you talking about?'

'My contract has 18 months to run.'

Ezra Norton was fuming, even though he knew Baume to be correct. Yet Norton was nothing if not shrewd and realised that if he could force Baume to resign of his own accord, the contract was null and void. Eric Baume was a man not short of pride and ego, so Norton believed he could quickly gain a resignation. 'I'm not paying you any bloody money, you'll have to work your contract out,' he shouted. 'Go down and work on the subs' (subeditors') desk with all the plebs.'

'Fine,' said Baume and immediately moved his things from the luxury of 'mahogany row' down to the smoky, cluttered confines of the paper's lower middle class.

Baume worked assiduously for the first few hours and then had a tea break with the rest of his new workmates, who only a few hours before were his underlings. 'Where are the cakes and scones?' Baume asked the others. The group of subs looked bemused. 'Don't you have cakes at tea break? Well, they do upstairs!' — 'How about expenses? What expenses do you get?' — 'None you say? Gosh, Ezra and the executives take more in expenses than you fellas make in salary!' — 'Talking about executives, did you hear the story about the chief accountant and the blonde from the typing pool. It happened while his wife was in hospital having a baby and Ezra was on that overseas trip. Oh, and talking of travelling, did you ever hear mention of that incident involving Ezra while he was in Paris?

Everybody in town was laughing about it.' Next day Ezra Norton strode up to Baume, threw a cheque at him and yelled, 'Here's your bloody money, now get out of this place within ten seconds'.

Baume was best-known for his radio and television show called 'This I Believe', in which he pontificated on the world's problems and solved them nearly as quickly as he pontificated. Notwithstanding the world at large, most of the problems of which Baume spoke were those with which Baume was personally familiar. One day Jim was with him in The Journalists Club when Baume got caught up playing the poker machines, a not uncommon occurrence for Eric Baume. By the time he had rushed out to drive to the television studio, Baume had lost a lot more than his lunch money. When Jim arrived home that night, he switched on the television and listened to his companion of that afternoon speaking on a subject that was near and dear to his heart. 'And I say to the Premier of New South Wales that poker machines must be banned from our State. We cannot continue to have working men and women destroying their life savings and having their children reduced to rags because wealthy clubs want to become wealthier. I repeat, ban them Mr Premier, BAN them. And THIS I believe!'

Sometimes, Baume would spend too much time in the club in front of the machines he so detested and too little time in preparation of his nightly broadcast. One evening he raced into the studio with just a minute to spare before the cameras started rolling. 'What are you going to talk about Eric?' screamed his producer. As he rushed through, Baume grabbed a paper from a desk. 'This,' he shouted back. As the credits began to roll up on the screens of the nation, Eric Baume, with a fake library as his backdrop, sat at a desk reading a paper. Unfortunately, what Baume didn't realise when he grabbed the paper was that it was not a national broadsheet, but a copy of a local paper from the Dubbo area of New South Wales that had been sent down from the country to a girl in the office because it happened to contain a photograph of a friend's wedding. Like most bush papers of the time, this was a six page hastily printed 'rag' which gave a page and a half of local news, results of the local rugby league games, the names of the finalists in the Country Women's Association baking contest, photos of weekend weddings and not much else. Baume looked over his glasses and began:

'I have here a wonderful editorial from my friend, the editor of a well-known country paper; a paper which covers the whole of the Central West of New South Wales. I want to read it to all you viewers — and I quote. "It is about time the Government began thinking seriously of allowing a subsidy for fertiliser for the wheat farmers of our area. The farmer needs assistance in improving his crops and this paper is asking ..."'

Slowly and deliberately, Baume waded through the editorial, bringing into the lounge rooms of the nation boring statistics on wheat quotas, petrol prices in the country and the difficulty in obtaining parts for broken harvesting equipment, until eventually he reached the last paragraph. Building to a crescendo he continued, 'There is hope due to the recent rain that the crops will be better than average next season. This would be helped greatly should the Government give serious consideration to a fertiliser subsidy.'

Eric Baume ripped off his glasses, banged his fist on the table and with his face turning a shade darker than the colour purple, yelled at the camera, 'The bush is the backbone of our nation. The Government will ignore the farmer to its peril'.

'And THIS I believe!'.

Since early days, when Jim joined as a copyboy on *Smith's Weekly*, cartoonist Stan Cross was his mentor. Cross advised him on such things as technique and gags and introduced Jim to people who would help with his career. For some years, Cross had drawn a comic strip called 'The Potts', which was a continuing saga of a battling lower-class Australian couple, slightly rough in their habits and in their speech. Mr and Mrs Potts's best friend was a tall bachelor with the interesting name of Whalesteeth. The comic strip was syndicated to papers around Australia and New Zealand and was quite popular. Nothing stays the same, however, and editors from various papers had suggested that as Australia began to swing from a working-class to a middle-class society it might be advisable for Stan Cross to change the image a bit. The sight of Mr Potts weaving his way home with a bottle in his back pocket may be accepted by the battlers of South Sydney but 'How would it play in Kew?' (a conservative suburb of Melbourne). Cross was getting on, and set in his ways; he told the editors what to do with their strip. The Potts was subsequently handed over to the young Jim Russell.

Jim adopted The Potts as his own — or maybe the Potts family adopted Jim. Whatever, Mr Potts became a pillar of the community, Mrs Potts joined the golf club and Whalesteeth was scrubbed up. Jim's format for a comic strip was based on simple fundamentals. Each of the three captions had to have a different 'camera' angle and the cartoon as a whole had to be regarded as a three-act play. The first act (or in this case, drawing) was the establishment, the second, the development and the third, the payoff or punchline. For example: Drawing (1) Mr Potts is walking towards the first tee where, in the background, his wife is about to hit the golf ball. Drawing (2) As Mrs Potts is about to swing, Mr Potts says, 'You can't hit off from there, dear, you're a metre in front of the markers'. Drawing (3) Mrs Potts looks up and replies, 'Shut up, this is my fourth shot'.

The strip 'worked' from the beginning, but deep down Jim knew there was something missing. Australians, though better educated and more conscious of the finer things of life than previously, were still Australians. The men continued to have a drink and a bet and the women still talked about them when they did. So, soon after 'The Potts' became Jim Russell's, Whalesteeth disappeared and a rascally reprobate of a relation named Uncle Dick came to visit them for a week. Six decades later, he is still there, creating trouble for all those he meets and enjoyment for millions. Over the years, Uncle Dick has borrowed money from all and sundry, not one cent of which he has paid back. He has promised countless girls that he would marry them but never once has he walked down the aisle (and he's taken back all the engagement rings as well) and the fines he has received, and not paid, would paper a wall. Uncle Dick always fancies himself as a great sportsman, constantly skiting about his prowess with bat, racquet and ball. Yet whenever he is challenged to a game by the Potts' grandchildren and their mates, the great all-rounder is bowled out for a duck, never holds a service game and drops every pass he receives. Uncle Dick has bent the truth, broken promises and smashed cars; he suffers from over-confidence and hangovers, but he makes us laugh. The world would be a poorer place if there was no Uncle Dick and those of his kind — some of whom we all know.

'The Potts' established Jim Russell's career, helped him buy his own home, led him to other media interests and allowed him to pursue his love of sport. Today 'The Potts' and Jim Russell are still together; 58 years of uninterrupted friendship — the longest running cartoon, drawn by one man, in the history of the world. If it hadn't been for the money that he has loaned to Uncle Dick over the years, Jim would be a very wealthy man today.

Radio was booming in the 1940s, especially after the war, and Jim moved into radio in those halcyon days. The names associated with the era ring like a bell in the ears of those of us who sat and listened, entranced by the famous voices that came over the airwaves: Roy Rene (Mo), Jack Davey, George Wallace, George Foster, Bob Dyer, Ada & Elsie, Harry Dearth, Kitty Bluett, John Dease, John Harper, Clif Cary, Alan McGilvray, Gwen Plumb and Eric Baume; this was history on the airwaves. Radio was then a comfortable medium; the easy-going link which straddled the bridge between the comical, melodious vaudeville of the past and the Orwellian future that was soon to be upon us with the advent of television.

The undisputed king of radio was Jack Davey: quizmaster, comic and all-round professional, who bestrode the medium like a colossus. 'Hi, ho everybody,' he used to call and Australia rolled about laughing. Davey was a New Zealander who came over to Australia as a crooner and worked the Hoyts Theatre circuit. Between songs, the quick-thinking Kiwi would mix in some topical patter and jokes, and it wasn't long before the talking became more popular than the singing. Davey was made for radio and he was soon snapped up by the commercial stations. Jim Russell worked on radio with Davey in such shows as 'Twenty Questions' and 'Leave It To The Girls', where he too swapped jokes and ad-libbed — but he always made certain that Davey, the star, received the last opportunity for the punchline. On the other hand, personalities like Gwen Plumb fell out with Davey because they tried to steal his thunder.

In 'Twenty Questions' (animal, vegetable and mineral) Jack Davey, as compere, knew the answers, as did the studio audience and those listening. The panel, of course, was in the dark and had to ask questions to get to the truth — though whether they eventually arrived at the correct answer within the allotted number of questions didn't really matter. Indeed, Davey often liked the panel to milk the questions, even if they knew the truth. For instance, when the answer was 'A pair of ladies' bloomers', Jim would hear the titter of shocked laughter from the audience and knew that the subject matter was, for those days, considered slightly risqué.

Russell: 'Jack, could I wear this?' (Roar of laughter from audience.)

Davey: 'No Jimmy you couldn't wear it. Wait a minute, there is nothing to stop you if you *really* wanted to, Jimmy.'

Russell: 'You'd be surprised at what I wear, Jack.'

Davey: 'Jimmy, nothing you do would surprise me.'

Russell: 'Okay then, would it surprise you if I stuck this garment on my head and danced around singing, "Mammy".' (Audience rocks with laughter.)

Davey: 'It would surprise me, Jimmy, but you have my permission to do so.'

On one program, Jim did get the best of Davey. The answer to the question was 'a monocle'. Davey began by saying , 'Oh, I see, jolly good. Yes I see, pip, pip whato, I see. The subject is mineral. You're first, Jim Russell.'

Jim knew Jack Davey pretty well, so when he heard Davey sending up an Eton accent and putting emphasis on the word I (eye), he thought quickly and had a stab. 'Is it a monocle, Jack?' Davey's jaw dropped as the audience cheered ... but it was almost impossible to one-up Jack Davey. 'Correct, Jimmy — what took you so long?'

The only time Davey was bettered came during a quiz show he was compering. The contestant was not too bright and was struggling for the answers. 'This is your last chance, if you miss this you're out,' said Davey. 'What is a sporran?'

The contestant nodded his head and answered confidently, 'It's that big hairy thing that hangs down between a Scotsman's legs.' Davey had no comeback, because like the rest of Australia he was laughing too much.

Jack Davey was good company and an extrovert, but he was a compulsive gambler. Just how much money he lost at baccarat and other gambling pursuits could not even be imagined. In desperation, Radio 2GB even hired a manager to look after him. One of the manager's most important jobs was to sign all Davey's cheques but this didn't deter Jack Davey. He continued betting as before and when he lost he would write out a cheque and say to his creditor, 'There's the cheque, get my manager to sign it'.

Though he made the transition to television, Davey didn't succeed in the new medium. He was fighting a battle with cancer and the jolly, happy-voiced king of radio looked tired and drawn and was soon bypassed on the box by his friendly rival, Bob Dyer. The last time Jim saw his friend was just before Jack was due to commence further treatment for the cancer. Jim remembers Jack stubbing out a cigarette and saying, 'I reckon this is the last one of these I'll ever have, Jimmy'. Jack Davey died a month later and a golden era ended.

Not long afterwards, Jim, too, moved to television, appearing on game shows in the early black-and-white days. They were a lot of fun and as the shows were not pre-recorded there were often many hilarious calamities. On Channel Seven, Jim was on the panel of a show based on the parlour game of Charades. In one of the early shows Jim was miming the old saying, 'A man reaches his greatest height, when he stoops to help a fellow man'. The panel members weren't quite used to each other and Jim had some difficulty getting the message across. On and on went Jim's mime with the panel making very little progress towards the answer and by the time somebody worked it out, Jim had been bent over for so long that he had to have physiotherapy for potential stress fractures of the back. From then on Jim tried to make sure that he was given the mimes that were not only easier but less dangerous — 'Hailing a cab' or 'Man smoking a pipe'.

In 1953, the Melbourne *Herald* came up with the idea of sending Jim, and 'The Potts', to Britain for the summer. This was Coronation year. As well as covering the great event, Jim also wrote and drew on cricket's Ashes series and the tennis at Wimbledon. Cartoons appeared in Australia of Mrs Potts cheering loudly and waving an Aussie flag as the royal coach drove by, of Mr Potts eating strawberries and cream at Wimbledon and of Uncle Dick at Lord's, the home of cricket, yelling at the top of his lungs, "Ave a go ya mug,' while well-dressed gentlemen in MCC ties fixed him with baneful glares and muttered, 'Tut, tut'.

Jim remembers his tour of Britain with great affection — but not everything went to plan. Along the way he was scheduled to cover the Third Cricket Test, at Old Trafford in Manchester, and Arthur Mailey had agreed to arrange accommodation for him. On arrival Jim found that no booking had been arranged in his name. Manchester was booked out because of the Test and Jim was in a real quandary until he ran into fellow journalist and former first-class cricketer, Dick Whitington, who offered to let Jim share his room. Unfortunately, Whitington only had a double bed in his room.

And so it was that, with much jocularity, Jim and Dick settled down for the night. The next morning an elderly waitress arriving with the breakfast tray for two looked aghast at the two men yarning away in the double bed. That evening Jim was able to arrange a room for himself in the same hotel and he ordered breakfast in bed for the next morning. Sure enough, the same elderly waitress delivered the tray. She looked at Jim, recognised him from the morning before and remarked, 'Oh, so yuz 'ave 'ad a little tiff 'ave yuz?'.

Due to his knowledge of the way that press people thought and worked, his sense of humour and his popularity with everyone he met, Jim was offered the job of Public Relations Officer for the Olympic village at the 1956 Melbourne Olympics. This proved to be a wonderful experience and Jim has been connected with the Australian team in one official capacity or another at every Olympic Games since then, with the exception of Moscow (1980), when he was ill. During that period he has come to know some of Australia's greatest sporting heroes and counts many of them, including Dawn Fraser and John Devitt, among his closest friends.

Jim loves all sports but his favourite game is tennis — although to describe tennis as 'his favourite game' is downgrading the something in Jim's life which has been his great relaxation, an obsession and a never-ending love. In his early days in journalism, Jim was asked by the sporting editor of *Smith's Weekly* to go to Sydney's White City courts to interview and draw caricatures of the great players who were on show in the Australian Championships. Jim was playing tennis in the district C-grade competition at that time and was enjoying himself, though it was little more than a fun hit on a Saturday afternoon. That first day at White City courts he saw the champions practising and stood in awe of the crunching power, the natural dexterity and the magnificent coordinated balance of the athletes involved.

To watch players such as Jack Crawford and Ellsworth Vines in action at close quarters was, for Jim, an experience of sporting ecstasy which made him realise that there was so much more to get from this game — and more to give as well.

From then on Jim pestered his editors to let him cover the tennis. He spoke to tennis officials, requesting that he be allowed to help them in their duties, he studied every on-court movement of the great players and copied these until he had, within his own limitations, perfected them. After a couple of years, Jim was an up-and-coming young administrator in his own right, a better than average A-grade player and a tennis scribe far ahead of the pack. Now, more than 70 years later, Jim is a world-renowned expert on the game, soon to put together a film on the history of the Davis Cup, the doyen of tennis journalism and a walking encyclopaedia on the game. Yet all the plaudits and honours he has received do not begin to reveal the good works he has effected behind the scenes, his far-sighted initiatives in helping the game to progress to the multi-million-dollar industry it is today — nor do they tell of the friendship and guidance Jim has so readily given to players, coaches and officials. World tennis very likely does not know the debt it owes to the sporting editor of *Smith's Weekly* who, one sunny Sydney day, sent a young reporter armed with a few crayons to a green and pleasant oasis called White City.

In 1939 Jim was sent via the combined resources of *The Telegraph* and *Argus* to write and draw cartoons on Australia's Davis Cup challenge rounds, to be played over two months in the United States. As was expected, Australia won through to the final, to face the United States on the Merion Cricket Club Courts in Philadelphia. Jim Russell was the only Australian sports journalist in the country at that time and became the sole Aussie media witness to what turned out to be the closest contest in Davis Cup history to that point. The interest in Australia was high and Jim's reports were read with great relish at the breakfast tables of the land. At the time of the final, Jim was doing radio work with NBC and these broadcasts too were picked up by the stations in Australia. So, while Bromwich and Quist were fighting it out in 'the land of the free', Jim Russell was becoming a household name in the 'wide brown land'.

What a Davis Cup tournament it was! America's Bobby Riggs caused an upset in the first rubber, when he beat Bromwich — the best player on either side. Then America's second 'seed', Frank Parker, disposed of Quist and Australia was down 2–0 with three to play. In the doubles, Quist and Bromwich played inspired tennis and clawed their way back, beating the American pair of Jack Kramer and Joe Hunt.

Now it came down to the reverse singles, in which Bromwich was expected to beat Parker and Quist was expected to struggle against Riggs. After the doubles, Bromwich had said to his partner, 'Look here, if you beat Riggs I reckon I can win the last one'. This was a view shared by most observers, so, in effect, the Quist–Riggs match was the 'decider'. It proved to have more twists and turns than a python's tail; eventually it stood at two sets all and the Cup to win. Riggs had the most natural ability of the two players but Quist was an unflappable character and kept scrambling Riggs's best shots back. The fifth set ebbed and flowed until finally the American cracked ... and, after Bromwich, true to his word, disposed of Parker in straight sets, Australia had won its first Davis Cup.

Adrian Quist became an instant Australian sporting hero and, later, was given an even higher 'honour', when his name took a most important place in the colourful, colloquial language of his country.

It was after the match between Quist and Riggs that Jim broke a cardinal rule of his journalistic career and deliberately misquoted a prime source. Shortly before the game began, Jim asked Bobby Riggs if he could be given a quote as soon as possible at the end of the game — and Riggs agreed. After the hurly-burly of the final set there were people all over the court and Jim found it impossible to get anywhere near the American. So he waved to the doorman, who knew of his connection with the Aussie team, walked into the Australian locker room, waited till the doorman's back was turned and slipped across to the American room just opposite. Jim heard Riggs storming down the passage, heard the door crash open and then ducked for cover as six tennis racquets crashed against the lockers. Riggs followed the racquets into the room and in a sentence laced with expletives, asked what Jim wanted. Bravely, Jim faced the vanquished tennis player and murmured softly, 'A quote, Bobby'.

'I'll give you a (*!$%!&) quote! You can tell your (*%!$"$) Aussie readers that, "I should be #%"$&!".'

Next day the paper's headlines told of the great Australian victory, and the lead story in the sports section read, 'Riggs yells, "I should be shot!".' And that was the moment in his career when Jim Russell was guilty of deliberately misquoting — 'shooting' was not exactly what Bobby Riggs had in mind for himself.

It was at the Merion Club that Jim and the captain of the Davis Cup Squad, Harry Hopman, had their first run-in. Over the years there were many more to come. Of all the people he has met, Jim found Harry Hopman the most difficult and, although Jim is almost the antithesis of a vindictive man, he remembers the various slights from Hopman as if they happened yesterday.

Jim recalls particularly the time he was passing through London and, with a few hours to spare, rang his two young friends, Lew Hoad and Ken Rosewall, who were in town preparing for Wimbledon. Realising that Jim was on his own, the 'tennis twins' invited him to their hotel room for dinner. Jim arrived and had a drink, before the boys ordered dinner, to be served in Lew's room, for their guest and themselves. As they were tucking into the soup, team captain Hopman walked in, greeted Jim warmly, chatted for a while then wished him good luck and left. About five minutes later, the phone rang and Lew answered, said a few words and left the room — returning shortly with a grin on his face but saying nothing. It was some time later that Jim, back in Australia, was at White City having a drink when Lew and Ken joined him.

'Do you remember the night we had dinner in my room in London and I had a phone call?' said Lew Hoad. Jim nodded. 'Well the call was from "Hop", demanding that I come and see him. "What's Russell doing with you blokes?" he asked me. "Having dinner," I replied. "What for?" he shouted. "Because he is a top tennis official and he has been very kind to Kenny and me."

'Hop glared and said, "Well get him out of there, now. And, by the way, I'm taking the cost of Russell's drinks and meal out of your allowances."'

Jim was upset when Lew Hoad had finished his story, but Lew grinned his famous crooked grin and remarked laconically, 'That's why we're here now, Jimmy, it's your turn to shout. Kenny and I are going to get that allowance back'.

There were other incidents in Jim's relationship with Harry Hopman which caused him disappointment and angst, yet when the two were together in a one-on-one situation, dealings were mostly harmonious. Moreover, Jim would never criticise Hopman's tennis theories or methods, either in the press or off the record. Hopman had the 'match points' on the board, and today Jim rates Hopman as the greatest motivator of people he has seen, in any field of endeavour. Jim also defends Hopman against the criticism that he was a poor selector (such as when he dropped Ken McGregor for Mervyn Rose and Rosewall for Rex Hartwig) — blaming instead Sir Norman Brookes for such monumental Davis Cup blunders.

Jim once turned the other cheek and acted as a character witness on Hopman's behalf when the latter was embroiled in a litigation case. Jim is sometimes sad when he thinks of Hopman's attitude towards him, but he remains sorry they did not resolve things before Hopman's death. When Jim remembers Harry Hopman he is philosophical. 'Hop's mood swings often let him down, but he was the greatest Davis Cup captain of all time, with a wonderful ability to recognise young talent. Yet Hop always wanted everything to be done his way and everybody to toe his line. The trouble with dictators is that they all believe they are benevolent.'

Jim had toured the world many times with sporting teams and as a journalist/cartoonist. He loved travel and knew the pitfalls of touring so, eventually, he started his own travel business. Through his agency he arranged group travel for sporting teams and sporting fans that became so successful that he started another agency and then another. This, along with his many other interests, kept him extremely busy — all of it better than selling papers at Belmore Station.

One of his employees was a young John Newcombe, who showed a great aptitude for the group travel business. However, Newcombe went and won Wimbledon, which Jim reckons was a stupid thing to do as 'Newk' at that point decided to concentrate full-time on tennis and the lucrative money that came with it, and ruined what could have been a great career in travel.

Jim was to become National President of the Australian Federation of Travel Agents, working assiduously to improve their arrangements with the carriers and with the hospitality industry.

Today, Jim continues to see a rosy future. In 1998 he decided to sell the house he has lived in for 37 years in the southern suburbs of Sydney, with its magnificent view of the Georges River, and has moved to a smaller place nearby. From there he plans to open another travel business and look for other entrepreneurial opportunities. He also aims to work at stabilising his comic strip of 58 years, which Jim sees as only in its infancy. In a rare lapse into ego, Jim offers the thought that it's getting better. He plans also to sit and watch the waves roll in while he polishes his novel and a film script — about three generations of Australians. That done he can begin his next book which has the centre court of Wimbledon as its focus. Finally, he will write his autobiography which in its own way will encapsulate much of the style of this century and what it means to be an Australian. What stories it will tell and what lessons it will teach!

Jim Russell though will never preach. He remains forever the optimist, the positive individual, always part of the team. He does not try to force his opinion onto others and resists the opportunity to lecture, learning his lesson from his time in England in 1953. During that summer in England, Jim spent many hours with a young Rupert Murdoch. They would talk and drink together, Jim finding Rupert to have a brilliant mind as well as being a very good listener — it is a fact of life that when one has a very good listener at one's elbow one is inclined to be a very good talker. One afternoon, the two walked out of the pub where they had been meeting, made a time for their next get-together and said goodbye. Murdoch stepped into his waiting, chauffeured Rolls Royce, while Russell headed for the underground to catch his train. It then dawned on Jim that, perhaps, *he* should be the one doing the listening.

The Australia Jim knew when he was growing up in Campsie has changed beyond all recognition, with large cities like Sydney now reaching far into the hinterland. Jim regrets this high concentration of our population in these cities, because it has come at the expense of the bush hamlets and small country towns, once so much part of our heritage. The Potts are thriving but Dad and Dave are dying! Yet despite all its changes and the advent of a new multiculturalism, Jim sees Australia, with its easy-going ways, as still a caring country; a country in these fast travelling, high-tech times, no longer isolated and certainly better educated. In his wise view unemployment remains the chronic modern disease.

For the last five years Jim and I have made it a ritual to meet for a drink on the first day of the annual cricket Test at the Sydney Cricket Ground. Though the place is crowded with both the famous and not so famous, there would be hardly a person that he doesn't know. Inevitably there are many he has at some time assisted and advised and many he has made laugh. Jim stands only a touch over five foot six inches in height, yet amid the milling throng of the Noble Bar he stands tall. I guess that's to be expected because Jimmy Russell has always stooped to help his fellow man.

NINE

MUSICAL CHAIRS

Administrators are much maligned in the game of cricket. As in so many other sports, cricket has its good its bad and its ordinary administrators. Most players are inherently critical of the 'back-room boys' — especially those in the back of the back room who are called 'selectors' — yet I have found over a lifetime in sport that most of these officials have their hearts in the right place, even if sometimes their brains are inclined to wander to areas which are confused and backward. There are three types of administrators ...

Those who sit quietly and say nothing because they have nothing to say.

Those who sit quietly and say nothing because they are frightened that if they do say anything it may be construed as contentious and they may get voted out at the next AGM, thus missing out on their free feeds at Sheffield Shield matches.

Those who have a lot to say, whether it is worth saying or not.

There were many times in my early years in cricket when I was part of a captive audience listening to speeches from the hierarchy of the sport. These people could give speeches on any subject; speeches of welcome, of goodbye, of recognition, of information and speeches on absolutely nothing at all. As a young man wanting to achieve fame on the cricket field, I had been taught by my father that part of the process was to sit politely and listen to those holding high office talk about the giants of the past. Then when the speech had eventually ended, like those who had just listened to a diatribe by Stalin in the Soviet Politburo, I was to jump to my feet and clap enthusiastically, making absolutely certain that I was not the first person to cease clapping. This was part of my cricket education, so my father explained. Let me tell you, I was well educated!

The president of the New South Wales Cricket Association in my early days was a man named Sydney Smith. Syd, whom I never referred to as anything but 'Mister Smith', was a nice old man who had gained a modicum of fame in his playing days. Apparently, he terrorised the batsmen in Sydney's third-grade competition by bowling full-tosses at them. Syd Smith was what used to be known as 'a delver of high lobs'. This type of bowling was quite popular in the middle of the 19th century and had been the cause of many a bearded batsman's undoing.

A delver of high lobs would saunter up to the wicket, toss the ball as high as he could into the air and, if he was accurate, the ball would pitch over the batsman's head and land on top of the bails. At worst, the ball would bounce so high after hitting the pitch that the poor old batter would have great difficulty keeping it down and would be forced to hit the ball into the air. As a result, he would be caught out by one of the fieldsmen, set cunningly by the 'delver' for such a purpose. However, with the advent of full-time cricket and the ability of batsmen to wait on the full-tosser and smash it into the adjoining farm, the delvers of high lobs began to disappear from the scene and by the end of World War I, the species had gone the same way as the Mohicans and the Dodo. Yet there remained in a small outpost of empire, around the Petersham area of Sydney, one Sydney Smith, who continued to ply the forgotten craft until he retired and became a cricket administrator.

I'm not sure how many speeches Syd Smith made in his time, but I would hazard a guess that the numbers would have reached somewhere in the vicinity of Alan Border's batting aggregate. He always spoke politely in a style which could best be described as a 'nostalgic monotone', though there was a degree of sincerity in his words. Yet, unfortunately, he told the same stories every time he spoke — at least he did every time I heard him. Syd has been dead for well over a quarter of a century and those of his generation, and most of the generation following, have moved on. His stories, once so well known, are now fading deep into the mists of time. So for the benefit of young players making their way up in the cricket world, allow me to tell Syd's favourite tale once again; hopefully, sitting in a retirement village somewhere there may be a battle-scarred old 'quickie' who will also read this and smile wanly when he recalls the story and the decent old man who told it so often.

Syd Smith was the manager of Warwick Armstrong's famous team to England in 1921, and in 1926 he managed the team captained by Herbie Collins. When the boat arrived at Southampton in 1921, the team was besieged by reporters and Smith was required to answer many questions from the news-hungry press corps. At the end of the conference, a young journalist came up to Smith and asked if he could have a word with him in private — a request that Smith granted.

When they were alone the reporter was quite nervous but finally stammered, 'Er ... Mr Smith, I didn't ... er ... understand one word you ... er ... said'.

'I didn't realise I was so incoherent,' Smith replied.

The young man was most embarrassed. 'Oh it was not you, sir,' he mumbled, 'the fault is entirely mine. You see, the cricket reporter from my paper is ill and the editor sent me down here to take his place. I am the music writer and I don't know the first thing about any sport, let alone cricket. Therefore, I was wondering if you would be kind enough to fill me in on some of the fundamentals of the game.'

Syd Smith was a kind man, so although his schedule at that stage of the trip was particularly busy, he took some time out to give the music writer a rudimentary lesson on the game of cricket.

In 1926, the Australian team arrived once more in Southampton and the press again came aboard to ask questions. In the vanguard of the group was the young man whom Syd had taken under his wing on the previous trip.

'Remember me, Mr Smith?' asked the man.

'Of course I do,' answered Syd, 'you're the music critic'.

'Well not exactly,' replied the reporter, grinning proudly. 'My boss was so pleased with the article I wrote after our interview four years ago that he made me the Sporting Editor!'

TEN

ON THE EDGE

Bill Lawton doesn't look like an Anglican minister,
at least not one from the Sydney diocese. His lean
good looks, greying semi crewcut and ambling gait
somehow don't fit the Calvinistic stereotype of his
clergy brethren. Bill is far more likely to be
mistaken for a character actor in old-time movies; a
face we recognise but whose name we can't quite
remember — a sort of downmarket Henry Fonda.

Bill is about to embark on a new phase of his
life's journey; a journey that began in the Australia
of the Depression. He began as an outcast, became
a member of the Establishment, went through a

number of transitions and returned to be a holy man to outcasts. Yet despite the twists and turns of the road, the signposts always pointed back to the edge of Australia's society. And though he once hated it he now feels comfortable there. But it has been a long journey and it is not yet over.

Bill recently wrote the following words in the book, *A Real Yet Perfect Communion*, published by St. Paul's Press.

At 6 a.m. the last of the working girls have moved on from their nightly vigil opposite St. John's Church, Darlinghurst Road (Kings Cross). I used to watch them, standing on that windy corner, pulling their jackets around their thin bodies. The last girl stares vacantly at one of the cars as it slows down in the congestion just before William Street. She will do just one more trick for one more fix, then move on. You get to know them in a distant sort of way; you are on each others' territory. The tall sombre spire of St. John's Church casts an incongruous shadow over Darlinghurst Road; it owns the space, yet itself is owned by people who would never venture inside — and I, too, am owned as the village priest, the local shaman, the almost holy man.

In a moment of longing, people find an out of the way corner of St. John's to shoot up: 'You will clean up won't you?' The question is ridiculous and you wonder why you have tried to claim back your territory in such a paternalistic way. Somehow, the interchange maintains distance, respectability, power.

My second Christmas Eve, all this was furthest from my mind, though the pattern of distance ingrained in priesthood lent itself to the mechanical formula endlessly recited, 'The Body of Christ — the Blood of Christ'. Suddenly she was there at the communion rail, the working girl I had watched for so long. She knelt and held out her hands, tears running down her face. I paused, breaking the routine, and held her. It was probably only for ten seconds and then the recitation began again, 'The Body of Christ — the Blood of Christ', but everything had changed in an instant. The Eucharist was filled with the presence of Christ; there was a mystery of inward transformation.

Two days later, as dusk fell, I was walking through Kings Cross, like every inner-city dweller, my eyes fixed on my destination. She stepped out of the shadows, called softly, 'Hello Bill' and kissed me gently on the cheek. It was a renewed touch of the chalice.

Bill Lawton was born in Sydney in 1934, the only child of Ruth and William (Bill) Lawton. Ruth's mother and Bill's father were both of Irish extraction (she from the north and he from the south) and while there were some English antecedents as well, it was the Irish part of their heritage that seemed to dominate their personalities. Ruth was Protestant and William Catholic. Between the two however, there were no Orange and Green battles as they were not interested in religion and never attended church. This was the time of the Great Depression and making ends meet seemed to be the raison d'être of all working class Australians. Soon after the birth of young Bill, the Lawtons rented a shop in the suburb of Hurstville and attempted to turn it into a mixed business but it was difficult to run any business in the mid 1930s, especially since most of their customers were out of work and their suppliers wouldn't supply unless the Lawtons put cash on the line. Thus the business folded and the two looked elsewhere to make a living.

Fortuitously, at around this time, an aunt was left some money and became a licensee of a couple of hotels; one at Wagga in the Riverina area and the other at Muswellbrook in the Hunter Region of New South Wales. Ruth took a job as a barmaid and Bill became the pub roustabout. The Lawton family lived on the premises and one of young Bill's first memories was being advised by his parents 'not to look right or left, just stare straight ahead'. (If Bill had followed this advice throughout his life, he may have lived far more comfortably, but his life would not have been nearly as interesting — or productive.) In the Depression even the pubs were struggling and Bill Senior moved north to earn a living. He stayed away for three years and to this day Bill does not know where his father went or what he did.

When it became obvious that her husband was not returning, Ruth was forced to take any menial job she could find so that she and young Bill could survive. In 1937, Ruth was employed as a cook on a banana plantation outside the small township of Beaudesert in south-west Queensland. Bill remembers little of Beaudesert except the image of huge banana palms towering towards the sky and, as a small boy, walking beneath them, lost and confused.

The following year Ruth left Queensland and took another job as cook on a sheep station in Narromine in western New South Wales. Their time in Narromine was short-lived, however, and soon Ruth and her young son were heading back to the city. This was a summer of catastrophic drought and there remains indelibly printed on Bill's memory a picture of dead sheep and a thirsty brown land covered with red dust. In the steam train coming back, he stared out the window for many hours and all he could see was a red blanket covering the landscape. Even in normally green Sydney there was red dust hanging over streets and parks and changing the colour of the sky. When Ruth and Bill arrived back in Sydney, they moved into two rooms in a large rambling boarding house in Norton Street, Leichhardt, and life was awful. Then, suddenly, Bill's father reappeared.

Years later, Bill heard from a family member that an aunt of his had ventured 'up north' and brought his wayward Dad back to the bosom of his family. The reunited couple and their son then moved into a rented terrace house in Paddington and once again the husband and wife tried their luck in the retail trade when they attempted to run a mixed business, this time in the beach suburb of Maroubra. Neither were cut out for a vocation that required regular hours and a disciplined lifestyle. The husband would spend lengthy lunch hours at the pub while the wife, angry at being left alone, would shut up the shop and go down to the hotel herself, taking her little son with her. While his mother was inside getting drunk, Bill would be forced to amuse himself for many hours while sitting on the steps of the pub. Once again the business was a failure, so early in the 1940s Bill's father joined the army.

Bill Lawton saw his father as an intruder in his life and remembers him with a mixture of resentment, humour and a sense of regret for an opportunity lost (to both of them). Yet Bill Lawton Senior was nothing if not a character. Though Bill's Dad was a sort of 'Aussie artful dodger', there remained in him the gift of the blarney and the ability to drift from crisis to crisis without ever becoming overstressed or worrying too much about what he was doing to those around him. And there was always refuge in a bottle when things got tough or when he was thirsty or for no particular reason at all. Bill's Dad would binge regularly and disappear for a couple of days, sometimes ending up at the local police station. Meanwhile, Bill's mother would also head for the bottle to forget the sins of her husband, and Bill would have to look after himself. Yet strangely, when Bill Senior eventually staggered home there were no loud arguments. Husband and wife would not speak. They would then remove themselves from each other's presence and, quietly and independently, get drunk. To the frightened son, on the edge of it all, the atmosphere crackled with tension and the silence was overwhelming.

Bill Senior spent most of his war career in an army camp just over the Blue Mountains outside the city of Bathurst and he spent his leave-time in the town with a mistress. So, although the war was long for the 'artful dodger', it was not particularly taxing and, no doubt, had its relaxing moments. Towards the end of the war Ruth and young 10-year-old Bill climbed into a taxi and headed for Bathurst. The cab halted outside a house in the town and Ruth got out. Meter ticking away, Bill sat quietly in the cab. Eventually, Ruth appeared, with Bill Senior in tow carrying his kitbag and a suitcase, and they all returned to a rented house at Harrow Road, Stanmore.

It seems unusual that a man with the selfish character of Bill Lawton Senior would simply do as he was told and meekly follow his wife's instructions. What Ruth held over her husband was for many years a mystery to young Bill, until one day an aunt hinted that, before the birth of Bill, Ruth had been pregnant and had lost the baby. Whether the unborn child had miscarried or whether the pregnancy had been deliberately terminated is unknown, though Bill suspected the latter. The Irish are into guilt as river-boat gamblers are into cards and it seems probable that both Ruth and Bill Senior never forgave themselves for the deed that was committed.

At the end of the war and for the rest of his life, Bill Senior was employed by the Department of Defence on a casual basis only, as his war record showed that he had gone 'absent without leave' and been arrested. (The Defence Department forbade former felons to work on a full-time basis.) Bill Lawton Senior died in 1962. He was a 'lurk man' typical of his breed, an Aussie character and probably a good bloke with whom to have a casual drink. A man streetwise and morally foolish, Bill Senior had the ability to contribute something to society and to make a better person of himself but he settled for the ways of those on the edge. If Bill Senior did anything right in his life it was that he gave to his only son the perfect example of how not to live. Bill dearly wanted to love his father but he never could, so he settled for learning by the example he was set.

Now, heading towards eternity, Bill has mellowed. He has known worse men that his father and come to understand and forgive them. So, occasionally he looks back and remembers a bloke who was not there much but who never harmed him physically and never *deliberately* harmed him mentally. And he recalls his father singing, in a light Irish tenor voice, popular old ballads like the poignant 'Two Little Girls In Blue'. And he smiles when he thinks of his Dad bursting forth with gleeful gusto about the frustrated lady who was left:

> *Waiting at the church, waiting at the church …*
> *I didn't know 'e'd left me in the lurch — my 'ow it did upset me.*
> *All at once 'e sent me round a note — 'ere's the very note,*
> *Vis is wot 'e wrote — 'Can't get away to marry you today,*
> *My wife won't let me.'*

Conversely, when she was not drunk, Ruth indulged her only son — though on a number of occasions she let slip that she would have preferred to have had a daughter. Nevertheless, Ruth gave Bill whatever she could and tried to make up for the fact that for most of his life he didn't have a father close at hand. Bill now believes that the guilt with which Ruth was burdened was probably the reason for this. Yet despite her indulgences and natural maternal love towards him, Bill does not recall his mother with any great affection, though he now understands that he learnt much more from her than he first realised. Ruth came from a family of alcoholics and was an alcoholic herself. Bill remembers his mother and her family sitting in the kitchen drinking demijohns of brown muscat, the air filled with the smell of cheap wine and raucous laughter. He recalls once hearing his mother and others playing strip poker and the roars of bawdy laughter that accompanied the loss of each hand. In particular, Bill remembers the house at Harrow Road, where the chip heater was broken and there was no hot water. The Lawtons shared the place with an aunt and her boyfriend, Elbie. Elbie worked in a foundry and managed to obtain various saleable items which fell from passing trucks, which he and Bill Senior would endeavour to 'fence' to anybody who was interested. On weekends, Elbie worked on a trawler and the house always stank of stale fish. Over five decades later, Bill can be quietly working in his study when he is suddenly overwhelmed by the smell of stale fish.

Despite her weakness for a drop of the hard stuff, Ruth was intelligent and set in her views. Long before it became fashionable, she was a hardcore republican and hated anything to do with the Establishment or the royal family. Bill remembers going to the movies and, as was the custom, 'God Save The King' would be played just after the lights went down. Ruth would then make a disparaging noise and sit firmly in her seat. Up would come an usherette, shine the torch on Ruth and say, 'Please be quiet, madam, and kindly stand up during the national anthem'.

Ruth would loudly reply, 'You and what army are going to make me?'.

This anti-Establishment feeling was inculcated into Bill at an early age. On his very first day at infants school, the class joined together to sing 'Rule Britannia' but the little five-year-old Lawton refused to do so. He was hauled out in front of the class and publicly spanked. Bill took the punishment as a martyr should and didn't cry. However, as he was walking home the dam of humiliation broke and he sobbed bitterly until he reached his front door.

None of Bill's early memories are pleasant. He moved house 12 times in six years. He lived with aunts and uncles and their de facto partners, he attempted to play with cousins who teased him or, worse still, ignored him. He witnessed inter-family feuds and mostly slept in the same bed as his mother. He can recall eating a meagre meal off a 'table' made of plywood on top of two cardboard boxes, there was no covering on the floor and the only place to sit was on empty packing cases. Then Ruth got a job which paid reasonably well and one day she came home with a small radio. The radio was a great boon to the lonely young boy, for Bill could listen to music and lose himself in *The Search For The Golden Boomerang* and *The Argonauts*. Sometimes he went to town with Ruth and saw how people lived and behaved away from the edge but he couldn't quite comprehend it and he came back to the smell of brown muscat, stale fish and body odour. Once he lived with an aunt who told him that he was illegitimate because he was not confirmed into the Roman Catholic Church. Thus, when he died he would be loaded into Hell's paddywagon and driven directly to the fiery furnaces without the benefit of a kind word or a comfort stop. Many years later, when Bill and his cousins had grown, they made a pact never to see each other again — because each time they got together the memories of things past were too painful.

Primary school was no better. Bill had no friends and to make matters worse, he had very little ball sense, couldn't run fast and didn't know how to swim. The other kids used to send him away when they told a dirty joke, jeering 'Lawton is a sissy'. The teachers told him he was dumb and that he had no future. Apart from one kind man who taught third class, Bill found that the teachers in his primary years were bullies and sadists who used the cane for any misdemeanour, from failing a maths test to flatulence. On school days the little boy dreaded the sun coming up. Young Bill Lawton had very little going for him — so he turned to books.

As a very small child, Bill's mother would read to him before he went to sleep. The stories, though, were never fairytales or childhood verse but pages from the classics. Ruth particularly liked Dickens and by the time he had reached the age of 10, Bill was devouring the works of the great writers on his own. He may have been failing maths and history in the classroom but if the truth be known, Bill was probably better read than the teachers who were failing him. Books were great. A boy could lose himself in books. Yet he needed something more than this, Bill needed a cause.

At one of Bill's many abodes lived a maternal uncle who was a zealous card-carrying communist. He left communist literature lying around the house, encouraging young Bill to read it and suddenly a whole new world opened up. Not only did he discover a new way of life but, more importantly, Bill had found a cause.

After leaving primary school, Bill graduated to Drummoyne Junior Technical School (where the students left after third year). 'Graduated' is probably the wrong word — nobody graduated to Drummoyne Tech. This was a place where young boys were sent when they were not good enough to go to any other school and where they filled in the time until they reached the age when the law said they could forgo formal education forever and move into that great Australian tertiary institution, 'the School of Hard Knocks'.

Though Bill didn't learn much at Drummoyne Tech, he was more than willing to teach others about the cause of international communism. By reading so much literature and propaganda, Bill found that he could competently string his words together when anybody was willing to listen and gradually he built-up a few followers — mainly those who were bored or friendless. At recess periods, Bill would take this small group of stragglers out onto the school cricket pitch and tell of the utopia that would soon be theirs. 'Come the revolution, comrades, the capitalists and their lackeys will be swept down the sewers of history and the proletariat will march on to world order and prosperity forever.' Commissar Lawton knew all the buzzwords and catchphrases. It mattered not that Russian peasants were being forced to leave the land, or that dissenters were arrested, tortured and murdered by the secret police — a few had to suffer for the benefit of all. What *did* matter was that Bill had a reason for his existence and for the first time he had also found a religion, with Marx as God and Stalin as Jesus Christ.

The only contact that Bill had with *real* religion came when Ruth's mother (Bill's grandmother) was dying. Realising that eternity was for a long time and touched by a spasm of guilt, the mother demanded that her daughter be baptised and, oh, while she was at it, she could do a bulk deal and have Bill baptised as well. Bill's grandma was Protestant, so Ruth and Bill were both brought into the flock of the Church of England — a group not as disciplined as the Roman Catholics, nor as pious as the Methodists or as hands-on as the 'Salvos' but, nevertheless, the right church to belong to if you wanted to make an impression in the higher echelons of Sydney society. Yet for people such as Ruth and Bill, it would not have mattered whether they took communion 10 times a day and could recite the Apostle's Creed by heart, they would always remain just a number on the roll of the church — after all, the two new members lived on the edge. Those that counted in the Anglican Church were as far away from Ruth and Bill as grand opera was from wrestling.

Bill may have been most proficient at shouting Communist manifestos from the cricket pitch at Drummoyne Tech but his class work wasn't improving. The teachers would look at Bill's work and shake their heads in dismay. And these teachers were extremely good judges of a child's future. After all, Bill had come to Drummoyne Tech from primary school burdened with an I.Q. test result which the examiners had told him placed him above the status of a moron, but not by much. When he failed the Intermediate Certificate, the teachers nodded sagely and said, 'Get a menial job in a factory young man and hang onto it because you are dumb'.

Thus, Bill applied for a job in a confectionery factory where he was required to pour syrup into a large vat for seven-and-a-half hours a day. As the supervisor was explaining the intricacies of this 'vocation' it suddenly dawned upon Bill that the teachers may be right — he had no future and little hope. Then, for the first time in his life Bill found the meaning of the word 'courage'. He turned and walked out of the factory, saying to himself as he did so, 'I'll show 'em. I'll *be* somebody'. So he returned to Drummoyne Tech for another year, sat for the Intermediate and passed. The teachers shook their heads in amazement. Bill was realising that there could be something better on offer down life's road. He knew, however, that if he was going to 'be somebody', he had to continue his education and sit for his Leaving Certificate.

Fort Street Boys' High School was one of the few selective high schools in the metropolitan area of Sydney. Over the years it had produced many pupils who became great intellectuals, sporting champions and people of influence in community affairs. Nevertheless, Fort Street was also required to take boys who lived in the immediate vicinity no matter what their academic qualities. Thus, the school enrolled a young man from 'the edge' who couldn't understand maths, couldn't run, bowl or tackle and who loudly preached a philosophy which advocated the destruction of a way of life that most of his fellow students respected and by which they hoped to make their fortunes. With little regret, Bill left Drummoyne Tech and moved to this new place of learning.

'Come in, Lawton,' called the Fort Street headmaster 'Minnie' Mearns, a few days before the first term began. Bill, there for an entrance interview, stood up and walked through the door to the headmaster's office while the headmaster walked around behind his desk. 'Keep your shoulders back son, you're a Fort Street boy now,' Mearns demanded. Mearns looked down at Bill Lawton's scholastic record which lay open in front of him. The headmaster frowned — it was not a document to admire. 'All right boy, let's see what your general knowledge is like!' Minnie Mearns then leaned back in his chair and asked, 'What made Great Britain great?'.

Without hesitation, Bill replied, 'Piracy on the high seas, sir.'

Minnie Mearn's chin nearly hit the desk. 'You will withdraw that answer immediately Lawton.'

'No, sir.'

'You will.'

'No sir.'

The headmaster blustered and bullied but the young lad stuck to his guns. When Bill was eventually ordered out of the office, he felt quite proud of himself. It is probably superfluous to note that Bill was never made a prefect.

It was a different experience for Bill at Fort Street. For the first time in his life he began to make friends and although he still struggled academically, he could see some structure in the subjects and realised that if he slogged away at his studies, he would improve. Selective schools had the best teachers and although Bill was there simply because of fortuitous geography, he came under the influence of a number of these high calibre men. For example, there was a Maths teacher who so inspired him that in one week Bill learned every theorem in the syllabus. Then there was an economics teacher named Goodman (nicknamed 'Benny') who revealed to Bill impressive theories which were the antithesis to those of Karl Marx. Theo Neuhous, an English teacher who later went into the church, showed Bill the intricate beauty of the English language and although Bill didn't like Neuhous as a person, he will be forever grateful to the man for some brilliant lectures on the Bible as literature.

It was at Fort Street that Christianity first touched Bill, although Bill and Scripture started off badly. In the 1950s, all children in state schools had one Scripture period a week. The school was divided into senior and junior groups and between Catholics and Protestants. Then along would come a priest and a minister who would set about converting the heathens. Soon after the war a group known as 'Open Air Campaigners' had suddenly found influence in Protestant religious circles and had taken over Scripture teaching in many suburbs of Sydney. At Fort Street each week, a well-known evangelist by the name of Jim Duffecy would appear, bringing with him large amounts of fire and brimstone, plus an imagination that would make Hans Christian Andersen seem bland. Even as an impressionable teenager, Bill Lawton would laugh at the stupidity of the man's pronouncements. Once, Duffecy told the story of the Israelites placing sheaves of wheat into the walls of Jericho and then blowing trumpets until the walls toppled over. At the end of the story the evangelist reached into his bag, pulled out a glass jar containing some plants and shouted in triumph to the class, 'And in this jar we have some of the original wheat which was placed in the walls of Jericho'. Bill was astounded by such hyperbole and found himself waiting for Duffecy to blow on one of the 'original' trumpets but the preacher failed to produce any. Perhaps the evangelist could have searched through economics teacher 'Benny' Goodman's cupboard and discovered a trumpet hidden away among the clarinets?

Then one week Duffecy did not appear and in his place stood the Anglican Dean of Sydney, Stuart Barton Babbage. Babbage, a former R.A.F chaplain, was a man with a most impressive bearing and resonant voice who told enthralling, believable stories. He became Bill Lawton's first role model. I want to be like him, thought the young man.

So impressed was Bill with Babbage's message that the following Sunday he went along to both the morning services at St. Augustine's Church, Stanmore. St Augustine's was what is known in Anglican parlance as a 'High Church' (a church close to the Roman Catholic tradition). The church was sparsely attended and young Bill Lawton was utterly mystified by the liturgy and the theatrics but, despite this, he went again the following week.

Within weeks, 16-year old Bill who, previously, didn't know a cassock from a curate, was teaching Sunday School, the only male in the choir and acting as a server at Communion (dressed in robes). His head was awhirl — from a nobody he was suddenly a heavy in the hierarchy; in a matter of weeks he had gone from the edge to well towards the centre. Though the minister had him running from one activity to another, Bill was still impressed with the feeling of love and 'churchiness' at St. Augustine's and he knew that he wanted to continue to be a part of spiritual formality. As this feeling grew it became a calling and as he read more about doctrine, he felt himself being drawn to the dogma and liturgy of the Roman Catholic Church. Bill spoke to Angus Tipping, the minister of St Augustine's, about these thoughts. 'Put your feelings on hold for awhile,' counselled Tipping and went on to suggest that Bill apply for entry to Moore College, the Anglican school for the training of clergy in Sydney. Bill took his advice and to the surprise of all, not the least Bill himself, was accepted. When Bill told his father of his new vocation, Bill Senior was neither proud nor disgusted — just mystified. Bill Senior shook his head and asked, 'If you've got to go into the church why don't you at least choose a real one?'. Obviously referring to the Catholic Church.

In his first year in Moore College, Bill Lawton was brilliant at ancient languages and topped the yearly exams — which says little for those who marked his I.Q. test, some years before. Paradoxically, as Bill grew in his understanding of the bible and Moore College's Anglican syllabus, he reaffirmed his loyalty to communism and his feeling that he should really be a Roman Catholic grew stronger. Then in 1956 the Russian tanks rolled into Budapest. Bill bailed out from the communist cause and has reviled communism ever since, though he still remains a member of the Labor Party, sitting unashamedly on the Left.

By the time he reached third year, Bill was the star of Moore College. Yet he was now totally convinced that he had chosen the wrong church and was seriously considering becoming a Roman Catholic priest. Bill believed that salvation could best be found through self-denial and that the submissive life of a monk was the way to earn God's grace.

Moore College courses were for a duration of three years, though when Bill passed his final exams, he was too young to go into a parish, so the College allowed him to continue for a fourth year. As Bill was the only student, there were no exams involved, thus he was left to his own devices. He grasped the opportunity of disciplined, private study and read widely, especially in the area of radical post war theology and avant-garde literature, and gradually discovered that he was moving away from the theology of Rome and becoming more comfortable with the beliefs of his Anglican teachers.

In 1958 Bill was ordained a deacon and for a time was a curate in a suburban parish. He was then offered a job as a lecturer at Moore College, and duly accepted.

However, Bill didn't always agree with some of the conservative teachings of Moore College — in particular finding the College's attitude to the priesting of women dated and insulting.

Despite this, he enjoyed the teaching, while the students liked Bill and benefited from his tutelage. Yet over a period of time a most surprising change had quietly occurred in his life (though nobody who knew him in his early days would believe it) — Bill Lawton had become an academic.

Bill may have left behind thoughts of becoming a Catholic monk, but his lifestyle wasn't far removed. He liked a drink but was careful about the amount he drank, because in his veins ran the blood of alcoholics. Bill had gone on a 'session' or two and he knew that if he wasn't careful he could fall into a trap that was waiting for him, sprung not so much by hops, malt and fermented grapes but by a hereditary curse. On the other hand, celibacy had been part and parcel of his day to day existence. He liked women but had never been out on a date with one. There were no sexual skeletons in Bill Lawton's closet. He had suffered no scandals and no heartache. He was never seduced and was never spurned. One evening at Moore College, he was giving some personal tuition to a young man named Barry Hugget. During the lesson Barry asked his tutor if he had a girlfriend, a question Bill answered in the negative. 'You need to meet some women, Bill,' Barry stated, with the authority of a man who knew some. 'What about I tee you up with a blind date.' Bill hesitatingly agreed. The blind date turned out to be an attractive, intelligent young woman named Margaret Dawson. They met in March and married in December. Barry Hugget was their best man and the present Archbishop of Sydney, Harry Goodhew, was their groomsman.

After the wedding, Bill's life changed radically. He and Margaret decided that they wanted six children which, in retrospect, was quite a hefty ambition for a young man who, until a few months before, had never even been out on a date. Bill left Moore College and embarked on parish life and the couple had three children in quick succession. After a break came a fourth child and then a fifth — a daughter who died after four days. Later they adopted a boy.

Bill and Margaret's first parish (for they were soon a team) was in outer Sydney; the tranquil semi-rural area of Dural — also taking in Galston, Kenthurst, Glenorie and Annangrove.

Well-bred families had lived here for generations and many of them believed, like the squatters of the 1800s, that this was their domain. Thus, newcomers were regarded with suspicion and in some cases outright hostility. So when the Lawtons decided to redecorate the church with Regency wallpaper and paint the pews off-white, the congregation stormed the barricades and quickly put a stop to the architectural ambitions of this trendy new priest who had lived all his life in the city. 'Keep Dural rural' was the catchcry of this area in the 1960s, though what a few rolls of striped wallpaper had to do with the conservation of flora and fauna, was something that Bill and Margaret Lawton failed to comprehend.

There were good times and bad times at Dural. With hindsight, Bill believes that many of the disagreements he had with sections of his flock were due to his own immaturity. The new minister was endeavouring to prove he was in control and was inclined to forget that he had spent nearly all his life 'on the edge', or in Moore College, and knew very little of how the other classes lived. For example, he ruffled congregational feathers by arriving extremely late for his very first service. (Bill had only just obtained a driver's licence and was struggling to work out the difference between the clutch and the brake and while concentrating on these difficult problems, drove the car into a ditch.) Then he had a row with the organist who, in musical terms, was also struggling with the clutch and the brake. On another occasion, Bill, Margaret and their three small children were invited home by some kindly parishioners. It had been raining and the ground was muddy so they left their shoes outside on the verandah. When they came out they found that the shoes had been chewed to pieces by the family dog. The Lawtons remained close friends with the parishioners but they never forgave the dog — turning the other cheek is not easy when you're standing in bare feet. Then there was the flag incident!

Politically, Bill remained left of centre and had inherited the philosophy of republicanism from his mother Ruth. Hanging on the wall not far from the Communion Table was a large Union Jack which dominated the forward vista of the church. Bill wanted it removed but the old families of the area would have none of it. One day repairmen were working in the church and somehow Bill arranged that the contentious flag be, accidentally, ripped. The Parish Council insisted that Bill send the flag away to be repaired but despite his 'constant efforts' Bill had great difficulty locating a repairer of Union Jacks. The flag remained torn and locked away and when asked by those concerned what was happening, Bill would just shake his head and say sadly, 'You can't find a good tradesman anywhere, these days'.

There were also sad times, like the summer of the bushfires when property and crops were lost and one terrible day when, while attending a church adventure camp, a young boy drowned. There was the time when his three year old daughter, Nicola, got lost and another occasion when she was rushed to hospital. At one stage, Bill himself became quite ill for some months and struggled to carry out his extensive parish duties, and he remembers with deep regret the drawn-out death of his good friend, Warwick Davies, the local Methodist parson. Yet as the weeks turned into months and the months to years, Bill matured and the family prospered in an almost idyllic playground of trees and space. Now, looking back, Bill recalls the time with a sense of nostalgia, yet he would have done it differently if he had his time over again. He wrote recently: 'Dural nurtured our spirits and deepened our experience of God. This made much else that was sad and trivial, seem bearable.'

From the sophisticated old-money area of north-west Sydney, the Lawtons moved to the smallest parish in rural Western Australia, although to describe it as small is probably a misnomer as it was 25 000 square miles — larger than Tasmania. The rectory was situated in the tiny township of Mullewa, a declining railway town in northern wheat belt country, where 1500 people 'lived at the far extremity, where filth, disease and alcoholism bred despair and apathy'. In his book, *Being Christian, Being Australian* (Lancer Books, 1988), Bill describes the starkness of the location, the plight of the people and his thoughts soon after his arrival:

Two tribes, black and white, were divided by the stench of an open sewer and by generations of suspicion and alienation. The abandoned Anglican church pointed severely heavenward, its sharp, alpine pitch proclaimed its English origin. In this town of soaring temperatures and minimal rainfall, it was built to withstand a European snowstorm. The large iron bell, rocking in the hot wind, summoned the dead. The existence of the Catholic and Anglican buildings were not symbols of some past golden age of faith; they were historic protests of a handful of former believers in the face of a long tradition of Australian hedonism.

The time at Mullewa was not easy for the Lawtons but it brought Bill back to society's edge, a place from which he had drifted away, though he was beginning to understand that 'the edge' was where he felt closer to and more comfortable with God. Mullewa taught Bill a lot and showed him how much he didn't know. For example, before he moved to the outback he couldn't change a tyre and, with macabre humour, Bill recalls how he learned to do so. He had been on a pastoral call a long way from base and on the way back across the rocky countryside he became lost and his vehicle became bogged in the soft sand of a dry creek bed. To make matters worse one of his tyres was going flat. he tried everything, but the vehicle wouldn't budge and the tyre kept getting flatter. The day was hot, Bill was running out of water and after digging away for an hour or so he eventually threw up his hands and sat down on the truck feeling sorry for himself. Then he noticed four crows sitting on the branch of a dead tree near the river bank. He can't say for sure that they were licking their lips but he is positive they were smiling. Suddenly the adrenalin began pumping and Bill began digging again. The tyre was replaced and eventually he made his way out of the creek bed and headed home. Necessity is the mother of invention. At the end of his stint at Mullewa, Bill could not claim a lengthy string of conversions but he was confident that should he ever wish to leave the church, he could hang out his shingle as an odd-job man.

In 1976, Bill once again moved away from 'the edge', returning to Moore College in the position of Dean of Students. Basically, this meant that Bill's main brief, apart from teaching, was to act as a counsellor and mentor to the students. The general opinion of those who came across Bill at the college was that he was a 'great bloke'. One of his ex-students stated, 'Bill was a tremendous teacher. He could sit with a plodder and patiently explain and re-explain the answer to a problem. Then he could move on and speak to an intellectual, conversing at lofty academic heights and the intellectual would go away more than satisfied. I wasn't particularly good at Greek but he helped me to such an extent that I topped the course.'

Bill Lawton stayed as Dean of Students at Moore College for 13 years — probably too long. Former student, Jeff Ware, now a school chaplain in Sydney, remembers Bill Lawton with great affection. 'Bill is one of life's great characters. He was a wonderful teacher and always there for his students but he wasn't your typical Anglican clergyman. I fondly remember Bill coming into one of my lectures at Moore dressed in a T-shirt and a pair of builder's shorts. He stood for a moment, then he looked out at the class

114

and said: "What am I doing here, standing at this lectern trying to force information into the brains of you dumb guys? I should be minister of a leafy, well-to-do parish, whiling away the time drinking cups of tea with little old ladies".'

As his time at Moore College passed, Bill found that he was having doubts about Anglican theological teaching and the direction in which the Anglican church, as a whole, was heading. He disagreed with the Sydney evangelicals' proclamations on the priesting of women and their attitude of 'we are right but we'll pray for those who are wrong'. Bill could never see God as an angry God, believing those who saw Him in this light missed the beauty and the love that He wants to show to humankind. Bill also disagreed with the emphasis that the 'powers that be' placed on the teaching of Paul, which sometimes seems to accentuate the Thou shalt Nots and which puts Jesus and the Gospels in a seemingly lesser position. Furthermore, because of the male-orientated ethos of Moore College, Bill felt that Margaret, who had always been a partner in his work, was now little more than an appendage to the Dean of Students. He realised this was wrong. His wife was a brilliant, dedicated woman in her own right and deserved to take a meaningful part in the work of God and the community. Therefore, Bill and Margaret sat down to rethink their relationship to each other and to others. They came to the conclusion that they wanted a mutual ministry that could maximise their skills and initiatives; a parish that was not in the mainstream of the Anglican church — a place where social justice was the focal point.

They decided to make a career move that would never have been envisaged in the early years of their marriage. So they took over the church of St. John's, Darlinghurst, the Parish of East Sydney, in the heart of Kings Cross — Australia's most difficult city parish. Bill Lawton was going back to 'the edge'.

Over the decades, the Parish of St. John's had built-up a tradition of involving itself in Christian outreach to the marginalised people of the community. Going back to the depression of the 1890s, the community of St. John's made a huge commitment to the unemployed and if a stranger should walk into the same church over 100 years later they could not help but notice the church windows which focus almost solely on charity. Up until the 1950s, 'the Cross', as it is known to all Sydneysiders, had always been a pleasant lively bohemian area which encouraged the avant-garde and the non-conformists, where the professional working girls walked their weary beat and where, for a price, you could obtain anything you wanted. Yet, in those days, it was a place the middle class could visit with a sense of excitement and a degree of safety. Then the Cross began to change as the massage parlours, strip joints and brothels came out into the open. Worse still, in the depraved shadowlands of the backstreets, child prostitution became a commodity and driving it all was the burgeoning drug trade.

When Bill and Margaret Lawton moved into the lovely old rectory in 1989, positioned almost at the hub of the Cross in Victoria Street, they found a parish in trouble. The previous two ministers had set a course towards social justice, being there for and helping the people who lived on 'the edge' (the homeless, the gay community, the prostitutes and those suffering from AIDS). These men had vision and understood that the answer to the problems of the Cross and Darlinghurst could not be found by conventional means but by showing that God's presence was everywhere: in the pubs and coffee lounges, in the porno shops, and in the gutters strewn with used syringes. They were men who, if challenged, would probably say that their theological beliefs were far closer to Universalism (the doctrine that all humankind will eventually be saved) rather than that of Sydney evangelical conservatism. However, to run a successful parish a priest must alienate as few parishioners as possible and he must avoid the pitfalls of life. Though Jesus Christ achieved the latter, even He could not carry out His duties without opposition and neither could those at the church of St. John's, and thus it fell apart.

Bill and Margaret discovered that those who remained in the parish were confused and withdrawn. Gossip and innuendo about the past was rife and there was little support or pastoral care coming from the area bishop or the powerful in the Sydney diocese. In the reduced congregation of St. John's, there were those who supported the previous minister and wanted his programs to be continued and extended, and others who wanted the new 'team' to sweep clean and start again. For despite its internal problems, there had been many initiatives over the past few years. A hostel had been set up as a stopping-off place for those suspected to be suffering from AIDS. People from other areas of the country could stay there while they were having their conditions assessed at hospitals close by. If they were found to be HIV positive they could continue to stay in the hostel until they found somewhere else to live while treatment continued. A call-in coffee shop, known as PJs, was set up and it became a meeting-place for the marginalised people of the area. Here street people would pop in and any evening would find transvestites, working girls, the homeless and the hopeless sitting down drinking coffee and talking. Sometimes these people requested counselling from the employees and volunteers of the parish, while at other times they would just sit quietly, drinking coffee and seeking a short-term refuge from the pain of the streets.

Johnny Martin attempts another six, but misses.

The exclusive Members Stand at the Burrell Creek Cricket Ground.

Doug McClelland with colleagues Rex Connor and Clyde Cameron.
Looking 'patrician' in the foreground is then-Prime Minister, Gough Whitlam.

Lorna and Doug McClelland being introduced to Pope John Paul II by Bob and
Hazel Hawke. Parliament House, Canberra, November 1986.

Jim Russell celebrates another Aussie win in the Davis Cup.

Jim Russell and his mentor, Stan Cross, talk about their
favourite family, 'The Potts'.

Ian 'Speed' Kennedy leaves court during the Anita Cobby murder trial.

AUSTRALIAN PEOPLE
AUSTRALIAN TALES

Kennedy passes the ball to number 10, Mark Ella, 'the Randwick magician'.

Standing on top of her mountain, Wendy reaches for the moon.

Wendy on the downhill run.

When Wendy laughed, the world laughed with her.

Bill Lawton and his 'first date', Margaret Lawton.

Pat Hughes in his uniform of 'Aussie Blue'.

When one person takes over from another, whether Prime Minister, football coach or parish priest, two common problems occur: comparisons with their predecessor and expectations which cannot be realised. Bill and Margaret Lawton decided to follow and confirm the positive practices and programs initiated by the former rector, though there were some which varied markedly from Lawton's previous convictions.

The paid staff at the church were dedicated and devoted, they knew the scene (one was a former prostitute) and they achieved results. However, no matter how good the team, it all comes back to the 'coach'. Bill was more than just a coach, he was a player/coach. He planned the tactics and led from the front. He quickly found that the biggest problem with his team was not the opposition (evil) but an insidious malady called 'burnout', for the main game at the Cross was played at night and the church ministry must follow. This was the time when the street people came out. Yet there was also much to be done in the day: administration, counselling, preparation for services etc., and so the hours were long and sleep was not always restful. At the battle front, the troops of God don't belong to a union.

In their early years at St. John's, Bill and Margaret got stuck into the job boots and all, expanding on the positive initiatives of their predecessors and introducing new ideas. First, the Sunday services were given a new lease of life and the congregation built-up quickly. A newspaper, *Krossways*, was established and became popular even among non-believers. Margaret, whose forte is counselling, made herself available and soon was besieged by a cross-section of the community who needed guidance. P.J.'s, which had been winding down, was closed and replaced by a people's club called 'Rough Edges'. Here people pop in whenever they like, read, play cards, yarn or just sit and meditate. A cup of tea or coffee cost 40c at Rough Edges and if customers can't afford to pay then they are required to wash a few dishes. This is not to help the profitability of the place — Scrooge would struggle to make a profit at 40c a cup — but the principle maintains the dignity of the customer and allows them to call in even when they are stony broke.

Any clergyman in the Cross and Darlinghurst area inevitably comes into contact with the gay/lesbian community. The relationship between the Lawtons and the gay community did not start out well, as not long after the couple arrived at St. John's a gay lobby group moved to take over the government funding of the church's interim hostel for AIDS sufferers. The lobby group eventually won control and the church lost the hostel which it had founded and which had helped many. As the years passed however, Bill's pastoral contacts with gays became much more significant and though he was never close to the gay hierarchy, the community as a whole respected his work. Bill did not necessarily agree with the lifestyle of some in this community but he always went above and beyond to support individuals in their search for love and acceptance. He was even accused by members of the Anglican establishment of being 'a gay lover'. One of the saddest parts of Bill's ministry at St. John's has been officiating at dozens of funerals for people who have died from AIDS. Many of the deceased were members of the congregation and some were friends.

After serving at the Cross for some years, Bill's spiritual journey began moving in a different direction. He had always seen the human Jesus as non-conformist; a man not afraid to speak out against the heavy-handedness of the ruling class and the high-handedness of the social establishment. Bill saw Jesus not only as the Son of God but as a healer of the people, a messiah from 'the edge'. So, at St. John's social justice became the dominating theme yet Bill tried never to lose sight of the traditional evangelical essence of the church, although some back in the Synod may have felt he was not placing enough emphasis on the Sydney evangelical line. Bill, who had always been regarded as one of the city's better orators, also began to change his style from the pulpit. His sermons became far more personal and far less judgmental, emphasising God's loving forgiveness. The Sunday services were structured for different sections of the community and Bill's themes showed how the Bible was relevant to modern living. Particularly popular was a series entitled 'Women Of Faith and Action', in which well known women such as author/broadcaster Caroline Jones, Aboriginal activist Faith Bandler and author Helen Garner stood at the pulpit (often for the first time) and spoke of their faith (or lack of it), their battles and their problems.

The Lawtons also discovered early on in their ministry just how varied the members of St. John's were. There was an immense amount of illiteracy in the parish and in some services 30 per cent of the congregation could not read. These people sat near worshippers who lived in the expensive high-rises of nearby Edgecliff, or old mansions of Woollahra and Bellevue Hill, and it made an interesting contrast. It must not be easy when a minister says, 'Take out your prayer books,' looks down and knows that a third of the congregation cannot read. Thus, courses in literacy were set up, the results of which were positive and gratifying.

St. John's, though, is not just an area for worship. It has other uses. Being situated almost in the centre of the Cross, it is one of the few places where there remains a modicum of quiet in this whirl of lights and life. St. John's is, therefore, a tempting place for those with other than spiritual thoughts on their mind. Bill would need a calculator to count the number of used syringes he has found in he grounds and on many occasions he has come across addicts shooting up. He tries to talk to these people and occasionally they respond but mostly they become aggressive and swear at him for interrupting the short term remedy to their long term craving. If they are belligerent, Bill just shrugs and asks politely if they would mind cleaning up when they are finished and sometimes they do. Once Bill came across a prostitute and her customer lying on a pew in the church — getting to know each other, in the biblical sense. Bill immediately ordered them out of the church and they went without hesitation. When Bill returned to the rectory he informed Margaret that he was guilty of 'clericus interruptus'.

Many of Bill's advisers from the parish have suggested that after sunset the church be locked and the iron gates of the grounds closed. Bill adamantly refuses to countenance such a suggestion. He believes that people should have a place to commune with God whenever they feel the need. And there is more to it. Bill knows that 'if we lock the gates, we are admitting defeat — we have lost the battle'.

Yet it is the unconventional, the illegal, and the sordid that makes this such a vital parish. For although Bill does not deny that many have found God in nature, music and other cultural pursuits, he sees God more clearly in the struggle of life. He witnesses the God on 'the edge', not the omnipotent vengeful God of the Old Testament but the broken Jesus on the Cross. Perhaps the Church is too preoccupied with cathedrals and bishops when God is concentrating his love on the back alleys and the torments of the junkies and the prostitutes.

This was brought home to Bill recently when he was walking through the Cross. Up ahead he saw two men fighting. It was a vicious encounter in which one of the combatants was receiving a terrible battering. The passers-by were giving the men a very wide berth and the chance of anyone attempting to pull them apart was about 1000–1, with the odds drifting out. Bill had no intention of interfering either but sometimes the decision is not always left to ourselves. Suddenly the minister, in his sixties, found himself bursting into the fray, imitating a boxing referee and metaphorically demanding that the fighters return to their corners. Neither man took the slightest notice. Knives, fists and feet were everywhere and foul, blasphemous language filled the air. Bill felt the most vulnerable he had ever felt in his life. More vulnerable than when he sat alone waiting on the pub steps; more vulnerable than when the examiners of the I.Q. test told him his future was limited; more vulnerable than being bogged in an outback creek bed. Bill was in a situation where he could quite easily be killed. Yet despite this vulnerability he felt closer to God than he had ever been — and he prayed. He didn't have time to pull out the prayer book and read the Nicene

Creed, or even the Lord's Prayer. Nevertheless, he prayed. And the fight stopped! The God of 'the edge' had answered. And at that moment, Bill knew beyond doubt that God answers prayers from the gutters, just as He answers those from Canterbury, Rome and the Anglican Diocese of Sydney. But perhaps the gutters get divine priority.

Bill looks younger than his 65 years; 'a mature attractive man', most women would say. Nine years at the Cross have aged him but it hasn't shown in his face. He looks back and realises that what he believed once may not necessarily be the truth. Bill once described Australians as hedonistic but he doesn't see us that way now. He finds that modern Australians are spiritual, as were the first Australians thousands of years ago — not religious or churchgoing, but spiritual. Bill talks with enthusiasm of officiating at baptisms in the surf, of couples in love taking wedding vows without the accoutrements of bridal regalia and the accompaniment of a large bridal party, of lips that touch the communion chalice without the formality of confirmation.

Though Bill believes in the hereafter, he never thinks of it — preferring to search for his own humanity which he still hasn't fully found. One day, Bill hopes to share eternity with God but he sees it simply as 'a place we'll go' — not a holy grail or the grand-final medal which is given to the champions. Bill doesn't know who the champions are — only God knows that — and maybe there will be some surprises when the time comes. In the meantime, Bill will travel his road in his special way and continue to keep The Cross at the Cross and everywhere else he can. And I reckon he will, as long as he can walk his turf and people move towards him from 'the edge' and say, with simple gratitude, 'Hello, Bill'.

Eleven

Advice From an Icon

In the 1950s New South Wales was the dominant force in first-class cricket, winning the Sheffield Shield eight times in 10 years. So strong were they at the time that it was not uncommon for a four-day game to be completed in three days or less, with 'the Blues' winning by an innings. One such game occurred in Adelaide in 1955 when New South Wales played South Australia.

The match finished soon after lunch on the third day and after stumps were drawn the two teams came together in the winning team's locker room to drink beer and to talk as cricketers are inclined to do of the game just completed, of games long gone, of characters of cricket now dropped, retired or dead, of umpires who couldn't tell an LBW from a batting glove, of fillies good enough to win at Flemington and of fillies that they happen to be taking out that evening. The yarning was in the time-honoured tradition of cricket, going back to days of Spofforth and sure to continue long after the days of Warne.

In the winning team at that particular game were two young colts beginning to make their name, Brian Booth and Warren Saunders. Not wishing to imbibe too early in the day (in Booth's case, not wishing to imbibe at all), the two youngsters decided on a game of tennis. So they walked around behind the grandstand to the Memorial Drive Tennis Club, borrowed some balls and a couple of racquets and began a 'boots and all' singles match on one of the perfectly prepared grass courts that then abounded in this magnificent sporting area of Adelaide.

Saunders and Booth were both excellent sportsmen. Booth would represent Australia in hockey at the 1956 Olympic Games and both were A-grade tennis players. The first set was a tough affair and every point was hard fought. With the score standing at 4–all, 30–15, on Booth's serve, Saunders noticed a man walking along the path that ran beside the courts. As the figure drew closer, he realised that it was none other than Sir Donald Bradman. Suddenly the young up-and-coming opener realised that he had a chance to impress the most powerful man in world cricket.

Saunders braced himself for the next serve, which forced him wide to his forehand, yet with natural anticipation and skill he managed to return cross court. Booth, though, knew before his opponent played the shot where the ball was heading and played the perfect drop shot over the net with Saunders well out of his ground — a certain winner. Not so! Saunders wasn't renowned for giving in easily and, what's more, he knew that 'The Don' was watching. He charged towards the ball which was just about to bounce for the second time and somehow managed to get his racquet underneath it, lobbing it over Booth's head. Booth turned and chased it, and with his back towards his opponent deftly returned it under his arm. Saunders chopped it off at the net. Booth lunged forward and lobbed it back. Still at the net, Saunders leapt high and smashed the ball at his opponent's feet. With the dexterity of a ballet dancer Booth blocked it back. Saunders hit for the open spaces, Booth returned it once again with a blinding forehand volley which with timing and power Saunders volleyed back — passing Booth down the backhand line. It was a rally that would have had the spectators at the centre court of Wimbledon jumping to their feet and spilling their strawberries and cream.

Bradman had not stopped but he had slowed his walk as he witnessed the rally. The point finally decided, the two combatants looked over at the man who averaged 99.94 in Test cricket and who, in his day, was also an A-grade tennis player and scratch golfer. The two players, knowing that they must have impressed the champion, greeted him as he walked past ...

'G'day, Sir Donald!'

The greatest living Australian raised his hand in a gesture of salutation and remarked, 'I'd have thought that you two would be better off practising your cricket'.

And The Don kept on walking.

TWELVE

TECHNICALLY CALLED INSURANCE

In my first days working in the insurance industry, I was told the old story of the builder's labourer who claimed workers' compensation for his back. The labourer declared that he was carrying bricks on a building site when his back seized up on him. Immediately, he began walking like a 95-year-old man, bent over and hobbling with one foot shuffling after the other. 'I'm crippled for life,' he told the investigator who worked for the insurance company which underwrote the particular policy. The investigator, who had seen a thousand 'compo backs', didn't believe the man and secretly followed him everywhere with a camera, however the man continued to walk with a hobbled gait when he visited the doctor, and remained inside his house for the rest of the time. Despite endless medical examinations and the untiring efforts of the investigator, the insurance company could find no substantial evidence to prove that the worker was faking.

In the meantime, the worker hired the best barrister in town and eventually the case went to court. The jury was mesmerised by the passionate oratory and well-rehearsed theatrics of the barrister who convinced them that the injury was caused by a greedy boss forcing the poor underpaid worker to carry a huge load of bricks that would have taxed the vertebrae of Clark Kent. The barrister claimed that, had it not been for this crippling affliction, the worker would have started his own multimillion-dollar building company, driven in the 'Round the World' car rally, won an Olympic Gold Medal for the discus and had sex nine times a night. So bewitched by the performance was the jury that the barrister asked for a payout four times more than expected and got it.

While the barrister and his client were celebrating in the barrister's chambers, the investigator walked in and said quietly to the 'injured' labourer, 'We know you're an imposter and no matter how long it takes or what it costs I'm going to prove it. So just be aware that I will be following you everywhere you go until I prove you are a fake and then you will go to jail for eight years. And don't try to hide, I'll find you'.

The barrister handed the investigator a glass of the best champagne and replied, 'Speaking on behalf of my client, sir, I wish to inform you that he has no intention of hiding. As a matter of fact, I will be only too pleased to give you his itinerary for the next week and a half'. The barrister took a sip of champagne and continued, 'Tomorrow he will be picked up at his house in a taxi and he will be taken to the International Airport. There he will board the first-class section of a plane bound for Paris. On arriving in Paris he will be taken by chauffeured limousine to a suite in the most expensive hotel on the Champs-Elysées. After resting his poor, sore back for three days he will be picked up by another limousine and driven slowly south to a little place called Lourdes. There he will await your arrival. The next day, with assistance from two nuns, he will hobble down to the Grotto, where, no doubt, you will follow him, with your camera at the ready. Then, sir, if you are watching carefully, you will witness a miracle. The greatest return to health since Lazarus rose from the dead 2000 years ago'.

I spent 27 years in the insurance industry, specialising in what is known as General Insurance, as distinct from Life Insurance (or 'Life Assurance', as it was then known). Most of this time I spent 'out on the road', which made for a pleasant and interesting life. Insurance folk are no different from any other people in commerce, except that they are not quite so well paid and they drink more. Over my three decades in the insurance game, I made a little money, many friends and had more than my share of laughs.

+ + +

Clive Nuttall and his wife Marilyn were clients of mine and for many years I was the broker who was responsible for their insurance portfolio. They owned a business on Pennant Hills Road, Pennant Hills, which sold prints, framed and unframed at the front of the shop, with a picture-framing business out the back. The business also ran a small fleet of vehicles.

One morning, I was on the road early, to keep an appointment with a client in Carlingford, when the traffic came to a halt on Pennant Hills Road. There was no movement for about 10 minutes and being a fairly impatient character, I stepped out of the vehicle and walked along the line of stalled traffic to see what was happening. Up ahead I could see there had been a two-car accident, although it didn't seem serious, and while I was watching both cars moved off the road to the parking area of a squash centre. Soon the traffic began flowing again.

Three minutes later, as I drove slowly passed the squash centre, I saw the drivers of the two damaged vehicles taking down details of each other's registration and licence and I recognised one of them as Clive Nuttall. I turned my car left into the parking area, found a spot and walked up to the two men who were huddled over the bonnet of one of the cars.

'Had a bit of a dingle, Clive?' I asked, stating the obvious.

'Oh, G'day Marksy,' he replied. 'Yes, a bit of a problem.'

Then Clive turned to the other man and introduced me, 'This is Neil Marks, my insurance broker'.

The man seemed a little startled but he put out his hand and I shook it. Clive then glared at his watch and, with the straightest of faces, he said, 'Gee, Marksy, you took your time getting here. At every other smash that I've had you arrived much more promptly than you did today'.

'I'm truly sorry, Clive. I promise to be less tardy in future,' I replied humbly.

I can still see the look of bewilderment on the other man's face as he muttered, 'Shit, I'm only insured with the NRMA'.

+ + +

General Insurance companies have a reputation for competing viciously for business yet, if the truth be told, they really can't do without each other. The reason for this state of affairs is 'reinsurance'. I won't go into the technicalities here, but let me give a simple example: You own a large factory which manufactures shoes. Through the XYZ Mutual, you insure against fire and other hazards. Your machinery, contents and stock is insured for replacement to the value of $5 million, your loss of income is insured for $3 million and your building is insured for $3.5 million. Therefore, the XYZ Mutual has a loss exposure of $11.5 million. Should there be a fire and the claim is declared a total loss, then the company is up for that amount for just one claim. A couple of these claims per year, and the shares of the XYZ Mutual would drop to about the same price as that of the company mining for diamonds in the Yarra River. So to overcome the large exposure for one claim, the XYZ transfers a proportion of the risk to other insurance companies — for which these other companies are given the same proportion of the premium.

Nowadays, insurance brokers dominate the general insurance market and parcel out the larger risks to the underwriters. However back in the 1950s and 1960s the insurance companies performed this duty themselves, through their Reinsurance (R/I) Departments. The men who ran these departments formed a closed shop with each other so that it became a type of secret society within the insurance industry, very likely with its own secret handshake.

One of the best R/I men in Sydney worked for the London Assurance — a character by the name of Roderick Arthur Short, known to all as 'Shorty'. They threw away the mould after Shorty was made. He brought in more business and placed more 'unplaceable' lines than anyone else in town. To the uninformed, the reason for Shorty's success was difficult to fathom, as Shorty spent little time in the office. He was always in the pub. Actually, this was the very reason that Shorty was so good at his job, for he was never in the pub on his own. Invariably he would be accompanied by other members of the 'R/I Lodge' and when they weren't drinking beer or talking sport, they were arranging business.

Just after lunch, one Friday afternoon, a broker rang the London Assurance and asked them to cover Building Number 4 of a large factory complex owned by Reichold Chemicals. Although it represented a big premium for the company in those pre-inflation times, there was no way it could hold a fire risk of some £300 000 on its own. The company's New South Wales manager, Cyril Hine, looked up his guidelines and found that Head Office permitted the company to hold only one-third of such risks. So he rushed down to where his R/I office was situated and asked to see Shorty, only to be told that he was still at lunch. 'Well get him to call me the moment he arrives,' demanded the boss.

Every 20 minutes for the next hour when Cyril Hine called down to the R/I Department the answer was the same. Finally, as the clock ticked past 3.30 he and the other executives started to worry. If there was an explosion at Reichold Chemicals over the weekend and if, by Monday morning, Building Number 4 was a pile of smouldering ashes, the London Assurance (New South Wales Branch) would be in very deep trouble. Cyril Hine grabbed the phone and, with shades of the Little Red Hen, he shouted, 'I'll arrange the reinsurance myself'.

Hine rang the man who was his equal at one of the largest insurance companies in town and requested that he take some of the risk. The manager replied that he would be more than happy to do so but he could not give authority without the permission of the R/I Department. Cyril muttered something about 'the tail wagging the dog' and was placed through to the company's R/I Dept. At the London Assurance all the personnel had their heads down over their work but all were listening intently as Hine spoke to Shorty's mate at the other company.

'My name is Hine. I am the manager of the London Assurance and because I'm a good friend of your manager's, I have decided to give your company the first opportunity of reinsurance for Building Number 4 at Reichold Chemicals.'

Cyril Hine frowned as he listened and the others could hear him saying, 'No, "Hine" with an "n". No, not hymn as in church. Hine rhyming with "fine". Sorry, Mr Short is unavailable at the moment.' (Shouting). 'I don't know where the hell Mr Short is, I wish I did. Now let's talk about Reichold Chemical. What's that? You wouldn't take it if they were paying a premium of 99 per cent in the hundred. Well you can go to buggery.' Slam!!! 'Get me the Albion!'

When the next call was answered, Hine screamed down the phone, 'Put me on to your manager.' Heads remained down in the London's R/I Dept, although ears remained open. 'Ron, Cyril Hine here. I'm giving you an opportunity to take as much as you want on Building Number 4 at Reichold Chemicals. What's that? You can't do anything without the approval of your R/I chief? (Sighing). Okay put me through. Reinsurance Department? I wish to place a line. My name is Cyril Hine, manager of the London Assurance and I ... No, Cyril is *not* spelt with an "S". C ... y ... r ... no, Mr Short is not here. All right, I'll get him to call you when he comes in.'

At this stage Cyril Hine's assistant manager and the assistant to the assistant had all grabbed a phone, though instead of wasting time talking to the 'heavies' they were going directly to the source. 'Reinsurance Department? My name is Wilson, I'm with London Assurance and I wish to place a line for Reich ... No, Mr Short is out at the moment. Anyway, he has nothing to do with it. I am now in charge of the London's reinsurance and ... Hello? Hello?'

As the clock moved past 4 pm the executives of the London Assurance were feeling deep concern, though some witnesses at the time have described this mood more as 'panic'. Eventually, Cyril Hine struck reinsurance 'oil'. 'You say you *will* take some of Reichold Chemicals Building Number 4? Wonderful ... Er, don't bother to thank me, it's my pleasure. The building is to be insured for £300 000 and I'm prepared to give you the opportunity of taking one-third. Look, I'm in a benevolent mood this afternoon ... you can take 50 per cent if you wish. Yes, that's right, £150 000 ... You'll take what? ... £500? ... Surely you can do better than that? ... You can't! ... All right, £500 it is.'

At around 4.35pm, in strolled Shorty, slightly the worse for wear but ready for action. The cavalry had arrived in the nick of time! By then, Cyril Hine's temper had disappeared, swamped by frustration and fatigue. He addressed Shorty in a polite and business-like manner. 'Oh, Mr Short, we are in the process of placing the reinsurance for Building Number 4 at Reichold Chemicals. Now that you have returned, we will leave the rest of the transaction to you.'

Shorty grinned and said, 'I know the risk. How much do you want reinsured?'

'Two hundred thousand pounds.'

'How much have you got covered?'

'It has been quite difficult,' replied Hine, 'but we are on the way.'

'How much?'

'Er, up to this point ... five hundred pounds.'

Shorty turned to one of his staff and said quietly, 'Get me the Queensland, Bankers and Traders and the Equitable.' The executives stood where they were, fingers crossed, and watched.

Those present that afternoon then witnessed a perfect example of the matey machinations of Sydney reinsurance as the brotherhood closed ranks. 'Is that you Charlie? Shorty here. What did you think of the game on Saturday? Souths were just too good weren't they? Building Four, Reichold. What will you take? Not enough. Make it fifty thousand. Thanks mate, see you at the usual spot Monday.'

'G'day, Mac, did you back that horse I tipped you? Good price wasn't it? Reichold, Building Four. Will you take sixty thousand? Okay. Thanks mate, my love to Valerie.'

By five-to-five, it had all been completed. Shorty turned around to Cyril Hine, passed him the slip of paper and stated calmly, 'You wanted to reinsure two hundred thousand didn't you Cyril? Well here's the documentation for one hundred and ninety nine thousand and five hundred pounds. I believe you attended to the rest yourself!'

Then Shorty picked up his briefcase and weaved his unsteady way home.

+ + +

The most overused term in the lexicon of insurance is the word 'technically'. It is used continually by both insurer and insuree and over the years has been the cause of many misunderstandings and gaffes. As a broker, I would present a storm damage claim to an underwriter, the claim form stating that during the recent fierce storms the rain had come through a faulty tile in the roof, poured into the living room, flooded the new Axminster carpet, warped the antique dining setting that was once the personal possession of Louis XIV, caused the paint to run from an original Rembrandt and drowned the family's pet Dalmatian. The claims manager would examine the claim and after much 'uumming' and 'aahhing' and pursing of lips he would state matter-of-factly, 'Technically, this is not a claim.'

'Why not?'

'Because the water did not find its own access through the roof. The roof tile was damaged *before* the storm. Therefore, technically, it is not a claim.'

I would nod and thank him for his wisdom. Then, as an afterthought, I would remind the claims manager that although my client paid a premium of only 700 dollars he was still an important part of the three million premium that our brokerage pays their organisation. What's more my client was on the executive committee of the Australian Workers' Union, was standing in the next Federal election for the safe Labor seat of East Sydney and was the second-best friend of Rupert Murdoch. To add to this, my client's wife was a rampant feminist and leader in affirmative action who continually asked me why executive positions in the insurance industry were so overwhelmingly dominated by males. Finally, it could be useful to note that my client was once a professional boxer who fought a draw with Tony Mundine and though a kindly man he had an uncontrollable temper. The Claims Manager would then suggest that we both discuss the claim with the State Manager. With much 'uumming' and 'aahhing' and pursing of lips, the manager agreed that, given certain circumstances in regard to the ferocity of the storm and overlooking for the moment certain factors which pre-dated the storm, it was quite within the realms of possibility that, technically, the damage could be construed as a claim. However, there was no possibility that the company would compensate for the cost of the broken tile or the interment of the pet Dalmatian.

Nevertheless, the boot was often on the other foot. Although the above story is *slightly* exaggerated, I have other examples of statements made on forms by claimants, all of which I have either seen or been told of by friends in various claims departments. Below are answers given by four different people for four entirely different claims.

1 Question: Who was at fault?

Answer: Technically I was going over the speed limit and technically I was drunk but the one who was really at fault was the lady in the old bomb in front who was driving too slow and forced me to smash into the back of her.

2 Question: Name of driver?

Answer: I was at the wheel but my mother-in-law was doing most of the work, verbally, from the back seat.

3 Question: What was the cause of the accident?

Answer: I was hit by a stationary post. I guess technically I was in the wrong but the post was placed on a part of the footpath that was too close to the road.

4 Question: How did the glass become broken?

Answer: Cricket ball hit through the window.

Question: Who was at fault?

Answer: My son and myself. He hit the ball but I am really to blame for not teaching him to roll his wrists when playing the sweep shot.

(On this one, no matter how the father tried to excuse the incident, there can be no doubt that it was the batsman who was, technically, in the wrong.)

+ + +

Jimmy Gillon was a very fine rugby league scrum half, who played for North Sydney in the early 1950s. So good was he that in 1952 he tied with the great Clive Churchill for the *Herald* Medal as the Best and Fairest player. Jimmy was also an enthusiastic insurance salesman and one of life's characters. He worked originally with a couple of companies and then went out on his own as a broker or, as it was sometimes termed in those days, 'Special Agent'.

Jimmy was working for the London Assurance when the General Manager for Australia was a man named Harold Moulton. Apparently, Moulton was a knowledgeable insurance man but he stuck to his office and left the lesser jobs to his underlings, who were all fearful of the somewhat remote and aloof Mr Moulton. He would stroll through the office every morning and evening and the staff would bid him good day, to which

Moulton would respond with a reply which, phonetically, sounded something like 'Harumph'. Jimmy Gillon did not have much to do with his GM, though Jimmy always wished him 'Good morning' and a few times had to deliver documents to his office. 'Harumph, thanks, er, er . . .'

'Gillon, sir. Jimmy Gillon.'

'That's right, Gillon.'

One Monday morning, about 10.30, Jimmy tired of sitting behind a desk and decided to stroll down and have a cup of coffee with his friend, whom everyone called 'Fonce', a bloke who owned a menswear store in Bond Street and who also ran a telephone SP bookmaking business on the weekends. This particular morning, Fonce's assistant hadn't shown up for work which made it difficult for the boss who, on Monday mornings, would dash round to some of his punting clients in the city to collect the winnings from the previous Saturday. When Jimmy arrived at the shop, Fonce asked him if he would keep an eye on the premises for 20 minutes or so. Jimmy agreed to do so. Why not? It was better than work!

Jimmy was sitting at the counter, sipping coffee and reading the paper, when a customer came in and walked to the tie rack. After a few moments Jimmy walked over, 'Can I help you, sir?' he asked.

'Harumph,' answered Harold Moulton, 'I'm looking for a tie to go with this suit I'm wearing.'

Jimmy Gillon froze. Moulton, however, turned back to the tie rack and continued to look through the ties on display, pulled one out and said, 'I like this, don't you?'.

To be a top rugby league scrum half a man has to be cocky, quick thinking and lucky; Jimmy was all of these. 'Yes sir, the blue in that tie goes with that suit very well, although maybe it could use a touch of red in it.' Jimmy pulled another tie from the rack. 'Here sir, try this.'

Harold Moulton held up the tie in front of his collar, looked in the mirror and nodded. 'You're right young man, it looks splendid.' He then lifted up the first tie and posed with it. 'Yet I still like this one.'

'You look great in both sir,' proclaimed the tie salesman. 'Why don't you take the two of them?'

'Both? Good heavens I can only wear one tie at a time.'

Moulton examined both ties again and then exclaimed, 'Dammit, why not? I'll take both. You're a smooth talker young man.'

Jimmy smiled respectfully and answered, 'Thank you sir, I'm here to help.'

Harold Moulton paid his money, collected his purchases and walked out of the shop a happy man.

Just before 9 am the next morning, Harold Moulton, wearing the tie with 'a touch of red', strode towards his office. 'Nice tie Mister Moulton.' Moulton stopped and looked at the blond-haired young man who seemed vaguely familiar.

'Harumph. Yes, I'm quite pleased with it myself. Thank you er, er . . . '

'Gillon, sir. Jimmy Gillon.'

+ + +

Later, Jimmy Gillon went out as a Special Agent, placing his life and superannuation business through Prudential Assurance. One evening he had signed up a newly married man for an Endowment cover with a Whole of Life, convertible option. Jimmy had completed the proposal form and was going through the questions on the health statement. These were easily answered as the young man had never succumbed to any ailment worse than pimples.

'Is your mother alive and is she in good health?' asked Jimmy.

'My mother is alive. She is 58 and in fine health,' answered the young man.

'Is your father alive and is he in good health?'

'My father is dead.'

'I'm sorry,' said Jimmy. 'How old was he when he died?'

'I was five at the time, so I guess he was around about 30.'

'What did he die of?' continued the persistent Gillon.

The man thought for awhile, then he shrugged his shoulders and answered, 'I'm not actually sure but I don't think it was anything serious'.

+ + +

I first went out on the road with a company called Sphere/Baloise (a merger between a British and a Swiss company), which set up offices in Sydney under the auspices of a special agency called Commonwealth Underwriters. It was only a small company and has long since gone the way of all small insurance companies and small fish — that is, being swallowed by a larger fish which is eventually swallowed by a whale. There is good news and bad news in being a 'rep' for a small company. The good news is that your bosses and fellow workers know who you are. The bad news is that out in the real world nobody knows either you or your company. To be honest, when I was working for Sphere/Baloise, not only had people never heard of us — they couldn't pronounce our name!

In a way I was lucky. I was given an insurance Tariff (a voluminous manual of instructions, rates and types of risks), a Vauxhall Velox motor car and some cards which read *Neil Marks — Insurance Inspector*. The boss opened the car-park door wished me 'Good luck' and off I went. I virtually started from scratch. It was not easy, though it was an interesting experience and people kept telling me that it was 'character building'.

The boss, a good bloke named Doug Thornton, had informed me that the Tariff was 'an insurance man's bible'. However, I must have been given the King James version because I hardly understood a word. I was shown the ropes by a wily old insurance inspector named Jack Catley whose first piece of advice was to, 'Chuck that bloody Tariff in the Harbour'.

One of my first clients was a man named Stewart, a 'business broker' in the inner suburb of Dulwich Hill. He was a realtor who specialised in transacting the sale of little mixed-businesses. The history of suburban life in Australia during and soon after the war is only now really beginning to be written and much mention is made of these 'corner shops', as modern historians refer to them.

I would call into Mr Stewart's office every Monday morning, he would give me a copy of the cover notes he had written the previous week and off I would go to Bardwell Park, Burwood, Croydon, Concord and suburbs even further afield, to complete the business and collect the premiums. They were usually very small stores, of one room with a residence at the back, and were mostly run by women whose husbands worked elsewhere. The goods for sale were sparse, the refrigeration was always breaking down and by the look of the dust that had gathered on the beetroot tins and jam jars, the produce had been through interesting times — though unlike wine, jam does not get better with age. These little shops often sold sandwiches on white doughy bread. 'What sort of sandwiches do you sell?' I'd ask, if I was in around lunchtime.

'Tomato, cheese and devon,' would come the answer. 'Nine pence each.'

'I'll have one sandwich with a combination please.'

'What! You want the three all on the one sandwich? Oh well, I guess you can if you like. That'll cost a bob.'

In the late 1950s and early 1960s, the corner shop was in its death throes with supermarkets coming into their own ('serve ya self stores' as they were first called) and fancy shopping malls were beginning to cast their ugly shadows across the suburban landscape. To add to this, the motor car was now becoming a working man's necessity, rather than a capitalist's plaything. No longer was there reason to walk to the shop; you could *drive* to the mall.

A decade before, the corner shop had been a place for small community gatherings. The folk who ran these stores, usually a married couple, were people of some prestige — pillars of the local church and treasurers of the tennis club. Sometimes, if I was a polite little boy, such people gave me half a bag of broken biscuits. I remember with special affection that their milkshakes were always fuller and, somehow, tastier than the milkbar next to the picture theatre. The male shopowner gushed with 'the good oil' for Saturday's races and his lady often acted as a marriage guidance counsellor for distraught housewives whose husbands thirsted for beer and lusted after the barmaids who served it. Yet only a few years later, as if hit by a plague, the corner shops disappeared from our neighbourhoods and from our lives. Now you will find only an occasional 'corner shop' set up on the tourist trails of our land, showing what it used to be like just as you see the remains of dinosaurs in museums. The tourists and the young 'Ooh' and 'Aah' and remark on how quaint it all is. Yet although there are biscuit tins with a coloured parakeet on the front, you can't buy bulk biscuits or dusty jam. These places serve only a nip of nostalgia and 10 pennyworth of yesterday's memories.

Friday was 'playday' for the insurance inspectors of Sydney and the reason for this was obvious. In most insurance companies the 'knights of the road' were required to present all their documentation and pick up their weekly agenda on Monday mornings. Friday has never been a productive day for any type of reps, as their clients are mostly too tied up with end-of-week activities to have any time to see them. Therefore, the inspectors would make a perfunctory call on some disinterested client at around 10.30 am and instantly retire to a bar until well after lunch. On Fridays, around the various clubs and pubs in the city and suburbs, insurance inspectors, assessors, investigators and sundry hangers-on would meet to discuss the vagaries of the industry, the difficulty of obtaining new business in a 'soft' market and what a bastard the boss was. Then, as a gesture to sobriety, they would drive slowly home, ring the office and ask for their messages, hint at how busy they had been, take a nap, wake up, eat dinner and escort their everloving spouses to the pictures. For those of us 'on the road', Friday was a pleasant day.

When I was with Jack Catley, we would meet a group of insurance men in a bowling club at Parramatta. As far as I can remember there were about seven or eight of us who began drinking at 11.30 am and began playing our own form of two-up around noon. Jack liked a drink though he always drank 'sevens' (small beers) and, because I was playing sport next day, I followed his lead, surreptitiously passing every second round. So at 2 pm Jack and I were the most sober of all and we had usually won the money, though it was never more than two or three quid. I well recall a young member of the group, a recently appointed inspector from the Insurance Company of North America, with a wife and baby to support, who was not only a very cheap drunk but also a very poor gambler. One Friday morning he had picked up his pay of about 18 pounds and by Friday afternoon he had lost the lot at two-up. I can still see the look in his eye as he said, 'Well I'd better go now'.

I followed him out to the car park and slipped him a fiver. 'This is only a loan,' he emphasised.

'Of course,' I answered. 'I'll see you next week.'

I saw him next week and the week after, but I never saw the fiver.

Among the group was an ex-cop, named Mick, who worked as an investigator of claims. Mick was an alcoholic, a cheat at two-up and what's more the rumour around the insurance world was that Mick 'could be spoken to' (took bribes). However, when the occasion demanded, Mick was probably the best investigator in the business and a raconteur of high calibre. I remember particularly the story he told about the fire at Botany ...

In the years just after the war, a lot of backyard factories sprang up around the suburbs, as the Australian economy began to swing back to peacetime mode. A man named Long had been an apprentice to a tailor as a lad and later worked with a large clothing company. In 1947 he rented an old factory in inner-suburban Botany, bought some second-hand machinery and started his own little manufacturing business, making ladies undergarments. Long's business never really got off the ground and a year later it was nothing but ashes and smouldering ruins. Long immediately contacted his insurance company.

Mick was called in to investigate and after checking the ruins and the records, quickly came to the conclusion that Long had attempted to defraud the company by starting the fire himself. At first, Long emphatically denied this. However, after a short time the ex-cop wore him down with the weight of evidence against him, threats of legal action and the real possibility of a jail term. Long then broke down and confessed. He admitted, tearfully, that he couldn't make ends meet, creditors were hounding him for money and with a wife and three kids to support he didn't know where to turn. So in a fit of depression he decided to burn down the factory and claim the insurance. Mick immediately arranged a meeting for Long and himself with the Claims Manager of the insurance company. At the meeting, the Claims Manager agreed to drop any civil action on the proviso that Long would sign a form releasing the company from any claim now or in the future.

After the meeting, feeling a little sorry for Long, who still had three kids and a wife to support but who was now destitute, Mick suggested that they go to a pub nearby where the poor man could drown his sorrows. After entering a fairly deserted pub, Mick laid a pound note on the bar and said, 'Let's drink it out' (in those days beer was ninepence a schooner). As the morning turned into afternoon and with only a few pence left on the counter, Long, very intoxicated, turned to the investigator and asked what it was that first made Mick suspicious.

'It was obvious,' Mick replied. 'You took a "fire only" cover and didn't include the extension for "storm and tempest and extraneous hazards", which costs very little in premium and are far more likely to happen than a fire.'

Long said nothing, so Mick asked the obvious. 'Tell me, mate, why didn't you at least include the extension for storm and tempest?'

Long shrugged his shoulders, took another sip of his beer and answered sadly, 'I didn't know how to start a tempest'.

As with all facets of commerce, insurance is now a far more complicated and sophisticated business than it once was. Every 'i' must be dotted and every 't' crossed — how different it was in the old days. Then promises were made to be kept and a handshake was as binding as a legal document. I remember a client of mine presenting a claim form about which there was some doubt and I was called into the Company Manager Max Husband's office. Though not lacking in ego, Husband was an old-fashioned insurance man and a gentleman. 'Neil, tell me about Mr X. Is he an honest man?' he asked.

I replied, 'Personally, Max, I've always found him reliable and a good bloke and have no reason to doubt him'.

'Then I reckon we should think seriously about paying the claim,' declared Max Husband.

Standing next to Max was the Assistant Manager of the company who looked at his boss and said cynically, 'Yes, but is this "good bloke" telling the truth?'

Max turned red. 'George, you heard Neil state that we are dealing with an honest man. And what is more he has signed a claim form which, as you well know, is a statutory declaration. This man is not going to perjure himself for a few hundred dollars or, indeed, for any amount.'

Husband threw the form across the desk to his assistant, 'Pay the claim,' he said.

I have since met people who would perjure themselves for a half-empty can of warm beer. Yet I have never forgotten the sentiments contained in Max Husband's comments so many years ago. Business may now be more technical and professional and it may have changed beyond all recognition from the time of Roderick Arthur Short and Jimmy Gillon — but people haven't changed. In the old days the most modern piece of equipment in the office was the telephone; computers were as far away as the planets. Since then we have landed machines on the planets and men on the moon. Computers, so we are told, are a far more important part of the office than those who run them. Computers can now give us endless information and even advice, they are the first thing turned on in the morning and the last thing turned off at night and we even have computers that are never turned off. Yet, no matter how they are programmed, computers know nothing of real values. They do not understand ethics, fairness, compassion or humour.

I'm glad to be out of the insurance game. I couldn't even read the old Tariff so I guess that now I would be quickly buried under an avalanche of computer information and washed out to sea while surfing the Internet. Therefore, I'll be content to occasionally remember the past, the old-fashioned industry that was kind to me and to recall some of the wonderful people I met. After three decades, all things considered, I can say that, 'technically', I enjoyed it.

THIRTEEN

CRIMS AND SCRUMS

When I was a kid growing up in suburban Sydney, I was told by my schoolteachers, 'If you get into trouble, call a policeman'. With the benefit of both hindsight and middle-aged cynicism, this seems (and seemed then) just one of those banal statements which sound profound but are no help whatsoever in day-to-day existence. I figured that if the school bully was belting hell out of me behind the ablutions block, I could call 'police' until the cows came home and then went out again, but the chances of seeing a policeman jump up from behind the urinals to grab the bully and shove him into the back of a paddy wagon before I lost the rest of my teeth were, at the very best, remote. Yet, as I look back, I remember policemen as huge blokes with kindly faces and voices with a laugh in them. The sight of them strolling down the street provoked feelings of respect, envy ... and a touch of fear as well. It is different now — and our society is the worse for that.

To quote police vernacular, the New South Wales Police Service has been 'doing it tough' lately. It has been tainted by the bogey of corruption. Policemen are 'dobbing' on fellow policemen and morale is lower than the cells beneath the old courthouse at Darlinghurst. In the meantime, a new Police Commissioner has been recruited from the United Kingdom to try and prevent what is left of a once great institution from gurgling down the plughole of public disillusionment. Whether the new Commissioner, Peter Ryan, or anyone else can help the situation is doubtful, for as time has passed our society has become less caring and people far more self-centred. Meanwhile, crime hasn't exactly knocked off for lunch

Ian 'Speed' Kennedy, has left the 'Force' for a while, taking two years' leave of absence without pay. In the circumstances of the times we live in, this may look suspicious, but I can assure you Detective Inspector Kennedy has not been 'sin-binned' for any perceived misdemeanour. He is simply taking an opportunity to pursue his other 'career' — rugby football. In fact Speed Kennedy has an unblemished record with the New South Wales Police Service and is a man untainted by scandal. It would probably be fair to say of him that he hasn't always followed the rule book to the letter, but it would also be reasonable to add that he is one of the State's most admired lawmen, thorough and brave — a copper's copper.

Ian Kennedy was born in Sydney in 1948 and if there is such a thing as a 'typical' Australian, I guess that Speed Kennedy is about as close as you'll get. For starters, he is related, on his mother's side, to Captain James Cook (not a bad start!). His forebears came from Scotland to Australia well before the turn of the century. His father fought at El Alamein and is one of those privileged Aussies belonging to the famous but ever-diminishing band of gallant soldiers known to the world as The Rats of Tobruk. Reg Kennedy, now 82, has lived a successful but unobtrusive life since returning from the war. He is proud of his family but like so many of his digger mates, he doesn't talk much about the war, which is a pity because there are tales that should be told.

For four generations the male members of the Kennedy family tended towards the police force as a career direction. Kennedy has no explanation for this — 'it just happened' — and his grandfather, uncle and a cousin all made their mark in the business of 'law enforcement'. It was therefore taken for granted that young Ian would follow in their footsteps. However, as a schoolboy, the lad yearned to go to Duntroon Military College and become a soldier. At Sydney High School he worked hard at his studies and at his rugby — with this military goal in mind — but, despite a good result in the external exam, Ian missed out.

It was at Sydney High that Ian Kennedy received the name 'Speed'. Before football practice one Thursday, a couple of pick-up teams were playing touch footy. The First XV five-eighth slipped through the defence with nobody to oppose him but the full back. The five-eighth looked around for support and saw it there in the shape of a young third-grade hooker named Kennedy. The ball carrier drew the fullback and sent a pass to Kennedy who caught it with nobody to beat and only 35 yards to run. And run he did, but not fast enough for the school's reigning football hero and, later, champion Wallaby and South Sydney centre, Phil Smith. Smith reached Kennedy in a few strides, slowed down and then ran behind him, calling 'Show us some speed, son. C'mon, Speed keep on going Speed.' The young lad with the ball tucked under his arm moved his legs as fast as possible but with Smith running behind and teasing him, Kennedy felt as if he was running through 35 yards of treacle. The rest of the players were rolling on the ground laughing and in the end Smith himself fell over in hysterics as Kennedy ploughed on to score the try. 'Good on you, Speed,' called one of his teammates and, like the treacle, the name stuck.

At the time Kennedy left school the Vietnam War was escalating and soon afterwards the Government brought in National Service, better known as 'conscription'. The names of all Australian males aged 20 went into a lottery. If your number came up you could be sent to Vietnam to fight and, of course, if you were unlucky in battle your number could be up again. Young Kennedy wanted to be a soldier, yet Duntroon had been denied him, so he waited expectantly for the news that he was being sent off to Vietnam, providing him with the chance to be accepted into an officers' training school. Fate, though, is a fickle fellow and his number never came up. So Speed Kennedy joined the New South Wales Police Service and the Randwick Rugby Club.

After his police training was completed, Constable Kennedy was given his first posting to the Darlinghurst and Kings Cross area of inner Sydney. If crime in Sydney could be equated to a swimming pool then 'the Cross' and 'Darlo' represented the deep end. For it was in this area that drug dealers pushed their murderous wares, illegal gambling dens operated and prostitution was the dominant industry. In the late 1960s and early 1970s the policeman who controlled this district was one of Sydney's best-known personalities — Frank 'Bumper' Farrell. Bumper was not only the town's toughest and best-known cop, he was also its best-known and toughest rugby league footballer. He played for Newtown in their halcyon days and when Bumper tucked the ball under his arm and charged forward, the crowd roared and the opposition players had nowhere to hide. Stories abound about Bumper's toughness on and off the field and if you were to go into a club where some old rugby league players are gathered at one end of the bar and a few old cops are reminiscing up the other end, you could very likely stop on the fringe of each group and hear the same name — 'Bumper Farrell'.

Once an opposition player accused Bumper of biting his ear off in the scrum. Now even in the tough old days of rugby league, this sort of offence was considered quite serious. Much front-page publicity was given to the incident and also to Bumper's pending appearance before the judiciary the following week. However, Bumper was found innocent when he showed that it would be impossible for him to bite off anybody's ear owing to the fact that his (false) teeth were hanging on a peg in the locker room.

Whatever methods he used, Bumper Farrell knew his police district like he knew Henson Park — and ran it with a combination of toughness and understanding. Though crime remained part and parcel of the area, it never got out of control and the general public could walk the streets with a reasonable degree of safety. Farrell used to call young Constable Kennedy 'Rah Rah' (because he was a rugby union player). As a rookie cop, Kennedy found Farrell a great help in his career. Though rough and ready in speech and demeanour, Bumper possessed 'people skills' before anyone understood what the term meant. On a number of occasions Kennedy saw Bumper pay the bail money of old Kings Cross characters and chronic drunks who were thrown in jail for minor offences. Once they were released, Bumper would ring their families. 'He's here again, Maisie, come down and take him home.' Farrell may not have always played by the rule book and was not averse to throwing a punch when he considered it necessary, but despite the possibility that his teeth might be hanging in the locker room, Bumper took his heart with him wherever he went.

Late one summer, Farrell's direct boss, Chief Inspector Lew Nyall, stormed into the station, and yelled at Kennedy, 'Where's Mr Farrell?'.

The young constable answered that he had no idea.

'Well tell him I want to see him urgently,' demanded Nyall.

A couple of days later the same thing happened. Once again Kennedy told the Chief Inspector that he had no idea where Inspector Farrell was at that moment. This went on for two weeks with the boss becoming angrier each day. Eventually, the missing policeman strolled into the station and shortly afterwards in came Chief Inspector Nyall.

'Where the hell have you been, Farrell?' screamed the boss, while everyone in the vicinity kept their heads down and got on with their work.

'On holidays,' replied Bumper, glancing through some papers on his desk.

'Holidays?' shouted his angry boss. 'I looked everywhere and I couldn't find your leave application form that all officers are supposed to complete when they are to go on holidays.'

'What leave form?' Bumper asked.

'The rules state that everyone must fill out forms, otherwise how are we supposed to know where you are?' argued the Chief Inspector.

Bumper looked up from his papers and gave his explanation, 'Hell, Lew, you could have asked anybody. Shit, every bastard in Sydney knows that Bumper Farrell always takes his holidays in February.'

Speed Kennedy enjoyed police work, although he began to have second thoughts one day when he was called to a seedy building in Kings Cross, euphemistically called a 'boarding house', where rooms were rented by the hour. Somebody had complained of a smell coming from one of the rooms and when Speed and his partner went in to investigate, they found a known prostitute mutilated on the bed. She had been dead for well over a week. Although Speed came to see the results of many heinous crimes afterwards, he will never forget the instant he walked through that door. Nor will he forget the painstaking efforts of the detectives assigned to the case as they methodically investigated the murder, mixing modern science and old-fashioned methods to solve the case. Eventually an American serviceman, on 'R & R' from Vietnam, was charged. (The murderer was given life imprisonment and served two years in Long Bay before being sent back to the USA to spend his next 20 years in Levenworth Prison.)

Not long afterwards, Kennedy put in a request that he be moved to Plain Clothes Division. From there, after gaining two-and-a-half years of invaluable experience in collar and tie, he moved to the CIB and realised an ambition to be a trainee detective.

During this time, Kennedy had grown to six foot four inches, weighed over 16 stone and had been building a career and a reputation for himself in rugby football, working his way up the ranks with Randwick's famous 'Galloping Greens'. At the club in this era were many players who are now regarded as 'greats': Phil Smith, John Brass, Russell Fairfax and Ken Catchpole among them.

In 1968, Speed was playing in the thirds and learning the trade. Sitting on the sidelines at Chatswood Oval one afternoon that season, he watched a

Randwick versus Gordon first-grade game that was one of the roughest, dirtiest games he had ever seen. Fists were flying in every ruck and scrum and in the thick of it was (in Speed's opinion) the toughest man ever to run onto a rugby field, Randwick's prop forward, Mick Rosenberg.

A lineout formed near the Gordon line, in front of the packed Trumper Stand, with Gordon fans booing the Randwick forwards and calling for the referee to take action. Then just as the ball was about to be thrown in, the home team's Warren Swan thumped Mick Rosenberg across the jaw (or, perhaps, vice versa) and it was on again. Like drunken sailors in a dockside pub, the two packs tore into each other and the referee could do nothing about it, except endeavour to blow the pea out of his whistle into the Trumper Stand. The crowd cheered and booed as the punches flew, and in the heat of the battle, the Gordon linesman charged into the melee and belted Randwick second-row forward Denis Cleary over the head with his thick wooden flag.

Anger can be infectious and following the linesman was the ball boy who, with the dexterity of a cover point fieldsman attempting a quick run out, threw the spare ball directly into Cleary's face. When eventually a semblance of order was restored to proceedings, the referee warned both sides and then sent from the field Denis Cleary and the linesman. Mick Rosenberg and the ball boy both, somehow, escaped punishment!!

After the game Randwick coach, Jack Hovey, approached Kennedy and informed him that he would be playing first-grade against Manly on the next weekend. 'And, Speed, you'll be marking Slaggy (Tony) Miller,' Hovey explained. The young cop was about to achieve another ambition and play first-grade rugby with the most famous club in Australia. And to make the game all the more significant, he was to line up against Australia's most capped international. Speed Kennedy knew that first grade wouldn't be easy because not only would he have to mark the great Miller but he would also have to keep his eye out for surprise attacks from parochial linesmen and zealous ballboys as well.

The big day came and Speed Kennedy ran onto Manly Oval to face the 'immortal' Slaggy Miller. 'Don't try anything stupid,' coach Hovey had advised. 'No matter what Slaggy does to you, leave him to Rosenberg.'

In the first lineout, Kennedy and Miller marked each other and though there was some eye-balling, not a word was said. Speed tensed to jump and then felt as if somebody had dropped a cannon ball on top of his right instep. The pain was not caused by a cannon ball, but by Slaggy Miller's stomping foot.

'Leave him to me,' Rosenberg whispered from behind.

Next lineout, Kennedy jumped, but before he had reached his full height he felt his jersey being tugged from behind, went into reverse and finished flat on his bum. 'Leave him to me, Speed,' came the message from the rear.

In the third lineout of the game Miller ankle-tapped Kennedy and this time he fell forward, flat on his face. That was enough for the fledgling second-rower and on gaining his feet he threw a punch at his tormentor's jaw. Slaggy Miller took it flush and smiled sweetly.

'Penalty against you No. 11, for punching,' called the ref.

'I told you to leave him to me,' said the voice again.

For the next 30 minutes it continued, Manly won nearly every lineout and Kennedy was either on his back looking at the sky, flat on his face or hopping around in agony on a bruised foot. Just before the half-time siren, Kennedy was tipped over once more; then, a second later, Slaggy Miller collapsed on top of him ... out cold.

At half-time Rosenberg came over to Kennedy and said, 'I told you I'd fix him, Speed'.

'Well, why didn't you do that before he made me look a complete bloody idiot?' asked the novice.

Rosenberg chewed on an orange as he gave the obvious explanation, 'Because the ref was standing right next to me and it took him 35 minutes to look the other way'.

Speed Kennedy played 12 years of first-grade rugby with Randwick and in that time he was a member of five premiership winning teams. In three of those (1976, 78 and 79) Speed was the captain. Many critics of the time believed Kennedy deserved higher honours, yet he never got the call for his State. Nevertheless, to have captained the greatest club team of the era to three premierships and to have played with the Ella brothers at the height of their flamboyant brilliance was an honour for which many lesser players would have gladly swapped their blue jersey. As a wise old digger once said, 'It means more to be a private in the Australian army than a general with the French'.

Looking back on those years, Speed Kennedy wonders how he managed to pursue both of his careers. While he was packing down against Reg Smith and Slaggy Miller, he was tracking some of the country's most-wanted criminals as a member of the CIB's Armed Holdup Squad. At that time the squad was led by Roger Rogerson, who in recent times gained notoriety from the NSW Government's investigations into police corruption. Despite everything, Kennedy believes that Rogerson was one of the smartest cops he has known, even though there was a minor personality clash between the two. Apparently, Rogerson wanted to be admired by all and run the squad as his own, and he didn't want to share this status with anybody. One day he asked members of the squad to his home for a barbecue on the following Saturday, and received mostly negative answers because those not on duty were 'going to watch Speed play footy'. Kennedy was getting the glamour — not only from the media but also from 'Roger's boys' and Rogerson didn't like it. From then onwards Kennedy and Rogerson kept each other at arm's length. These days, when Kennedy talks about Rogerson, he just shakes his head. 'At his top, Roger was a hell of a cop. There were few better.'

It was while he was attached to the Armed Holdup Squad that Kennedy received the Police Bravery Medal. An underworld stooge had given police a tip-off that a gang led by well-known criminal Butch Byrnes, who was out from Long Bay Gaol on the 'work release' system, intended to hold up the security van from the South Sydney Junior Leagues Club in Kingsford. The amount of money collected at the club over the weekend was substantial and, the following week, the Holdup Squad staked out the area between the club and the bank. There were cops in parked cars along the route, in coffee shops, behind curtains, on the first floors of houses and at just about any other vantage point available. It seemed the whole of Kingsford knew what was happening and as he sat at the back of a real estate agent's shop, with a view of the club, Kennedy could not help thinking that surely Butch and his boys must know it as well.

Nevertheless, as the security van pulled up outside the club, a sedan stopped a few yards behind it. Everybody was ready to go, nerves tingling, adrenalin pumping. They waited, nothing happened and after the van had delivered the cash and driven away, so did the sedan. Obviously, it was a trial run only. Next week the van stopped and so did the sedan. This time, however, the four occupants of the car pulled balaclavas over their heads, opened the doors, drew out guns and raced towards the guards ...

Suddenly, dozens of cops appeared from their hiding places and the gang members, realising they were outnumbered, began shooting as they headed back to the sedan. Led by Kennedy, police returned fire as they rushed across the road towards the vehicle. Butch Byrnes went down, struck by the hail of bullets, and died within a few minutes. The other bandits managed to get to the car and it roared off down Anzac Parade towards the suburb of Maroubra, although within metres its tyres were shot out by police sharpshooters. The car kept going — clanging along on its rims. Meanwhile, Kennedy and about 12 cops had clambered into, and onto, the old security Kombi van and set off in pursuit.

Bullets filled the air like a lethal summer hailstorm as the fugitives returned the police fire. Within a couple of minutes it was all over and the bandits surrendered. The next day a newspaper headlined: 'Shoot-out at the Kingsford Corral'.

As he thinks back on the day now, Speed Kennedy can laugh, notwithstanding the danger that existed. And in a macabre way, it *was* funny … an old bomb, its driver with his foot flat to the floor, struggling along on metal rims, and behind, the clapped-out armour-clad 'Kombi' chugging along with police leaning out of every aperture firing away as if it was 'cracker night'. The press alluded to the movie about *The Gunfight at the OK Corral*, yet Speed believes that in many ways there was just as much similarity to the *Keystone Kops*.

Later in his career, Kennedy moved to the Drug Squad and then to the Homicide Division. By then, after 15 years in the force, he had experienced all the tough divisions and possessed a CV that any ambitious cop would envy. Homicide was the area of police work that Speed Kennedy enjoyed above all others. To bring a murderer to justice gave him great satisfaction. He enjoyed the investigation and the thrill of the chase — though the investigation was often painstaking and the chase was often slowed to a halt for weeks at a time. Murders in every-day life are not as you see on the screen and many are related to some domestic problem: husband kills wife's lover or wife-basher belts spouse once too often. Of course, there are also numerous murders related to the criminal world, such as when a drug dealer moves in on another's territory. Kennedy found that most murders are solved by informers giving assistance to the authorities or by accomplices 'squealing' in the hope of getting a lighter sentence by putting the blame on another. In the real world there is very little honour among thieves.

Kennedy was in charge of investigations into the Anita Cobby murder and solved it by the well-tested methods — seek out information, bring in the suspects, question them thoroughly and build up the proof. Almost always, he says, one of the murderers decides he's had enough, blames his cohorts and the confession spills out.

As much as he loved his work, Speed found it difficult to go home and forget life's seamy side and some of the abnormal people who make up this darker sphere of society. To provide balance and an escape Speed Kennedy threw himself into the game of rugby football and into the lifestyle that goes with it. He found that the camaraderie of 'the team' and the macho normality of footballers helped him forget for a while that, soon enough, he would be out there bringing to justice murderers who had taken the lives of innocent people. Rugby was not only an important part of Kennedy's life, it was also a safety valve for his personality and helped relieve the stress that came with the job. And, as his reputation grew as a tough second-row forward and, later, captain of a great club, Kennedy also found that it helped in his day-to-day police career. Young cops looked at him with respect the way he had once looked at Bumper Farrell, and as his fame spread, the informers and the criminals soon realised that Speed Kennedy was an old-fashioned cop who was not to be messed with.

The Kennedy style was to remain detached from his cases and to go about his work in a calm and dispassionate manner — yet every now and then the mask slipped and his true feelings came out. On one occasion Kennedy was in a courtroom at the trial of a particularly vicious criminal. During a cross-examination of an elderly woman, the man in the dock shouted vile sexual phrases, made bizarre threats on the woman's life and looked as if he might attack her. He was grabbed by the police and the magistrate ordered that he be placed in a straitjacket. The witness was badly disturbed by what happened and had to be led from the witness box to give her time to recover.

After the struggling prisoner was eventually placed in the straitjacket, he turned his head and spat in the eye of the young policeman who was guarding him. The cop saw red and had to be restrained from hitting the prisoner. Kennedy spoke to the young man and advised him to keep his self-control. Nevertheless, the policeman was extremely angry and wanted revenge, so Kennedy took the youngster aside and explained that a policeman's lot was not a happy one and that there are occasions when situations are unfair but that he must learn to 'keep his cool' and 'cop it sweet'. When the mature and experienced Inspector Kennedy finished his lecture, he moved back to his seat, passing close to the prisoner, who repeated his action of a moment before and spat straight in Speed's eye. That was the last the prisoner remembered for some hours as an uppercut that travelled from the floor connected with his stubbled chin.

I'm in big trouble here, thought Kennedy, after the prisoner collapsed to the floor. Yet, strangely enough, neither the judge nor any other official in the courtroom saw what happened. Somehow, they were all looking away at the time! Later, when he reflected on the incident, Kennedy realised that he had no right to feel proud of the fact that he knocked out a man who was constrained by a straitjacket ... but, then again, he didn't feel too bad about it either.

Even in the most serious of situations that can confront the guardian of the law there are often moments of humour. Russell 'Mad Dog' Cox, for many years 'Australia's Most Wanted', was the only man to break out of Katingal (Sydney) Maximum Security Prison. On the night of his escape, nobody in the fortress-like prison witnessed Cox's manoeuvres, except a woman living opposite the gaol who glanced up from the television and saw a man walking on the roof. She immediately rang the police. Within moments, a squad from within the prison was organised, though by this time Cox had clambered down from the roof and was heading across the yard towards the outside wall. The police set off in pursuit and were not far behind when one of the pursuers shouted 'Duck!' and hit the ground. The others followed suit but no bullets were heard and within seconds they were off and after the fugitive once more. But by this time Cox had scaled the wall and made his getaway in a waiting car.

When an investigation of the event was held sometime later, it was discovered that there had been a slight misunderstanding. Apparently, nobody had called 'Duck!' What had actually happened was that one of the policemen who was chasing Cox (and those helping in the escape) across the yard had fallen, twisted his ankle and in his pain and frustration at falling over had screamed out, 'Fuck!'. It was many months before Cox was apprehended.

In January 1997, Kennedy was offered the job of Head Coach for the sport of rugby at the Australian Institute of Sport (A.I.S.) (he had been coaching the Australian Under–21s in an honorary capacity for three years previously). It was a tempting offer, for he loved the sport dearly and saw the opportunity to put the benefit of his vast experience back into the game. Yet it was impossible to perform two jobs at once; he had to decide between solving crimes and packing scrums. So Speed compromised — took leave of absence from the Service and began his job at the Institute. As I write these words he has still not decided in which direction his future lies.

When Kennedy looks back on his time in the New South Wales Police Service, he is both proud and disappointed: Proud of being a cop, proud of some of his achievements and disappointed that he could not have done more. Allied to this is a feeling of disillusionment about the changing culture of the community.

Speed believes that many people are now cynical about those who make the laws — and cynical about those who see that the laws are enforced — and he realises that there is now a belief endemic in society that the perpetrator of the crime has more rights than the victim. Speed Kennedy wonders aloud whether youngsters today have the role models of yesteryear and if they do, are they the right role models? Speed well remembers his own mentors — his father and two grandfathers, cops such as Bumper Farrell, George Marshall and John Burke (Speed's partner when on the Holdup Squad), teachers such as Bob Outerside and Geoff Mould (mentor to the Ella brothers, Russell Fairfax and David Knox), coaches such as Jack

Hovey and Bob Dwyer, footballers such as Ken Catchpole, Reg Smith, Slaggy Miller and Greg Davis (the bravest player that Speed ever met) and great characters of life such as Jeff Sayle and Mick Rosenberg. Speed Kennedy is forever thankful that he lived in an era in which he was lucky enough to know such men.

At 50, Kennedy is contented with his lot and will let the future decide in which direction his life will take him. He is happily married with three sons — Brad (aged 28) from his first marriage (a second son died at the age of four) and two boys Matthew (11) and Scott (9) from his second marriage. Both his younger sons are determined that they will play for Australia at something. Matthew is profoundly deaf, though it hasn't affected his zest for life or his competitiveness, and the way he has handled this disability has taught his father to be a better parent and more understanding of others.

Since joining the AIS, Speed has begun to stamp his personality on the game and the signs are there that he could achieve success in the area of administration comparable to what he achieved as coach of the Australian Under–21 team. For a rugby buff to watch these youngsters in action is to see an Australian side reminiscent of the Wallabies of old, as the ball zips along the backline to the wing and the backing up comes as natural as breathing.

Unlike our national coaches of recent times, Kennedy doesn't just give lip service to the 'running game' . . . but genuinely believes in it. He also believes in Australia and sees his brief with young footballers as much more than the basic requirement of instilling in them the fundamentals and the slick moves. He sees too an obligation to imbue in his charges a pride in the jersey, a sense of mateship and a love of their country. This is what he grew up with and learnt from his father and grandfather and from the role models of his past who believed in those values — values which many now consider old-fashioned but which, for all that, still seem to work.

Ian Speed Kennedy, policeman–footballer is now a role model himself; a bloke who has done his best to make his country a better and safer place in which to live. And whatever path his career takes in the future, there is little doubt he will continue to do just that. Captain Cook, wherever he may sail today, would be very proud of him.

FOURTEEN

POSSESSION IS NO TENTHS OF THE LAW

When I first met Herself she knew nothing about the game of cricket. She played tennis at a fairly high standard (she still possesses a wicked cross-court volley that could leave Pete Sampras for dead) and, living in Adelaide, she followed Australian Rules Football. Her father, Ken Pearce, was a keen follower of all sport and cricket was high on his list but his daughter was an attractive young lady with an interesting life to lead and couldn't have cared less about Les Favell's batting average or who won the Sheffield Shield — she had other fish to fry.

Then we were married and Herself moved from the city of Chappells to the cosmopolitan city by the Harbour. From that point, she attended cricket matches endlessly, making hundreds of cups of tea at Waitara Oval, spending many a Saturday to the accompanying sound of leather on willow and enduring on many a Saturday night the raucous noise of macho laughter from the lounge room as her husband and his team celebrated their win, guzzled beer and ate the sandwiches that she had made to 'be sure you boys have a lining on your stomachs and don't get too drunk'. The sandwiches were always tasty, though on awakening next morning with leprechauns endeavouring to escape from my head by use of pneumatic drills and gremlins churning inside my tummy in a gremlin-hydrafoil, I cannot recall any evidence of the 'lining' being much use.

As time sauntered by and the family grew, Herself came to know the people who make up the community of cricket and she began to look at the game in a different light. She realised that 'point' was not just something you reprimanded your children for doing 'because it is rude,' and that an in-swinger was not just the trendy Eastern Suburbs bimbo who was always pictured in the social pages. Eventually the time came when, during Ashes tours, I would hear the television being switched on at 2 am — after I had switched it off at 1:15 and had crashed into oblivion. 'What's the score?' I would turn over and mumble.

'Four for one hundred and ninety,' she would answer. 'Bevo just got out playing an awful shot, but Tugger's still there, batting well.'

These days, Herself has come to know many of the the players and their families and she wants them all to do well. She has come to understand a few of the nuances of this complicated game, laughed at some of its funny happenings and been privy to a few of its dramas. Yet I must make it clear that my wife is nowhere near to being a fanatic about the game nor even a student of same — she merely enjoys cricket's atmosphere and people and it must be admitted that over a day's play she sees far more of the *Herald* crossword than she does of the happenings in the middle.

As a New South Wales selector, I am required to arrive at the ground about an hour and a half before the game begins, to look at the pitch and decide who will be made twelfth man. Recently I arose early, completed my daily ablutions, dressed and was ready to journey to the Sydney Cricket Ground for the match against Victoria when Herself opened her eyes, lifted her head from the pillow and informed me that she had decided to accompany me to the game. I explained that it would be a long day because I had to inspect the wicket and then ruin the day for some ambitious young player by telling him that he would not be taking part in the match. My wife explained that she would fill in the hours by reading the paper and completing the crossword — so off we drove to Moore Park.

Unlike test matches and one-day games, the gates at Sheffield Shield matches do not open until half-an-hour before the game is due to start but, because I have official duties to perform, the turnstile operators allow me through when I arrive and always turn a blind eye when my wife sneaks in behind. This particular day I moved straight to the Blues' locker room for a discussion with captain and coach while Herself walked up the stairs and sat in the top deck of the Members' Stand. As I walked out onto the arena a little later, I looked around and the only person I could see in the 45 000 capacity stadium was Herself sitting in the Members' Stand, hunched over a crossword (three across: 'Lonely' or 'Deserted').

At 10:30 am the gates opened and a few people trickled through the turnstiles. Herself was still poring over her puzzle when she heard a man clear his throat nearby. She looked up distractedly and noticed an elderly man carrying a hamper staring directly at her. 'Can I help you?' she asked.

He replied immediatelly, 'Madam, you are sitting in my seat.'

'I beg your pardon?'

'I said you are sitting in my seat.'

Herself looked round the grandstand, there was not another person in sight. 'Have you reserved this seat?'

'No but I always sit here, so would you mind moving?'

In a situation such as this, Herself's husband would have immediately made his feelings known by telling the man where he could go, what he could do with his seat and where he could shove his hamper. However, as mentioned, Herself hails from Adelaide and was brought up to be a lady and to respect her elders, so she apologised and moved two rows down. A few moments later the man was joined by a friend who, apparently, was also accustomed to sitting in the same seat. From her position two rows in front, Herself heard the first man say. 'When I arrived, that lady was sitting in my seat.'

She could hear the questioning tone in the voice as his mate asked, "How could that happen, Bob? You are *always* the first person through the gate!'

Herself kept her eyes on the crossword (15 down: 'Comfortable in own environment').

FIFTEEN

THE BEST OF A FEW

I stopped at a pub down in Cooma,

(I'd just spent five hours in my car),

While buying a beer from the barmaid,

I spoke to a bloke at the bar.

As happens, we soon began yarning,

Like blokes in a pub often do,

I talked of my days in the city

And dropped famous names that I knew.

I spoke of known heroes and legends
And boorishly bashed on his ear,
He let me continue my boasting,
Stayed silent and sipped on his beer.
I talked of Les Darcy and Melba,
Our first settlers' lives of travail,
I then paused for breath — he grinned wryly
And told me this wonderful tale.

'You think you know real Aussie heroes,
Explorers and legends of sport,
Burke, Wills, Henry Parkes and Don Bradman,
Ned Kelly and Margaret Court?
You could name me others, you say, sir?
Well for you do I have some news
Of one you may never hear mentioned,
A bloke by the name of Pat Hughes.

'You scoff at my rash declaration?
Well we all have differing views.
You say I've had too much to drink, sir!
Let me tell you the tale of Pat Hughes.
Young Pat Hughes was dashing and handsome,
He looked a bit like Errol Flynn,
Pat was ... hold on now, I'm digressing ...
I'll go back in time and begin.

'A man by the name of John Nicholls,
Accountant in old London Town,
Engaged in a bit of embezzling,
So jury and judge sent him down.
But this was the seventeen hundreds,
For minor crimes men had to pay,
So the Crown transported John Nicholls
And bound him for Botany Bay.

'So John was shoved down in the dungeon
Of a boat, with chains round his feet,
Sailed with Captain Phillip's flotilla,
(Old ships — later called "The First Fleet").
And John stepped ashore at Port Jackson,
As Albion's flag was unfurled,

Not knowing that one day his grandchild,
Would help save old Albion's world.

'John served out his time as a convict,
He found a nice girl whom he wed,
Was granted some acres at Prospect,
Toiled hard on his farm and then bred.
Like Nicholls, his children were clever,
The Lord forgave John for his sins,
And Pat Hughes was Nicholl's great-grandson,
And that's where my story begins.

'Pat Hughes first saw daylight in Cooma,
But didn't stay long in the cold,
The Hugheses then moved up to Sydney,
A town for the robust and bold.
Young Pat shone at surfing and rugby,
But life often springs a surprise,
For Destiny's diary was calling,
And Pat's heart was high in the skies.

'He attended Air Force Staff College,
Though outdated, Pat didn't care,
He flew only tortoise-like bi-planes,
But Pat Hughes was up in the air.
In London the "RAF" was recruiting,
He applied in May thirty-eight,
And then he set off for old England,
That moment Pat settled his fate.

'Pat was a natural-born flyer,
Knew tactics, manoeuvres and bombs.
Instead of Pat learning from others,
He found he was teaching the Poms!
His uniform never was British,
He always wore Aussie-style blue,
His accent was typically Sydney,
Not, "pip-pip old chap, toodeloo".

'A dog, name of Butch, was Pat's mascot,
He followed his mate everywhere,
And sometimes when no-one was watching,

Pat took old Butch up in the air.
But training and fun days were ending,
In Europe the Nazis had won,
Then Hitler's eyes turned upon England,
The Battle of Britain begun.

'Soon Pat became surrogate leader,
Though no braid was sewn on his arm,
To Hell men would follow this Aussie,
A skipper with toughness and charm.
He led by his own brave example,
He bent them like slaves to his will:
("If we lose there'll be no tomorrow,
The name of the game is to kill.")

'"Get close to the bastards, I tell you,
So close that propellers can kiss,
Then give 'em your whole ammunition,
I promise you boys, you can't miss.
For we have the home-ground advantage,
The Spitfire's the very best plane,
But if by some chance you should crash it,
Then bail out, and go up again."

'The future of freedom was doubtful,
For three months the world held its breath,
As daring lads soared into battle
And flew with their co-pilot, Death.
They fought without thought of survival
Limbs weary, nerves tattered and torn,
Not knowing if they'd be returning,
Or if they'd be dead the next morn.

'T'was high over verdant south England,
The stage where this drama was played,
The sky was alight with the carnage,
And down on the ground people prayed.
Pat moved his plane closer and closer,
He looked his foe full in the eyes,
The gun would deliver his message,
Pat Hughes was the king of the skies.

'The Luftwaffe started to worry,
They'd not lost a battle before,
They started to learn what defeat meant,
There's no second prize in a war!
"They've run out of planes," said H. Goering,
(Though he was a bit of a clown),
"Must be ghosts up there," said his airmen,
'Cause somebody's shooting us down!"

'While battle was raging Pat married,
Sweet Kathy caused Pat's heart to sing,
They both lived their lives for the moment,
Who knew what tomorrow would bring?
Though Pat was the idol of females,
His pretty young bride didn't mind,
With Pat on her arm she'd go strolling,
While dear old Butch trotted behind.

'But even the toughest feel pressure,
When playing a game they daren't lose,
And rumours were constantly flying,
"The Doc reckons Pat's on the booze!"
Pat had a few beers, that's admitted,
I guess you and I'd do the same,
When each single sortie spells danger,
And killing's the name of the game.

'But Pat never cared about rumours,
He continued as he began,
And his squadron cheerfully followed,
The kid that they called "the old man".
In eight weeks he'd shot fourteen Germans,
This grand "old man", aged twenty-four,
Of all the RAF's publicised heroes,
Pat Hughes was on top of the score.

'On September seventh, a battle
Saw Pat up and into the chase,
"Get close to the bastard," he whispered,
But "the bastard" blew up in his face.
He nose-dived, cartwheeling and turning,
"Hey, Pat's going down," someone cried.

The Spitfire spun round in its torment
Smashed deep in the ground and Pat died.

'Pat's wife had a bad premonition,
When that morning Butch disappeared,
Then later that day Kathy heard it,
The news that she always had feared.
The squadron looked hard for the Airedale,
They called and they whistled in vain,
That day they lost leader and mascot,
For Butch was not heard of again.

'The battle went on 'til November,
A Czech was claimed No.1 Ace,
Though Pat died in early September,
He still ended up in third place.
The tide to the British was turning,
The Germans were now on the run,
Then Hitler's hate turned towards Russia,
The Battle of Britain was won.

'You quiz me on who was the greatest!
That's something we'd all like to know.
The Ace of the Battle of Britain —
The Czech, Bader, Townsend, or Doe?
When I posed this question to vet'rans,
They seemed to have total recall,
With no hesitation they answered,
"Pat Hughes was the best of them all".

'Pat's medal from Buckingham Palace,
Was awarded posthumously,
He lies in a churchyard in Yorkshire
And lives in the hearts of the free.
You ask me what happened to Butch, sir?
A riddle I cannot explain.
P'haps he died of a dog's broken heart,
Or perished with Pat in the plane.

'The rest, as they say, sir, is hist'ry,
Misty times, six decades ago,
Now rockets can fly without pilots,

And Spitfires are only for show.
But if you should journey to Britain,
I'll tell you, sir, what you will see,
A land green and cold — but it's lovely,
A sky often grey — but it's free.

'I hope Pat is somewhere up yonder,
Above in the heavenly blue,
And knows his account is in credit,
That many owe much to so few.
So let's lift our glass up to heroes,
Great people, whomever we choose.
We'll then have a toast to Australia!
And let's have a beer for Pat Hughes.'

I had one more drink then I left him,
For I had some clients to phone,
I stood in the cold Cooma evening
And felt very sad and alone.
We often feel we are important
We think times are tough, though they're not,
For compared to those gone before us,
Our deeds hardly matter a jot.

'Our lives were not meant to be easy',
A saying oft-used though profound,
For some life is lengthy but boring,
They stay with their feet on the ground.
For others adventure is calling,
They gamble; they win or they lose,
We can stay on safe terra firma
Or fly to the stars — like Pat Hughes.

SIXTEEN

THE PAT I 'KNEW'

I have always had a fascination with the Battle of Britain. I was only a baby when the battle was being waged, though later I read of it and as the war dragged on I eventually became old enough to understand a little of what had taken place. While I was in my first year of school I recall planes flying low over our house and when I heard the drone of an engine, I'd stop whatever I was doing and rush out to gaze at the wonderful machine flying above. The same sort of thing would happen whenever I saw a man in airforce blue. I would surreptitiously manoeuvre myself close to him, hoping, in a magical way, that some of his aura would rub off onto me, because although the army and navy argued it fiercely, airmen were the glamour boys of the services. This was the era of propaganda and the stories in the press and even the songs on the radio told of the daring deeds of our fighting men and the romance of life in the forces. I would listen for hours to the tunes of the time on my little mantel radio but the songs which I liked best were those with a flying theme. (*He Wants To Be An Airman Like His Dad* ... *Comin' In On A Wing And A Prayer* ... and my favourite *Silver Wings In The Moonlight*.) Those old tunes are now long gone and like so many of our war heroes, forgotten.

The Battle of Britain was fought with the most modern weapons then known to humankind. Yet, looking at it now with the benefit of hindsight, there seems to be something 'Arthurian' in the way the combatants went about the business of fighting. I guess at heart I am a romantic, for to me, the one versus one 'dogfight' thousands of feet in the air, somehow suggests a medieval joust. Although these fights were to the death, there still remained a semblance of fair play in the duel, a hint of ethics and a modicum of respect between opposing pilots. This tradition began in the first war yet, although exciting and in the romantic style of the knights of old, these individual skirmishes between the Red Baron and others of his ilk had no bearing on the outcome of the war in general or any battle in particular. Yet romanticise it as we may, the Battle of Britain was entirely different from the aerial altercations fought out between airmen a quarter of a century before.

This battle was a fight for not only the survival of a nation but the survival of most of the free world as well. Even though it was fought by just a handful of warriors it was, undoubtedly, the most important battle of the 20th century. If Britain HAD been defeated in the air, then an invasion was inevitable; should Germany have won the ensuing land battle, the whole world certainly would have been changed, for the worse. The Americans and their Allies would have had no base from which to launch an attack on Nazi-occupied Europe and it is quite within the realms of possibility that Hitler's scientists would have invented the atom bomb before the Americans. Thus the Battle of Britain was the pivotal point of the war and although long years remained before the war was finally won, it gave the Allies the breathing space they needed. For the duration of the war, tiny Britain remained the bastion of freedom, situated only 22 miles from where their enemy gathered, poised to attack.

Reading a book by Royal Australian Air Force historian Dennis Newton, *A Few of The Few*, I was intrigued by the record of a man named Pat

Hughes, whose deeds in the Battle of Britain were spectacular to say the least. I contacted Newton and a couple of Aussies who fought in the battle to gain more information on Hughes. I also interviewed Pat's only living brother, Bill, who told me tales of Pat's childhood and early manhood. Pat was one of twelve children, coincidently the same number of children as their forefather from the 'First Fleet', John Nicholls, fathered. Pat's own father was a postman in Cooma who achieved a minor sort of fame at the time by being recognised as the best bush balladist in the Snowy River area of NSW. Bill showed me some of his father's verses which were indeed excellent and deserving of greater exposure.

When we travelled to the United Kingdom in the early 1990s, I wrote to a number of Battle of Britain pilots who had flown with Pat or who knew of him. Most of these men contacted me, verified what others had told me and, on occasions, filled in missing gaps. Particularly helpful was Bob Doe, the Battle of Britain's greatest living ace. We shared a wonderful afternoon with Bob and his wife, Betty, looking out on their magnificent garden in West Sussex. On the table in front of us was a bottle of scotch whisky and around the walls of his old-fashioned house were dramatic paintings of Bob's Spitfire in action. As the afternoon moved into evening and the bottle of scotch moved towards empty, we studied Bob's log, looked at old photographs and yarned about Pat Hughes, Bob's own flying career and the Battle of Britain. Listening to Bob Doe, I was taken back to the late summer and autumn of 1940 when a few young men, a few Spitfires and a newfangled invention called radar stood between the free peoples of the world and the 'abyss of a new dark age'.

I had intended to write my story of Pat Hughes in prose — but I was fascinated by the examples that Bill Hughes had shown me of his father's verse. So I chose that route. The facts in the story, as far as I have been able to ascertain, are true, and though a few queries do remain, I have not deliberately engaged in any form of poetic licence. The disappearance of the dog, Butch, remains the biggest mystery — and when I asked members of Pat's squadron whether it was possible that Pat had taken the dog into the battle with him, most rejected the idea. However, a number of them remembered the dog going up on training flights in larger planes. One commented, 'Did Butch ever go up into battle? Certainly not! The cockpit was far too small.' Then he paused for a moment and laughed. 'But with Pat, you never know.'

The one thing in absolutely no doubt was Pat's ability as a fighter pilot. Everyone with whom I spoke was adamant that Pat Hughes was the greatest they had ever seen. One finished our talk this way: 'Pat Hughes was a superb flyer and a wonderful gentleman. Please give my kindest regards to his family. It's over 50 years ago now, but tell them I still think of him often and always with admiration.'

Pat's widow, Kathy, married after the war and had a family. She died about ten years ago. Not long before her death Kathy sent Pat's D.F.C. to Bill Hughes, saying that she now believed Pat's medal belonged to Australia. Recently the medal was shown for a short period of time, along with other medals, in the Australian War Museum. It has since been returned to Bill and Pat's deeds remain, officially, unheralded.

Our skies are now filled with aircraft — huge bulky things carrying hundreds of people at a time around our country … and the world. They are ugly-looking machines which accost our ears and pollute the atmosphere. But sometimes when I go for a stroll at late dusk I hear the drone of a little plane heading towards its home somewhere in the bush. And if it's a clear night I look up in the hope that I might catch a glint of those silver wings in the moonlight. Then I offer up a prayer of thanks for Pat Hughes and the few who flew with him.

SEVENTEEN

DINNY, DOLL AND A GOLDEN BOW

I guess I was lucky. I grew up in the best city in the best country in the world — that is, of course, if you believe that anyone who grows up in a *city* can be described as lucky. Yet if fate happens to have decreed that a city is where you must spend those character-forming years from early infancy to post puberty, I reckon Sydney is as good as any you will find on this particular planet. I still live in Sydney, though over the last decade I have travelled and seen some of the world and come to realise that though cultures vary, people don't. Yet each time I return I know how fortunate I am. Sydney is where

I want to be. The following observations sum up my own feelings. The words are not mine (though I wish they were). They were written by Sydney journalist and author 'Buzz' Kennedy:

I have been in many of the world's great cities — wonderful London, fascinating New York, beautiful Paris, dreadful Los Angeles, raffish old and antiseptic new Singapore, the mystical experience that is Jerusalem and many more, but Sydney is my one true love. Of all other cities Rome tugs most strongly at my heart strings but Sydney plays upon them with a golden bow.

I will tell you here of my growing up in Sydney — not a chronological autobiography of youth or some parade of past peccadillos. Not even an opportunity taken to denigrate those acquaintances of my early days who have since shot past me on the ladder of fame and the bank balance of fortune. I ask that the reader be tolerant and permit me to roam a little, to recall incidents long gone — of the time when Sydney was a pretty and vivacious teenager, showing signs of emerging potential, yet still something of a tomboy with a style of her own. This was the era of Sydney's youthful years, before she grew into a beautiful, cosmopolitan, sophisticated woman (though less uninhibited than before). Sydney in the 1990s is admired and envied, a 'beautiful woman' among cities though she is not yet regarded as 'a lady'. I hope she never will be.

'Rabbits and clothes props!'

I can hear the words now, shouted in a hoarse voice somewhere down the street. During and after World War II old men rattled around the streets of my neighbourhood in a horse and cart selling this odd combination.

The rabbits were for eating and the clothes props, large wooden poles with a fork cut at the end of them, were used by the lady of the house, to push the rope clothes line up into the air — thereby ensuring that the wet garments gained every opportunity of being caressed by the prevailing breezes.

The cart, pulled by a broken-down old horse, did not have access to refrigeration — something that had only recently become popular, though few fridges had yet reached Randwick, where I lived. So the time to purchase a rabbit was in winter, early in the morning. If you stuck to that strategy, you and your family had a better than even money chance of avoiding food-poisoning. A summer afternoon purchase shortened the odds somewhat. The best guide of all was to keep your eyes on the dogs. When you saw the local mongrels following the cart with tails wagging, then it was time to dash outside and buy a couple of bunnies for dinner. If though, as the cart rattled up the road, you saw Fido and his mates with their paws over their noses, it was probably then best to search the pantry for a tin of baked beans.

Any historian researching this era would be amazed at the number of clothes props bought. Surely each household could need only one clothes prop per line? Furthermore, the props were made from sturdy gum trees and would last at least as long as the rope line — yet each week it seemed the same householders would rush out to buy another prop ... and the following week, another. The reason for this was vandalism. In our area a gang of the local kids, of which, with much guilt, I'll admit to being a member, would surreptitiously cut the forks off the top of the props, thus rendering them inoperable. What the housewives didn't know was that the 'V', which formed the fork, was absolutely perfect for use as a slingshot — a weapon which in those days in Randwick was as important as bows and arrows had been to the men of Sherwood Forest. I record for posterity that the ideal firing mechanism to attach to these sturdy pieces of wood, was the device used by ladies as a link between stockings and corsets, known throughout the lingerie trade as 'suspenders'. These suspenders were not easily obtained during the war years, though my aunt, who was in her early 20s and very attractive, seemed to be able to get them from somewhere. When I was living at my grandmother's house, I would get up early in the morning and sneak in to my aunt's bedroom and steal her suspenders while she was asleep. Sometimes, though, this plan went awry, as my aunt would go out on dates with American servicemen who were in town on leave and the Yanks often got to the suspenders before I did.

While my father was in the army, my mother, brother and I lived with my three aunts and my grandparents — in their home in Chepstow Street, Randwick. While she was living in the home in Chepstow Street, my Aunty Betty (not the one with the suspenders!) met and fell in love with a digger named Bill Hope who was one of life's characters. I'm not sure how 'Bet' and Bill became acquainted, but soon after they met, Bill was shunted off to the Middle East with a mission, so he informed me, to assassinate Rommel and annihilate the whole of the Africa Corps. To the best of my knowledge, Bill failed to accomplish either task.

Later, when the Japanese were moving south, Prime Minister Curtin recalled the troops from the Middle East and Bill was sent to New Guinea. When he wasn't locked in mortal combat with Rommel or Tojo, he was locked in romantic embrace with Bet in the lounge room at Chepstow Street. Bill played the ukulele and accompanied himself in a voice which in those days was known as a 'whispering tenor' — though in Bill's case it was far more whispering than tenor. Nevertheless, many of his ballads were most moving. Such plaintive melodies as *Jada, Jada, Jing, Jing, Jing*, would make a heavyweight wrestler cry, although my favourite was a poignant, melancholy lovesong which contained the soul-wrenching lyrics:

Back in Nagasaki — where the men all chew tobaccy
And the women wicky wacky woo.

Bill was always good for a joke and he would tell me of his time at Shore School, in North Sydney, where he was good mates with Errol Flynn, before Errol was expelled from that illustrious institution.

'Did you notice those swords Errol used in the movie?' Bill said to me when I was seven and had just returned home one day from a Flynn movie. 'Well he bought them with all the money he borrowed from me and never bloody well returned.'

Later when I was an adult, I would have a drink with Bill (not a difficult task) and he would tell me stories of his war days. 'We arrived in the Middle East and within three hours we had our first casualty,' he began.

'Stuka?' I suggested.

'No, one of our unit broke his leg by falling down the stairs of an Alexandria brothel, blind drunk.'

I laughed and said, 'Oh well, blokes will be blokes'.

Bill replied in all seriousness, 'Yeah, but *this* bloke was the chaplain'.

My worst memories of growing up in Sydney were of times spent travelling on trams. Gee I hated the trams! When they went at pace, which was not often, they swayed from side to side and your tummy swayed with them. When they went slowly, they jerked, which meant that you spent most of the time in the lap of the person opposite. Even when you travelled by car the trams still dominated your journey because the cars had to stop every time the trams did and your tyres were perpetually skidding on the tramlines. There used to be an old saying, 'He shot through like a Bondi tram'. Believe me, if 'he' shot through like a Bondi tram, it would take him two days before he even reached the edge of the metropolitan area — and what's more his tummy would feel like it had just taken on board a three-course barium meal.

The only good thing about trams was that they got you to town — and town was where everybody wanted to go. The suburbs in those war days, and early postwar days, were only dormitories. There were no department stores in the suburbs and every local shop was small and under a different roof. You bought the meat, papers and milk at Martin's or Peter's Corner, but to *really* shop, you went to town.

'Fares, please,' called the tram conductor and you could bet London to a brick that the passenger would hand the money over and say 'St James'.

St James was a station at the corner of Hyde Park which never seemed very busy — certainly not as busy as Central or Town Hall. In tram-fare terms, 'St James' was a euphemism for David Jones the department store which stood right opposite St James Station. David Jones was known to all as 'DJs' and whether you used the full name or the initials it was synonymous with Sydney. David Jones was Australia's oldest store, opened in the very early days of the colony — the original store was probably built by convicts. In the 1940s and early 50s it was the emporium of the people — a population that was moving swiftly from working to middle class. David Jones was to Sydney in those days a name to drop, a place to meet and a link with the past. It also had the biggest restaurant in town, where the waitresses were immaculate and prissy and where a string combo played selections from *The Merry Widow* or *Iolanthe*. The food was ordinary but the decor was olde-worlde and it was the place to be seen if it happened you couldn't afford Sydney's two plushest restaurants, *Romanos* or *Princes*.

I was never allowed to go to DJs unless I promised to be on my best behaviour. Later, it was one of the first restaurants to introduce the self-service style of 'grab a tray and help yourself' — very modern, very American! Well, in a way it was, yet I reckon we lost something when it happened. Soon afterwards, DJs and other large department stores began moving to the suburbs, to malls with all shops under one roof. The trams have long gone now, too, though buses still ply those routes. But the money is now taken by little machines and nobody ever says, 'Fares please'. As a matter of fact, these days most people are far too busy to even say, 'Thank you'.

I can't leave my jottings on restaurants without mentioning the most popular chain of all in those days — Sargents. I loved Sargents' restaurants (though, strictly speaking, to call these pie shops 'restaurants' is like calling bullfighting 'culture'): chunky meat pie, gravy, peas, and a cuppa tea — one shilling and sixpence. Mind you, if you were a person of independent means you could lash out and have pie, gravy, peas, a cuppa *plus* steam pudding with custard — two bob. Okay, I'll admit there was no string combo and even if there had been, you wouldn't have been able to hear it over the rattle of the plates but that didn't matter because you were eating the best pies in creation. Sargents' restaurants have gone now, and if you go to any shopping centre today you can have your choice of many pies — steak and onion or steak and mushroom or steak, onion and mushroom, et al. You can also go to the tennis and have your choice of Rafter, Philippoussis and a churlish little fellow called Woodsomething — but they can't play tennis like Rosewall and they can't play like Hoad. Likewise, you can have all the steak, mushroom and onion pies you want, but they'll never taste like Sargents.

The first of my possessions as a kid (at least, the first I remember) was a bag of marbles that was given to me by some relative who had himself collected them over the years. They were beautiful marbles, perfectly round and smooth, with wonderful colours inside their glassy exteriors. I loved playing with them. I'd place them in a circle, then sit in the middle and pretend I was the leader of a wagon train surrounded by Red Indians and my job was to shoot each of 'them ornery varmints' out of the circle so as to save myself and the settlers. I had five minutes to achieve this feat. After a while, I became fairly proficient at this life-and-death game and eight out of ten times we survived and the wagons would roll on safely to California. I used to fire my taw (aiming marble) in a manner then known as 'cunny knuckle': that is, taw placed on the second knuckle of the pointing finger and flicked off by the thumb. I would kneel on one knee, close my left eye, flick the taw and it would cruise across the carpet like an Exocet missile and *crash* — another redskin would bite the dust. In the lounge room of my home I became particularly accurate and by the time I had reached primary school age I almost never missed.

I was about nine when I moved into Randwick Primary School. Like Judy Garland in Oz I gazed on a whole new world. There were marbles everywhere. Kids were playing Big Ring, Little Ring, Shoot in the Middle, Follow the Leader and other games of which I had never heard. I felt like an alcoholic at 'happy hour'. I have many weaknesses in my character but shyness is not one of them and soon I'd elbowed my way into a game of Little Ring and more than held my own. After a few days, I began scooping the pool; soon I even became a little bored. This was 'Amateur Hour', the opposition were easy beats and I never actually *won* any of the other kids' marbles — I just won the games.

'You're not bad, Marksy, why don't you try The Big Ring?' said one of the players. Whether he was pointing me towards a grander future or just getting rid of me, I'm not quite sure.

The Big Ring, as it was known (not to be confused with the game of marbles by the same name) was where the real action was happening. Remembering those days I still feel a sense of awe at the imagination and initiative of ten-and-eleven-year old boys. The Big Ring was marbles at its professional best, organised by a tough-looking boy whose father, I believe, ran a two-up school. The whole structure was akin to a combination of a two-up game and the bookmakers' ring at Randwick Racecourse. The rules of the game were basic. There were two lines drawn six yards apart (though I may be out by a yard). On the back line were three marbles and behind the marbles would sit the owner or 'bookmaker'.

'Three up 'ere,' the bookie would cry and the shooters — 'punters' — would reply, 'I'll 'ave a go,' and with their favourite taw, attempt to hit the three marbles while standing behind the other line. There was only one other rule — the shooter, if he missed, could have his taw returned in return for handing over another, providing the bookmaker agreed that the other marble was acceptable. A favourite taw was, after all, a punter's means of livelihood.

My favourite taw was a dark and brown 'conny agate'. This taw was most efficient at humming across the lounge-room carpet but on the cracked old asphalt at Randwick school the journey was not so easy. 'Three up 'ere,' the bookie shouted and I walked over and yelled back, 'I'll 'ave a go'. I kneeled down, closed my left eye and in my cunny-knuckle style, I flicked. The taw was heading straight for the target and then suddenly took an enormous turn to the left, a break which would have delighted Shane Warne.

'Wanna another go?' called the bookie. I had another go and this time the marble spun to the 'off' and missed by six inches. Then there came upon me a dramatic revelation which over the years has occurred to many apostles of gambling — punting is a mug's game. The way to make marbles is to become a bookmaker.

Next day, there I was sitting behind three marbles from my beloved collection and shouting 'Three up 'ere'. The first punter who accepted my offer missed the target and then walked away, however when I looked down I found that his taw was a 'bottle-o'. (A 'bottle-o' was an out-of-shape piece of glass which was banned from The Big Ring and all reputable marble fraternities. To use a bottle-o at marbles was like using Monopoly money at the races.)

'Hey, you can't use this, give me a real marble,' I yelled.

'Whaddya gunna do about it?' he replied.

That stumped me. He was in fifth class and large, I was in third class and though solid in build, comparatively small in height. I yelled, 'You broke the rules'.

The Big Ring was quiet and everyone was looking at me. I made a lunge at him and almost in tears I shouted, 'Gimme my marble'. He leaned forward and cracked me behind the ear. Nobody moved. I swung a roundhouse right that missed his belt buckle by six inches. Whack! I felt a pain across my right cheek, the tears began to roll but I swung at him again, hitting him on the side of the neck.

'What's the trouble?' Appearing from nowhere and standing in between us was the tough-looking bloke who ran The Big Ring.

I held out the marble. 'He shot this bottle-o at me.'

'No I didn't,' lied my opponent.

The leader looked at us both and then said, 'Give us a look at yer other marbles'. I handed him my bag. He looked carefully at my beautiful collection and handed them back to me.

He walked over to my opponent and said, 'There is only one place this little kid would a got a bottle-o from, Robbo, and that's from you, you #$%@!'

The tough-looking bloke then grabbed the boy by the hair with his left hand and hit him across the ear with his right. As Robbo reeled back, the leader crashed another right into the solar plexus. Robbo fell to the ground and began to vomit. The leader walked over, put a hand in the puking boy's pocket, pulled out a marble and threw it to me. Then he turned to Robbo and said in a voice just above a whisper, 'You're banned from The Big Ring and if you go runnin' to Mr Ryan and tell 'im what I done, I'll belt the shitter out o' ya.'

At this stage I didn't know whether I was a clown, a coward or a hero. Then the leader walked up to me, ruffled his hand through my hair and stated, 'Ya don't throw yer punches very good but at least ya throw 'em.'

I nodded, not quite knowing what to do or say. 'Gimme two marbles,' he said. I nervously passed him two of my best conny agates. He took them and grinned. 'To be a bookie in The Big Ring, the rule is ya gotta pay me six marbles but two'll do for you.' He turned away and the activity in the ring started again. I hadn't realised that before you worked The Big Ring at Randwick Primary it was a prerequisite to obtain a licence.

I would like to say that after this inauspicious beginning, I went on to make my marble fame and fortune, however such is not the case. 'Three up 'ere,' I cried out once again. I heard a voice, 'I'll 'ave a go' and looked up to see a boy everyone referred to as 'Dinny'. In the years I have been connected with sport, I have never used the term 'champion' lightly, yet without a moment of hesitation I will state that in Dinny I came face to face with a champion worthy of such an epithet. After watching him in action I very quickly found out what I didn't know about the game. First of all, when you're in the 'marble big time' like Dinny, you fire with the taw from the top of your pointing finger, so that the fingernail just touches the marble. To fire cunny-knuckle, as I did, was tantamount to riding side-saddle in the Melbourne Cup. What's more, you never roll marbles along the ground, you fire them from a height and you hit the target on the full. Moreover, you use the rules to your greatest advantage. Dinny had his feet behind the line but he leaned his torso forward and stretched out his arm, so that he seemed to be almost on top of my poor little marbles, and then he let rip.

It was like the systematic bombing of Dresden in World War II! My marbles were flying all over the Randwick Primary playground as Dinny ruined me in eight minutes, leaving me marble destitute. I will never see his like again! In my memory, Dinny to marbles is what Minnesota Fats is to pool. He was magnificent and even though he was ending my career in pro marbles, I could only sit and watch in awe. Dinny could flick his taw through the eye of a needle, he could knock the private parts off a frenzied blowfly from 15 paces. If he'd been born in Old Testament times there's little doubt Dinny would have killed Goliath with a conny agate.

The only comfort I had left was that my brown and blue taw, which had saved many a wagon train in the lounge room, was still in my pocket. 'Three up 'ere,' I heard, as I dejectedly walked away. Why not? In for a penny, in for a pound! I took my brown and blue beauty from my pocket.

'I'll 'ave a go,' I called to the bookmaker. I stood with my feet behind the line, I leaned my torso forward, stretched out my arm as far as it would reach and from the top of my finger I fired my taw — and it hit the bookie in the middle of the forehead.

Randwick Primary was situated on the corner of Alison Road and Cowper Street and as my paternal grandma lived in Cowper Street I often took the opportunity of staying at her place for a while as a relief from the large but fairly crowded house in Chepstow Street. Grandfather Marks had died at the age of 36, mourned by few from what I can gather. Thus my grandma (known to her family as 'Ma') was a widow and remained contentedly so for the rest of her life, although there were any number of men who would have been more than happy to reintroduce her to conjugal bliss if she'd given them the nod. She was a real character, standing four foot ten inches in the highest of heels. An intelligent, confident character, she never stepped back in a verbal confrontation and was always prepared to tell people what she really thought. Many a time I heard her arguing the point — with everyone from the local member to her miserly landlord. She always won. She was an old vaudevillian (working under her single name of Eileen O'Neill), who had starred on a number of the vaudeville circuits in Australia and overseas, with an act called *Tom Rees and His Doll*. Ma was the doll. According to family lore, it was a class act which topped the bill on a number of occasions. The act would begin with the spotlight falling on a large box in which Ma was encased, dressed as a doll. Tom Rees would come onto the stage, open the box and out would step Ma, to walk with stilted steps around the stage like a wind-up doll. Tom would then play some sweet music on his clarinet and the doll would come to life and so besotted with the music was this 'toy', that she picked up the musical instruments, which just happened to be scattered over the stage, and played them. There is nobody alive now who really remembers the act, and family members (who were very young at the time) differ on the number of instruments that Ma played. It appears, however, that she played at least four (possibly seven) in the act, and she was a virtuoso on the cornet and violin. Whatever the exact details of the act, there seems little doubt that when *Tom Rees and His Doll* were in town, the theatre was always full and at the instant the four foot ten inch 'doll' hit the high note on the cornet at the conclusion of *Oh You Beautiful Doll*, the audience would stand as one.

Ma, because of her size and the name of her act, was always known as 'Doll' to her contemporaries in the theatre. In the course of her career she toured the world and worked with such famous names as Roy Rene ('Mo'), Gus Bluett and Gladys Moncrieff, though her best mates in show business were Nellie Colley and Queenie Paul. Nellie was a down-to-earth Australian and she and Ma were room-mates on one trip to South Africa. I recall meeting Nellie one day at Cowper Street when she came to visit Ma for afternoon tea. I regret to this day that I didn't write down the stories they told. But at the time I was only about seven, annoyed that I had to sit inside and talk to an old lady instead of being out in the fresh air playing footy. Yet a couple of the comments from that afternoon have remained in the recesses of my mind.

'You're a nice kid,' I remember Nellie saying to me.

'Thank you, Miss Colley.'

'Call me Nellie. Your grandma and I used to be room-mates — though I spent a lot of nights in other rooms. Hey Doll, what was the name of that bloke I had the big crush on in Cape Town?'

'The chorus boy, Nellie?'

'Chorus boy, was he? Hell, I always thought he was a conjurer.'

The Prince Edward Theatre in Elizabeth Street was a movie theatre, although different from all the others in Sydney. It could better be described as a combination movie theatre and part-time vaudeville palace. The Prince Edward had its own band, its own organist and would feature a different act every couple of weeks. It showed a newsreel but no B movies. The band, the act and the organist would make up the first part of the program and the main movie would be the finale. When I was about 11 years of age my godfather, Os Taylor, suggested that he shout Ma and I to a matinee at the Prince Edward. 'What's on?' I asked.

'*Whispering Smith*,' he answered. I was pleased about this because some kids at school had recommended the movie, with Alan Ladd starring as a gunslinger who never missed and whose six-shooter never ran out of ammunition. It was not, though, a movie that my middle-aged Ma would have been beating down the doors to see. Os explained his reasoning. 'Your Ma will be more interested in the first part of the show because Nellie Colley and Queenie Paul are performing.'

Ma gave me permission to wag school that day (an event not without precedent) and off we went in the tram. 'Fares please.'

'One adult and a child to the stop after St James, thank you.'

We handed our tickets to the uniformed usherette and were shown to seats in the very front of the stalls — not the place to watch Alan Ladd but certainly the connoisseur's position for Colley and Paul. I was looking for the ice-cream boy when the lights dimmed and I heard a rumbling from under the floor. Suddenly, like lava spewing from a volcano, an organ burst out of the bowels of the theatre, with an attractive woman seated up front thumping keys and pumping handles. (That evening, when I'd returned home to Cowper Street, I explained my day's adventures to my aunt. 'Gee, I had a great day Aunty Gyps. I saw the fastest gun in the west, Nellie singing and Noreen Hennessy on the Were-till-izer.')

Noreen Hennessy played some tuneful melodies, though as my lack of musicality was matched only by my lack of understanding of mathematics, I leaned over and asked Ma if the lady was a top-class organist. 'She is a magnificent organist but I do hope she doesn't sing,' Ma answered. As if on cue, Ms Hennessy announced that she would like to sing a Jerome Kern medley. 'I will begin with *Smoke Gets In Your Eyes*,' she told a breathless audience.

They asked me how I knew, my true love was true – oo – oo
I of course replied something deep inside cannot be deny – i – i – ed

'Pitiful,' Ma whispered.

After the smoke had eventually cleared from Noreen's eyes and tonsils and she and the organ disappeared back into the theatre's bowels, the curtains opened and there stood the band leader, Lewis, and his orchestra, dressed in tuxedos. I can't remember much about the act except there was a West Indian man on a double bass singing like Louis Armstrong. Then Lewis took the microphone and announced 'The Prince Edward is proud to present two of Australia's greatest entertainers. Let's have a great hand for Miss Queenie Paul and Miss Nellie Colley.'

Queenie, befitting her name, was dressed regally in a flowing lilac evening gown and carried a lilac handkerchief about the size of a small tablecloth which, throughout her career, Ma later told me, was her prop and trademark. Nellie, carrying a cane, was dressed in her trademark men's tails and a top hat. They began with a duet, then Nellie sang about *The Man*

who Broke the Bank at Monte Carlo and brought the house down with
Burlington Bertie:

I'm Burlington Bertie, I rise at ten-thirty
And saunter along like a toff.
I walk down The Strand with my gloves on my hand,
Then I walk back again with them off.

In contrast to Nellie strutting all over the stage, Queenie with her
pleasant soprano voice stood quietly in front of the microphone,
pronouncing the words as if she was being tested for an elocution
examination and, at the appropriate times, waving her tablecloth:

You are my honey, honeysuckle, I am the bee,
I'd like to kiss the honey sweet from those red lips you see.

(What lyrics! Andrew Lloyd Webber, eat your heart out.)

Even though I was 11 and desperate for the movie to begin, I somehow
understood that I was watching two wonderful Australians, products of an era
of the theatre that was almost dead — overtaken by radio, cinema and, later,
by television. Yet these wonderful old troupers carried on. An era might be
dead, but here were two survivors — consummate artists who would continue
to tread the boards until the boards were gone ... or they were. Queenie:
ladylike and controlled, not stretching to reach the high notes as she once did,
yet the audience heard every word and when requested, they lovingly sang
along with her. Nellie: bouncy and brassy, the epitome of vaudeville's halcyon
days, who could deliver a song as if she was doing it off-the-cuff for the first
time, who milked an audience with the ease and confidence that came from
God-given talent, charisma and more than 40 years of experience. Nellie was
an artist's artist. She slapped on the greasepaint, placed the top hat at a jaunty
angle, grabbed her cane and night after night went out to entertain — not for
the money or even for the applause but just for the love of it.

Nellie and Queenie and their ilk are long gone now. I doubt there are any
tapes or videos of them and if there are any old records around, I've not
heard them. They remain no more than wistful memories to the fading
number of people who once saw them. And they continue to evoke a sense
of nostalgia in a middle-aged man who, as a boy, once went to the Prince
Edward Theatre to see *Whispering Smith*.

Towards the end of their act that day, Nellie Colley peered over the
footlights, saw Ma in the front row and called, 'That's Eileen O'Neill out

there. How are you, Doll?' Queenie Paul shaded her eyes from the glare, waved and said, 'It's been a long time, Doll.'

I nearly jumped out of my seat but Ma just smiled and said, 'Hello Nellie. Hello Queenie. You're both in good form.'

Nellie grinned broadly, 'Grab a cornet from the orchestra and hop up with us.'

Ma shook her head and replied, 'The old days are well and truly gone for me, girls.'

Nellie laughed, 'True Doll, but you're the only one in the theatre who knows it. The stupid buggers are still paying us money for an act that's 40 years old.'

Nellie Colley looked up to the lighting man and called, 'Give this lady a spotlight'. She took off her top hat and pointed it at Ma. Ma rose to her full height. 'Ladies and gentleman,' called Nellie, 'a big hand for Doll O'Neill, a good friend and once one of the great acts in the business.'

There was some polite applause as the bright light shone on Ma. Then from up the back of the stalls a man called, 'Stand up, love'.

Ma turned swiftly in the direction of the man and in a voice full of scorn replied, 'I *am* standing'.

In the meantime, Nellie had been in consultation with Queenie and the band leader. After Ma had resumed her seat, the band struck a note. 'Remember this one, Doll?' asked Nellie. Then she and Queenie sang another duet.

Oh, you beautiful doll, you great big beautiful doll,
If you ever leave me how my heart would ache,
I wanna squeeze you but I feel you'd break,
Oh-oh-oh-oh-oh you beautiful doll.

(And the audience stood as one. Well I did anyway!)

When Ma's husband died she had to go back on the stage to keep the family going. Later, when she retired (for the last time), she rented out two rooms to supplement a rather paltry income. One of them was taken by Os Taylor, a well-known man in sport in the Randwick district. Os had been my father's mentor and had encouraged him in his successful sporting career and when I was born my parents asked Os to be my godfather.

During the war each family was issued with a book of 'ration coupons' which restricted the amount of supplies to each household. Times were tough, though the sacrifices of the people of Sydney in the early 40s could hardly be compared to the Siege of Leningrad and I can never remember being hungry or cold. Still, everything is relative and when beer is unobtainable in Australia then times are indeed at rock bottom. It didn't matter a jot to me then, yet as I sit at my desk now recording that diabolical historical fact, a chill runs up my spine and my mouth goes dry. To Os Taylor, who was badly wounded in World War I, the lack of amber liquid in the Harbour City was a disgrace — a crime, in fact, and if he could have laid his hands on the perpetrators of this calamity then blood would have flowed in the streets. Yet Os was not without initiative, so he decided to make his own. He obtained a recipe from a friend, dug some old bottles out of the shed and set to work.

At this time in Sydney the making of 'home-brew' was very fashionable and there was quite a market emerging for bottles and corks. The secret, the makers claimed, was not so much in the formula but in the length of time you left the brew to settle. Nevertheless, Aussies being the beer-loving citizens that they are, thirst often conquered patience, and most of the home-brews were not given much time 'to settle' and when the cork was removed they were certainly not given any time to breathe.

'Nice drop this, George, what year is it?'

'Yesterday.'

'Yesterday eh — am or pm?'

Os, though, was determined to make the best home-brew possible, so he let the liquid settle under Ma's laundry tubs for awhile. When I stayed at Cowper Street I used to sleep in the same room as my great-grandmother — known to all as 'Gay'. One evening, Ma and Aunty Gyps had gone to play housie and Os was out playing cards. Gay and I were on our own listening to the radio.

Crack!!!!

'Did you hear a noise?' asked Gay.

'Yes I did.'

Crack!!! Crack!!!!

Gay shouted, 'That's bullets.' Then she screamed, 'Aaghh, aaghh, the Japs have arrived. Get under my bed.'

I jumped out of my bed and dived under Gay's. It was dark and I could smell urine, which was reasonable enough because Gay was over 80, blind and couldn't get around very well, so she kept a potty under the bed for obvious reasons. As a gesture to hygiene, the potty was covered by a lovely lace doyley. There was silence, I wasn't game to breathe. Above me I heard Gay turn the radio off. More silence. Ten minutes passed.

Crack!!!!

'Are you all right?' whispered Gay.

I felt no pain. There was no blood. Thank the Lord the Japs were poor shots.

Crack!!! Crack!!!!

Missed again. I stuck my head out from under the bed. 'Are you sure they're bullets, Gay?'

'Just keep quiet and don't let them know we're here.'

There were no more bullets for an hour or so and, eventually, with Gay shaking above me, I dozed off with only the potty to keep me company. I don't know how long I slept, but I woke quickly when I heard Gay calling, 'Neil, it's all right now, Os is home'.

I crawled from under the bed and walked down to the laundry where I had heard some movement and there was Os mopping up a mass of foaming liquid from the floor. He looked up as I walked in. 'There's been an accident,' he stated morosely. Then I heard, 'Crack!!!!' as another cork popped from a bottle and more home-brew gushed onto the linoleum.

Radio, referred to by most as 'wireless,' was the medium of that era and the serials of the time, such as 'Mrs Obbs', 'Martin's Corner' and, of course, 'Blue Hills', were the 'soapies' of their day. I listened fascinated to them each evening, though not with the same grim fascination as the adults listened to the news. Early in the war, the news was never good — and if we had known the real truth it was a lot worse than we were told. Still, it didn't effect the way Mrs 'Obbs and Mrs Bottomley chatted endlessly over the back fence.

These days television has stolen most of radio's thunder, leaving the latter as a popular medium but one which is becoming more and more restricted to news, talk and music (I use the term 'music' in its loosest sense). In the 1940s, the stars of Sydney radio were comedians, quiz-show comperes, actors and actresses, singers, bands and even race callers. There were never any 'talkers' of the ilk of today's Laws, Jones and Carlton. There were only 'announcers'. An announcer's job was to announce: 'The next record is Brahms' Lullaby played by the London Philharmonic Orchestra conducted by Sir Benjamin Bottlebrush.' ... 'This program is brought to you by Munchie Biscuits, found at all good grocers.'

The listeners rarely knew the announcer's name and the radio station didn't seem to care about the announcer's grammar, pronunciation or syntax, so long as the voice was rich and mellow. (In a newsflash one afternoon an announcer stated, 'Earlier today, a tram ran into a lorry on the corner of Cleveland Street and Anzac Parade but nobody has suffered any serious misdemeanour.) There was, though, one exception to this rule and his name was John Harper ...

John Harper worked on Station 2KY on the 9 am to noon shift and was known as 'Old Gravel Voice'. On the surface, Harper didn't do anything different from any other announcer on radio. He read advertisements and played music, yet John Harper allowed his personality to come through, refusing to be regimented or cloned. Thinking about it now, I'm inclined to believe that Harper didn't like his job very much. He didn't read the advertisements, he growled them. If he had a hangover he would never behave 'professionally' but would get terse and angry and sometimes a swear word would even slip out. Monday was always a good day to listen to Old Gravel Voice. If he was happy, he had had a good weekend at the races; if he was terse and angry, the bookies had fleeced him or he had a hangover, or both.

The popular singing trio, The Andrew Sisters, was anathema to John Harper. 'Oh no, here they are again. Those ridiculous Andrews women to shout Boggle Wuggle Biggle Boy or some stupid name like that.' As soon as *Boogie Woogie Bugle Boy* had finished, the microphone would be silent for a moment and listeners would wait in anticipation. Then, smash!!!, the 78 rpm record would hit the floor. 'Now let me tell you about June Millinery,' Harper would continue happily. On another occasion he announced, 'The next song will be *Don't Fence Me In*, with Bing Crosby doing the singing and the overpaid Andrews women doing the shouting.' The song ended ... smash!!!. There was a few seconds silence, then Harper came back on air saying, 'You'll be pleased to know that the part of the record in which Bing sings is completely intact but the section in which the Andrews women shout is broken into little pieces'.

Gravel Voice Harper left the airwaves decades ago, yet in his time he made the mundane entertaining — and he broadcast to Australians in the Australian language. I still smile when I play old Andrews Sisters' tapes; I still recall June Millinery; I still buy Kinkara Tea because that's what Old Gravel Voice told me to do. John Harper was himself, he didn't *have* to be professional, he *was* — without even trying.

Towards the end of the war, the State Government asked the citizens of Sydney to open their homes to American servicemen who were here on leave. Ma became quite patriotic and offered her home to any GI who might be interested. Her offer was taken up by a young sergeant named Leo from (I think) somewhere in the Midwest. He was a skinny young man with glasses, very quiet and polite. He didn't seem much like a soldier to me, though for all I know he could have been a member of the first landing party at Guadalcanal and Iwo Jima. He swam at Coogee and Bondi and walked around the Botanical Gardens. Sometimes he'd hop in a tram or train and disappear for many hours. One day he took me to Taronga Park Zoo. We travelled across by ferry, walked around the zoo for a few hours and Leo bought me pies and ice-creams. I backed up for seconds (it was a well-known fact that the Yanks were loaded, so I made the most of it).

On the way home, Leo struck up a conversation with a man on the ferry who asked him if he had seen much of Sydney. 'Yeah, I guess I've seen a fair bit,' Leo replied.

'What do you think of it?' asked the man.

Leo didn't reply immediately, then he said laconically, 'Well, sir, I haven't seen too many cities, but I've seen some and there ain't none to compare with the beauty of this'.

That was the first time I ever really looked at my own city. Even now I sometimes forget to look. It's not until I show visitors around that I realise how lucky we are.

Yet I don't believe an occasional attack of indifference is an affliction that effects me alone. There are so many beautiful places in the world and the people who live there often miss the forests and only notice a few old straggly trees. I remember some friends of ours in Somerset taking us on a trip to a place called Watchet Harbour. Around the lovely lanes and byways of the West Country they drove us, beside the greenest of countryside, through the most attractive villages with thatched cottages and cute country pubs. As we passed I desperately wanted to call out 'Stop here,' for we had nothing like it back home. However, they continued on, extolling the glories of Watchet Harbour with ever-increasing enthusiasm.

When at last we arrived at this place we had heard so much about, we stopped the car by an old wall and gazed out on the 'great harbour'. What we saw was about half as big as the centre court at Wimbledon with a few old boats bogged up to their gunwales in mud. I looked everywhere for water and came to the conclusion that if I really wanted to find any my only option was to open the bonnet of my friend's car and peer into the radiator.

'You realise that when the tide is in, Watchet Harbour can take ships up to 3000 tons,' our friend explained proudly.

'Fancy that!' I murmured, resisting the temptation to say, 'Hell mate, in Sydney they park the QE2 at the end of Pitt Street'.

Still, I shouldn't be too smart. We were showing our American friends, Richie and Patti Moed, around Sydney on their first visit not so long back and as we stood at the very top of South Head, I lifted my arm towards the distance and declared proudly, 'There you have the magnificent Sydney skyline'. At that instant, I suddenly remembered that they lived in Manhattan. Without pausing for breath, I continued, 'Er, and if you turn quickly to your right, folks, you will see the glorious beach and harbour area of Manly'.

We can all be biased. Yet our home town will always be our home town, the place where we spent 'the best years of our life', a time when the sun was perpetually shining and the only tears that were shed were tears of laughter.

But, I was lucky to grow up in Sydney, lucky to know her people and to experience the vibrancy of her adolescence. These days, grown and changing in her ways, she can sometimes make me angry. Yet whenever beautiful Sydney decides to take out her golden bow ... just like old Buzz Kennedy, my heartstrings will be ever available.

Eighteen

Gamblers and Drunks

I used to play grade cricket with a bloke who was a pretty good batsman. He probably should have represented New South Wales but was unlucky to have played in a very strong era and didn't quite make it. As this man is still well and truly alive, I will not reveal his name. Nor will I refer to him by his nickname for, in the world of cricket where almost everyone has a 'nom de guerre', he could be recognised far more quickly than he would be if I called him by the name that is recorded on his birth certificate. So I will ascribe to him the pseudonym 'Rusty'. For the record, Rusty is still going strong and spends much of his time helping young cricketers hone their skills, hoping that some day one or more of them will wear the blue cap he never wore.

Rusty was an excellent sportsman who was also very proficient at rugby. He was popular with teammates, quick with a quip and always willing to perform a favour, though he did have one glaring weakness — he could not keep away from the racecourse or the TAB. Rusty was a prisoner of the punt. Whether it was the Melbourne Cup or the Menangle Park Trots, Rusty's money would be on some sure thing, and in the days before mobile phones I remember seeing Rusty standing outside cricket grounds in public phone booths, wearing his pads and gloves, bat leaning against the door, ringing his SP bookie. 'Howzat!' would come the yell from the ground and one of the batting team would be forced to race outside into the street and shout, 'Tom's out Rusty, you're in'.

'Fred, I'll call you at the drinks break or when I get out, whichever comes first,' Rusty would yell into the phone before he slammed it down. Then he would grab his trusty bat, rush through the gate, onto the oval and walk quickly to the crease. 'Centre thanks, ump.'

In his mid–20s, Rusty became engaged to be married which, as many older cricketers would agree, is an inappropriate move for a young batsman with potential and also the last thing any keen punter should even contemplate. Like most women, his fiancée fell in love with Rusty for the man he was and then, the moment the ring was placed on the finger, set about changing him. She informed Rusty that his punting was a real problem and he should desist forthwith. Rusty didn't altogether agree with her. He found punting a great satisfaction and an immense joy when he won; it was only when he lost that Rusty realised he had a problem. Nevertheless, in the interests of true love and peace, Rusty promised his ever-loving fiancée that he would join an organisation called 'Gamblers' Anonymous'.

After receiving a vast amount of literature from Gamblers' Anonymous, Rusty sallied forth to his first meeting one Friday evening. The meeting was to be held near Central Railway, in a less than salubrious area of Sydney, and when he was in the general vicinity Rusty couldn't find the exact address. Looking disorientated Rusty was 'rescued' by a lady in a Salvation Army uniform who asked if she could be of help.

'Yes, I have to go to a meeting and I'm not sure of the address,' said Rusty.

'I know of the meeting because I happen to be going there myself,' she replied. 'Follow me, brother.'

Rusty followed the lady to a small hall where a couple of dozen disreputable characters were sitting on wooden benches. He gazed around nervously and felt embarrassed — this was a situation vastly different from the casual camaraderie of cricket's locker rooms or the comforting rush and bustle of the betting ring. A few moments later, the woman who had directed him to the premises walked to the front of the hall, raised her hand and began to speak.

'Ladies and gentlemen, my name is Kitty. Most of us know why we are present tonight but for those who are visiting for the first time, let me state categorically that you are not about to be criticised or lectured. We are all here to talk over a common problem and thus to help each other by knowing we are not alone in our troubles. Now has anyone anything to say?'

There was dead silence. Rusty's eyes stared at the cracked old floorboards. 'Take your time friends,' continued the lady. 'Is there anyone who wants to tell us of his problem or make a confession?'

Rusty felt a movement beside him and he lifted his eyes up to see a man, sporting four days of stubble on his face, raising his hand. The leader nodded and said, 'Yes Andrew?'

The man stood up and in an intoxicated voice croaked, 'My name is Andy Thompson and I'm an alcoholic.'

'Hell', Rusty whispered to himself, 'I'm in the wrong place.'

Rusty stood up with the intention of heading for the door but before he could move, the leader pointed to him and called, 'Is there something you wish to say, brother?'.

Rusty shook his head and replied, 'I don't think I could be of much help, sister. I have no trouble staying sober. *My* problem is staying solvent.'

He walked out of the hall into the evening and suddenly remembered that it was Friday. At that moment an empty cab cruised past, Rusty hailed it, jumped into the back seat and shouted to the driver, 'Mate, take me to Harold Park Trots'.

Nineteen

The Moon in Her Hand

Every person on this earth is given a gift. Some are given many, though sometimes the gifts are wasted. And every now and then we meet someone whose gifts cannot possibly be overlooked, whose personality is such that they simply cannot be ignored — a person who draws people into their orbit as the sun draws the planets. On *this* planet, Wendy O'Donohue was such a person. She gave out love as summer gives out sunshine and the love was returned a thousandfold. Of the many people to whom I spoke, none said they 'liked' Wendy. 'Like' was never used ... the word 'love' dominated the conversation. Wendy was not well known in the sense that she was a household name in her country. But she was very special. For a brief time, in the winter of 1997, most of the world came to know of Wendy and a few of her friends, as millions of prayers were raised on their behalf and many silent toasts drunk. Wendy O'Donohue would have been embarrassed had she known of this, although she would have been delighted that people were enjoying a drink. If it had been possible, Wendy would surely have joined them. I first came to meet Wendy O'Donohue through Helen Gleeson, then I came to know her through friends and family.

+ + +

In July 1993, I was travelling with Herself in Europe, on one of those organised bus tours that have the potential to turn into a trip into hell — with a dictatorial egotist as the guide and a group of ear-thrashing teetotallers as your companions. On the other hand, such experiences can be journeys of eye-opening adventure on which you accompany people of like mind, people of humour and incessant thirsts. We were lucky; our trip was of the latter variety — leaving us with good friends and delightful memories.

'May I join you?' Helen asked.

My wife and I were sitting with two other Aussies in the bustling square which is situated beneath the beautiful, brooding Cologne Cathedral in Western Germany. A few metres down the road, the Rhine flowed swiftly as we ate bratwurst, drank beer and sat in the warm midday sun. We were pleased to welcome a fellow Aussie to share in the German fare. We yarned, laughed, soaked up the atmosphere and then for the rest of the trip the five of us were inseparable.

Widowed for seven years, Helen travelled alone. She was a small, vivacious lady who worked as the deputy principal of a Catholic High School and lived at Pakenham in Victoria, a town about an hour and a quarter's drive east of Melbourne. Though Helen was fighting an ailment that meant she was required to take regular doses of cortisone during the trip, she bounced around the tourist trails of Europe with a vibrancy and enthusiasm that was contagious and with a sense of humour which made us laugh. She took my teasing with a smile and responded in kind, feeling sorry for my wife who spent most of the trip apologising for the ill-mannered yobbo attired in the floppy white hat, stubbies and Resch's Beer T-shirt, who was continually making an idiot of himself with his fellow travellers and leaving an awful impression of Australians with the natives.

We kept in touch with Helen after the trip, trading rude letters and talking occasionally on the phone. Then in October 1995, we received a call from Helen's son, Marc, asking us to a belated wedding reception at his home in Sydney to celebrate the wedding of Helen to Tom O'Donohue, an ex-television engineer of some renown, who had retired from business and become a 'yachtie'. Tom, a widower, and Helen had met some months before, gone on a trip to the Greek Islands in Tom's boat and decided to 'love honour and obey' in the Catholic Cathedral of The Holy Spirit which is tucked well away from suspicious Islamic eyes in the backblocks of Istanbul.

It was a pleasant Sunday afternoon in Balmain when we toasted Tom and Helen. The wine and champagne flowed, though there was more than enough beer to satisfy we purists. I was feeling quite mellow when the blushing bride came over to me accompanied by a tall attractive lady in her mid–30s. 'Marksy, I'd like you to meet my new daughter, Wendy,' announced Helen. 'She works in Thredbo and wants to talk to you about it.'

'Hi, Marksy, I've heard about you,' said Wendy, coming straight to the point and flashing a smile that I remember thinking at the time was open and Australian, though well realising it must have originated from kinfolk of Killarney. 'You're tied up with New South Wales cricket, aren't you?'

'Well yes, in an unpopular way. I'm a selector,' I replied.

'Would the team be interested in coming to Thredbo for their pre-season training and using our magnificent sporting facilities?'

'I, er, I've never heard it suggested.'

'Come down and have a look. Once you've seen it you'll jump at the chance.'

She held me with a stare that was part business and part good humour. I hedged. 'I'll certainly mention it. I'll give you a call, Wendy.'

She grinned and we went on to other things — her relationship with her new stepmother; how she and her new stepbrother Marc had hit it off instantly. Shining through her conversation was the love she had for her family. I got us both a drink and we continued talking about Thredbo, skiing (of which I knew little), cricket (of which Wendy knew less), people whom we both regarded as characters and of other things, interesting but inconsequential. When we left Balmain that evening, Herself remarked, 'Wasn't Tom's daughter, Wendy, a nice girl?' I agreed, as I recalled her wavy red hair, her soft (but insistent) sell and her smile from the Emerald Isle.

To my shame, I must admit that I did not mention Thredbo to anyone of influence in the New South Wales Cricket Association (NSWCA), though now I regret my oversight. I was busy — and, anyway, the NSWCA is a professional organisation and supposedly knows what it is doing. Sitting here now, writing this story, I feel guilty about not responding to the request of that day and wish that I had initiated some discussion on the subject — if only to meet Wendy again.

THE ADOLESCENT COLLECTOR

Tom O'Donohue married Rosemary Hoare in 1958. Rosemary was 19 and Tom was 23. A year later a daughter, Wendy, was born. There were five children from the union of Tom and Rosemary, four girls and a boy; the fourth daughter died at the age of 11 months.

Wendy was an intelligent, chubby infant with freckles, red hair and a face which did nothing to disprove her Irish ancestry. She was the epicentre of her parents' lives and, even at an early age, the centre of attraction with others. There was a sense of fun and light-hearted mischievousness in her burgeoning personality — *a joie de vivre* in the way she toddled about her small world. She was also a lucky child in that she was born into a secure and loving home in which she was allowed the freedom to stretch her horizons without the inhibiting hurdles of over-protection and adult censorship.

Wendy's father, Tom, an ambitious young engineer making a name for himself in the early days of television, was sometimes forced to spend long hours at work as his career gained momentum. Her mother, Rosemary, was a therapy radiographer. When Wendy arrived Rosemary decided that the best course to follow was that of a full-time Mum — a job she performed with singular dedication and enormous success. Wendy didn't realise it until later but, even then, the roles her parents were to play in her life had been mapped out. Tom was to be her adviser in business affairs, the mentor in her career and the idol of her life. Rosemary was her closest confidante in personal matters and matters of the heart ... and also her best friend.

Sometime ago, in Melbourne, I asked Tom how he would describe Wendy as an infant. Around us played Bridget aged three, the youngest daughter of Martin and Judy O'Donohue (Wendy's brother and sister-in-law) who chattered away and at each lull in the adult conversation told of her recent adventures, making sure that the stranger from Sydney was brought into the conversation — not only so that her stories reached as many ears as possible but also, I believe, to make him feel that he was part of the family. 'How would I describe Wendy?' Tom repeated. 'Well, I could show you some photos of her at three but I really don't have to. Look at Bridget over there and her elder sister, Molly, and you'll see Wendy at that age. They are like her in personality as well.' I looked over at Bridget, the little red-headed girl with freckles who was pulling the ears off a large toy dog and I remembered the words of the old song:

Did ya mither kim from Oyland,
Cause there's somethin in ya Oyrish?
And that bit of Oyland steals me heart away.

In 1963, five-year-old Wendy began her education at St Bridget's Catholic Primary School, at Greythorne in Melbourne. On first days at school, some children shy away from entering the portals, clinging to mummy's leg, not wanting to leave the security of the environment they know. But, as she did for the rest of her life, little Wendy O'Donohue positively marched into this new adventure, seemingly delighting in the challenge. It was virtually from this day (and forever after) that Wendy began her hobby as a collector. In fact, it was a lot more than a hobby, it was a lifelong passion which eventually made her an expert in her particular field. Wendy O'Donohue collected friends.

It was at St Bridget's that Wendy met Gab Bennett and a friendship began that was to last for the rest of their lives — a friendship that was to take them to the wild cafes of Rome, the frosty ski slopes of Switzerland, across the Nullarbor in a broken-down car and to an Irish gaol.

At primary school Gab Bennett watched as a red-haired girl collected friends around her and was drawn too into the orbit. Gab's original impression of Wendy was that of a child with a smile in her eyes, who organised the other girls into games, and who took control without dominating. As Gab was to learn, this was to be the pattern of living as Wendy flew through life with her many mates following in the slipstream.

One day Wendy arrived late to school and there was no smile in her eyes. She did not organise the kids that day, just sat in a corner on her own. As is the way with young children, Gab did not know how to handle her friend's unusual attitude, so she stayed away. Then at lunchtime she saw Wendy sitting on her own, crying. Gab went over and asked what was wrong and Wendy managed to reply between sobs, 'My little sister died this morning'. The next day Wendy was laughing and organising once again though it was some time before the smile returned to her eyes.

When primary school ended, Tom and Rosemary sent Wendy to Siena College, a Catholic girls' school near their North Balwyn home. Gab Bennett's parents did the same with their daughter. At Siena, Wendy's friend-collecting hobby came into its own and soon Sally Keegan and Ann Harrison were added and it wasn't long before they joined Gab on the 'executive committee' of the ever-expanding club. Soon Wendy was organising groups of girls, not only at school but in holiday time as well. Tom and Rosemary owned a small weekender near the bay town of Sorrento on the Mornington Peninsula of Victoria. Wendy often gathered her friends together and took them there to stay for long weekends and school holidays. Friends such as Gab and Ann Harrison were amazed at how readily they were taken into the family circle, just as if they were Tom and Rosemary's own children and extra sisters for Wendy, Martin, Peta Mary and Janet. When the senior O'Donohues could not find time to go to the Sorrento house themselves, they had no problem letting Wendy and her guests take over the place without any parental supervision. This was an eye-opener for Wendy's friends, many of whom were protected Catholic schoolgirls, constantly warned by their elders of the ways of the flesh and the Devil. Suddenly these teenagers were alone to pursue a freedom they had only dreamed about, to go where they wished, eat and drink what they liked and, wonder of wonders, to be able to mix with members of the opposite sex. Wendy accepted all this as normal but her friends felt like Alice stepping through the looking glass.

Gab Bennett thinks often of the times she spent at Sorrento and the forbidden fruits that were tasted, though by modern standards of teenage behaviour the fruits were perhaps modest. Yet to impressionable girls who were crashing through puberty the experience of those days was an entrance to adult life. Gab recalls Wendy's brother, Martin, and a couple of his mates teasing Wendy and others in the group, making the girls feel sophisticated and worldly. She chuckles as she remembers her adolescent intimacy with Wendy when the pair sat in front of a mirror and compared pimples. One weekend, a group of the girls decided to experiment with alcohol and after much searching managed to obtain two small bottles of bitters, which were shared between them. Later, they all claimed that they got drunk, although the likelihood was that it was more imagination than inebriation. Nevertheless, to the girls who shared both the house at Sorrento and the warmness of Wendy's friendship, those days are remembered as golden and though the era has long-passed the pages are constantly re-opened in this section of their scrapbook of memories.

At Siena College, Wendy was never regarded as a top scholar though she was most certainly a top sportswoman and a person of influence on campus. In her final year, Wendy was elected Sports Captain and Vice-Captain of the school. Sister Rosemary Lewins, the principal of Siena at the time, remembers Wendy with admiration and affection. 'Wendy was different from many of the girls I taught. She had a maturity without ego and an ability to treat everyone as an equal, yet with respect. She could stand up and address adult forums without the slightest sign of nerves, yet she remained a student's student. I must say there was a touch of mischievousness in her but you couldn't help admiring her for it, plus it added to her personality. She was a born leader with so many friends and she was greatly loved.'

At holiday time Wendy and her friends didn't restrict themselves to the house at Sorrento and there were other happy times spent at a farm run by Wendy's aunt in country Victoria. Here they rode, picnicked and worked around the property, laughing and learning as the days flew by. At night they often sat beneath the moon while Wendy played a guitar, sang Janis Ian songs and impersonated Liza Minnelli. Naturally, Wendy's aunt felt responsible for the girls and though most of the time they were given free rein, she was insistent that her young charges must not eat with the shearers. Auntie Kath was not going to allow decent young Catholic women to become tainted by rough-living, coarsely spoken roustabouts who lusted after any female who didn't say 'baa' and wasn't dead. This greatly disappointed the girls who were at that stage in their lives when male company was considered a most desirable experience. Yet despite the pleas, their host, Wendy, refused to disobey her aunt's order. Wendy remained firm and forbade her friends to eat with the shearers. However, Aunt Kath hadn't mentioned anything about *drinking* with them!

In Wendy's early years at Siena College Tom O'Donohue won a raffle in which the first prize was two airline tickets to Perth. Wendy perceived in this windfall a wonderful opportunity. In Germany, in a town called Darmstadt, Tom had friends who had recently visited Australia and who had struck up a rapport with Wendy, who was learning German at school. Geographically, the Alps were not far from Darmstadt. 'How about it Dad?' she asked. 'You could exchange the two interstate tickets for one overseas return and it would be great for my education!'

Not for the first time, Tom was twisted around the teenager's finger and sometime later Wendy flew to Germany. She had a splendid holiday and came home more mature and, no doubt, better educated. While she was away Wendy was bitten by that most dangerous of predators, the 'travel bug', and contracted a chronic disease called 'wanderlust'. This is a disease for which there is no cure and from which she never recovered. For this Wendy was ever thankful.

FAR AWAY PLACES

After passing her final exams at High School, Wendy decided to tackle a teaching degree, opting for the subject of Physical Education — a course which suited her well. Once graduated, she was appointed to a teaching position at Mitchum Technical High School, where she taught for two years. As with everything she did, Wendy threw herself into the job, taking children on excursions to the farm and organising them in games, hikes and bike trips. However, at the end of two years there was a stirring inside Wendy. The travel disease, from which Wendy had been in remission, flared up again. It was time to leave the family, throw on the backpack and head for far-away places with strange sounding names. Life was to be lived, adventure was calling and there were friends waiting to be made.

Gab Bennett was Wendy's travelling companion on this backpackers' sojourn, a wonderful adventure for two 20 year olds. The girls travelled the Continent in an old Kombi van and when they returned to the UK, they travelled through Britain by foot and thumb. Winter on the slopes of Austria and Switzerland was invigorating and Wendy became a skier of high calibre, more than matching the experienced and often over-confident Europeans. Wendy would climb to the summit, look down to the valley below, and turn to Gab, shouting in schoolgirl French 'On y va' ('Let's go'), before pushing her stocks into the snow and heading off. Down she would rush, taking the most hazardous path — a weaving figure alone on the snow, challenging the mountain, racing the wind.

Wendy's favourite time for skiing was late at night when the moon was full and shining at its brightest. (There is a picture of Wendy taken on a mountain top holding her arm in the air; by a clever piece of camera work it appears that she is holding the moon in her hand.) To see the lights of an alpine village twinkling below stimulated Wendy, the frosty night air pumped the blood through her veins and at the bottom in the valley, the après-ski scene was in full swing, the schnapps and red wine flowing and the parties stretching 'till dawn. Skiing done, Wendy would shed her ski gear and join the partying. She would sing and laugh and, sometimes, dance on the tables. (The great West Indian cricketer, Learie Constantine, was once asked why he so often hit the ball into the air and he replied, 'Because there is more room up there.') Wendy danced on tables because it was fun and because, in crowded nightclubs and ski resorts she, like Learie, found there was more room up there.

Before Wendy and Gab returned to Australia, they toured Ireland to meet the people and to give Wendy an opportunity to explore the home of her ancestors. The Kombi van had long been dispensed with and Gab and Wendy resorted to hitchhiking. One day they had left Londonderry and were heading to Dublin to stay in a well-known hostelry called 'O'Donohue's Hotel'. It was Easter time, snow had recently fallen and lifts were hard to come by on the back roads that ran by the stone-fenced farms. Eventually they were picked up by a couple of tough-looking characters in an Escort panel van, who introduced themselves as Pat and Mike. Wendy and Gab laughed and told the two men that there were many jokes told at home in which both Pat and Mike figured as the front men. The two Irishmen just grinned and told the girls to climb in the back of the van. This was not as easy as it sounded, for the van was filled with newspapers, all of which had the heading, *Sinn Fein*.

'Why all the papers?' Wendy asked. Mike answered without hesitation, 'Well now, it would be seemin' obvious, even to Australians, that we are members of the IRA. And we are deliverin' the truth of our cause to all our friends who want to be livin' on the road to Dublin. Now I'm sure you girls won't be mindin' at all if we stop every now and again to hear news of our heroic comrade, Bobby Sands, who is about starvin' himself for the cause.' (This was an era of particularly heavy confrontation between the Protestant Loyalists and the IRA in Northern Ireland. Bobby Sands was a member of the IRA who had been captured and had gone on a hunger strike in a Belfast gaol as a protest against the perceived injustices of the pro-British Loyalists.)

'We do not be havin' a radio in this vehicle,' continued Mike, 'so we will have to be stoppin' along the way to see how our friend, Bobby, is doin'.' Sure enough, within a few minutes the vehicle halted at a pub en route and the IRA members and hitchhikers hopped out and went inside.

Apparently Pat and Mike really *were* the names of the two Irishmen. In the pub they were instantly surrounded by the local cadre of the IRA and told of the condition of the latest Irish martyr. Copies of *Sinn Fein* were delivered and much Guinness was drunk in the course of the next 40 minutes. Naturally, the two Australian girls joined in the drinking part of the proceedings. Then off they went for a few more miles until again the vehicle stopped at a pub. More news was obtained, more papers delivered and more Guinness consumed. The process was repeated a third, fourth and fifth time — though, after the third stop, Gab and Wendy decided to ease up on the Guinness. Not so Pat and Mike, who were becoming increasingly intoxicated as they progressed. On the sixth stop of this IRA pub crawl, the two men began singing mournful Irish ballads and shouting slogans. When Pat got behind the wheel, the vehicle began slewing all over the road, at which point Gab leaned through the window and suggested that it may be in the interests of all if she was to drive. To this kind offer Pat and Mike readily agreed. As the car neared the border, Gab noticed lights following and in a matter of minutes a vehicle came up beside, bearing on its side the word 'Garda' — the police.

A uniformed man wound down the window and called to Gab, 'And I'd be liking to be hav'n a little look at your licence if it wouldn't be too much trible'. Gab pulled the Escort to the side of the road and within seconds five other vehicles surrounded them. Although Gab carried her licence everywhere she went, it happened to be at the bottom of her backpack and took about ten minutes for her to dig it out. In the meantime, Pat, Mike and Wendy had been forced out of the car and were being interrogated by the Garda and others — whom the girls later found out were members of Britain's MI5.

The situation was serious. Gab was accused of being a driver for the IRA and Wendy of being an accomplice. The scene, however, had a touch of Inspector Clousseau about it; Mike was so drunk that he was slumped across the front of the Escort, calling for the beatification of Bobby Sands, while Pat seemed resigned to the situation and it would not have surprised the girls one bit if he had broken into an encore of *I'll Take You Home Again Kathleen*, which he had been softly crooning in the back of the panel van. The incident was scary, but Wendy was taking it all in and, to Gab, she seemed to be on the verge of laughing. The two girls were eventually taken to a nearby prison and interrogated but the various stickers of Aussie flags and bounding kangaroos on their backpacks were enough to prove their innocence.

The Garda discharged them in a typical Irish fashion. 'Well now, you two would be being from Australia, so we are releasin' ya, but don't yaselves go gettin' tied up with such rascals agin. Tell me now, would ya be knowin' the O'Briens from Brisbane as they happen to be cousins of moyn?' Wendy and Gab reached Dublin and soon afterwards returned to Australia. Later, they used to wonder what happened to Pat and Mike.

Not long after her first backpacker experience, Wendy decided to have a wider look at her own country. She talked three friends into travelling with her, bought an old Hillman and set off across the Nullarbor. Accompanying the four young tourists was a pile of luggage and Wendy's little dog; it was a little short of first-class luxury. But, somehow, they made it to Perth and nobody was more relieved than the dog.

Wendy worked in Melbourne for a time and then, bitten by the 'bug' headed overseas. Wendy's friends were increasing the more she travelled and when she returned she made sure that the 'overseas' group was introduced to the 'at home' group and that the groups became one. One of her closest friends was 'Tod' Lewin whom Wendy met at a bar in Portugal. They struck up a rapport when they began chatting over a drink and the rapport turned into friendship when later that evening they danced on the table. 'Wendy had so many assets,' Tod later explained, 'but her loyalty, combined with the fact that she was non-judgemental, were, to me, her most endearing features. Wendy never had acquaintances, she only had friends.'

Warren and Jan Townsend became her friends too, meeting her in circumstances that could only happen to Wendy. She had flown from London to Katmandu and, while waiting for a transit flight, sat down with the Townsends and struck up a conversation. After a quarter of an hour, Wendy excused herself and went to change some travellers cheques at the airport, only to find the money exchange booth was closed. She had a credit card but there were no agencies that would take the card there. She looked in her purse and found a couple of British pounds and a few coins — barely enough to buy a curry. She was stuck in a strange country with no money and no way of obtaining any. Typically, she laughed when she walked back to the Townsends and explained the situation.

'How much do you want?' asked Warren.

'Oh, I couldn't take money from you people, I've only known you for ten minutes,' Wendy replied.

Warren Townsend passed her A$150 dollars worth of local currency and waved away any arguments. When asked if they had concerns about ever getting the money back from a stranger, Jan Townsend left no doubts. 'Of course not — it was Wendy!'

The money was returned and another friendship secured. Wendy later stated, 'It was fun being with the Townsends, plus it was like taking your own bank everywhere you went.'

Wendy's sojourns overseas had to be funded, so she worked her way around the world in numerous jobs — her favourite being a six-months stint in Switzerland as a ski instructor to English-speaking ski novices. Her schoolmate, Sally Keegan, travelled with Wendy on a number of occasions and asked her once why she collected so many friends. 'Because you can't learn everything from just one person,' Wendy answered. 'There are different facets of your life and you can gain something from everybody you meet.' Wendy was a listener and in this world there are very few genuine listeners. Because of her natural humility, she never quite realised how much others learned from *her*.

Wendy was tall and vibrant and she enjoyed the company of men. Though she could never be described as 'beautiful', she was certainly 'attractive' and had no trouble attracting members of the opposite sex. There were a few relationships which lasted for a time and one or two which broke her heart when they ended. Nonetheless, life was an adventure for Wendy and although she couldn't stand suffering pain and even less the thought of inflicting it, she came through the worst of these times and enjoyed the best of them. Yet, as she reached her late 30s there was a stirring in her. She had watched her two nieces, Molly and Bridget, grow from tiny babies to children and Wendy absolutely doted on them. She had dressed as a clown at her nieces' birthday parties, bought them expensive presents and spoilt them in a manner that the child-care textbooks insist is radically wrong.

One day, Wendy had a serious conversation with her stepmother, Helen, and confessed that she wanted to have children. Apparently a former flame had come back into her life, an interest that over the years had never been quite extinguished. Could it wait? It was 1997, Wendy was 38 and most successful. There was much for her to think about — challenges to be faced, mountains to climb.

THE THREAD IN THREDBO

Wendy made intelligent use of her love of travel, establishing a career for herself in the travel/hospitality industry. She was appointed Victorian Tourist Manager of the R.A.C.V. (the large insurance company involved in many facets of Australian life) and moved back into the family house at North Balwyn with Tom, Rosemary and her siblings — a place where laughter echoed and where love had always been the order of the day. Later, she rented a flat nearer to her office in the central business district of Melbourne. When the moment came for her to leave home she turned and waved, opened the car door ... and began to weep. Rosemary was standing on the porch watching her daughter leave and she too began crying. Wendy jumped from the vehicle, raced over and embraced her mother. Tears fell by the pint and in a few seconds sobbing began as the two clung to each other. At that moment, Tom walked by. 'What's wrong?' he asked.

'Wendy is leaving home,' sobbed Rosemary.

'I'm leaving,' Wendy managed to gasp, between sobs of her own.

The bemused Tom O'Donohue shook his head and replied, 'Why the fuss? Hell, you're only moving a couple of suburbs away and you'll be here tomorrow night for dinner.'

Wendy and Rosemary gave Tom a withering look and continued their crying. Tom shrugged his shoulders and went inside to read the paper.

Wendy was remarkably successful in her post at the R.A.C.V. but the call of the mountains was very much in her heart and when she read of a position available as Chief Executive for the Thredbo Chamber of Commerce, she applied.

Tricia Hecker, a member of the board of the Chamber of Commerce at the time was given the brief of interviewing the applicants. Twenty-four people applied; Wendy O'Donohue was the first. Tricia remembers the interview well and laughs when she recalls that before the interview was half-over, she was talking as if Wendy already had the job while Wendy was discussing innovative plans for 18 months hence. The other 23 applicants never had a chance. Eight years later, Tricia made an interesting comment when she reflected on the interview. 'Even then I couldn't say "no" to Wendy and there was something in her personality that made me want to gain her respect.' Tricia smiled, shook her head and continued, 'No, I guess it was more than just *gaining* Wendy's respect — I wanted to earn it.'

The fact of Australia's large expanse of snow-clad mountains is often overlooked on the tourist brochures. It surprises many people to learn that the area of Australia's snowfields is larger than the country of Switzerland. Thredbo is situated in a valley that lies beneath the Crackenback Mountain in the New South Wales snowfields. The Thredbo River flows cold and clear through the valley, splitting it in two. For countless millennia the area was left to its native flora and fauna, the peace of the place disturbed only 30 000 years ago, when the Ngarigu tribe moved into the district to hunt for the large bogong moths which breed in spring. The tribe stayed for the summer season but when the chill of early autumn came, the Aboriginals moved back to the warmer area of the plains. One hundred and fifty years ago the white man appeared there, using the valley as part of a stock route between the Monaro and Gippsland. Later in the 1800s, property owners negotiated leases with the Government which allowed grazing on the cool green mountainsides during summer months, while the rest of the country sweltered.

Organised skiing first began in Australia at Charlotte's Pass (not far from Thredbo) around 1907 and continued in a minor way until the end of World War II. Then the Australian Government engaged in one of the most ambitious engineering feats in the history of the world — a plan for hydro-electricity known as the 'Snowy Mountains Scheme'. Rivers were dammed, old towns drowned, new towns built and thousands of experts from overseas moved into the Snowy River area to work on the scheme. Many of these workers settled in Australia and added much to the culture of our land. One such man was hydrologer Tony Sponar, from Czechoslovakia, who, driving one day along the newly built dirt track which connected the town of Jindabyne with Khancoban, looked up and saw the snow lying steep and deep on the lovely Crackenback Mountain. Down below he saw the peaceful Thredbo Valley with the river gurgling along. Tony Sponar was a skier and he had seen such places in Europe, and realised instinctively that here was a 'special place' for a village and a ski field. Within a short time, Sponar arranged a lease for 1000 hectares from the National Parks Authority, organised a small consortium of investors and set about implementing a plan to build ski fields and a village.

The amount required to establish a ski resort from scratch proved too much for this consortium of salaried professionals, so the lease, and the dream, was sold to the large Lend Lease company. The managing director of the company, Dick Dusseldorp, was himself something of a visionary and a man highly respected in Australian business circles. To him, Sporan's idea embraced not only a business proposition but shaped up as a labour of love and a favourite toy. Lend Lease set up a company called Kosciusko–Thredbo Pty Ltd (known as 'K–T') to organise and administer the village; 40 years later K–T is still running the show. The mechanics of the arrangement are simple. As owners of the major lease, K–T re-leases various areas of the 1000 hectares to others — that is, to lodge owners, retail shop proprietors, restaurateurs etc. The company also looks after many of the facilities, such as maintenance, the fire brigade and garbage disposal and has the final say on the type of buildings that are constructed.

Thredbo stands comfortably with its environment. Viewed from the top of the mountain it is a pleasing place to the eye although it tends towards being something of an architectural hotchpotch when seen from the ground. Nevertheless, there exists a feeling that is very different from other Australian small towns, an ambience of an overseas alpine village, probably more Colorado than Austrian Alps. Thredbo has an atmosphere of easygoing busyness and a sense that great fun is to be had here if the visitor is prepared to go and get it. The village now has all the facilities, plus ski fields which have the longest runs in Australia and that can match it with the best in the world. This was the Thredbo that Wendy O'Donohue fell in love with when she took up her position with the Chamber of Commerce. Thredbo indeed had much going for it when Wendy first arrived ... but not nearly as much as when she left.

Wendy had sailed through life, facing challenges and in the main succeeding, gaining a reputation for flair and foresight. There was no reason at all why she couldn't take on the challenges of Thredbo and come out on top once again. Well as it turned out she did and she didn't!

Despite blossoming into a 'special place' for snow sports and sophisticated vacations, Thredbo was actually a small village with a small-village mentality. At the height of the season the resort bulged at the seams, yet it had a regular population of only 300. Endeavouring to influence the everyday life of the village and plan for its future were three disparate organisations: The company (K–T Pty Ltd), who needed to make money to keep their shareholders happy; the Chamber of Commerce (representing the businesspeople of the village) who were desperate to bring people into the place; and the National Parks Authority which generally was doing its best to keep people out. Although her major responsibility was to the rent-paying live-in people of the village, Wendy knew she had to straddle the fine line between commerce and aesthetics. They needed each other, and if one group was to be put off-side then the whole system could be thrown into disarray, with people gossiping of 'them and us' and retiring to their bunkers to hide behind sandbags of self-interest. To make matters more difficult, the Chamber of Commerce was a freewheeling organisation heading in many directions at once, trying to do the best by all but fighting elements of self-interest every step of the way.

The Chamber of Commerce's main problem revolved around the lodge owners, who were dependent upon bookings for their daily bread. Most of these people were willing to give and take for the good of the whole. There were, however, one or two non-team players, whose sole aim seemed to be to make sure that any decision made would be to their own advantage. Wendy found herself endeavouring to not only pull opposing groups together but to also do her best to halt the vicious bloodletting of a civil war. She did this magnificently, drawing people into an orbit of friendship and common interest (something that Wendy did so well as an 'amateur') and turning formal meetings, that had previously been discordant free-for-alls, into a union of minds. She also swept away the 'them and us' attitude, progressively building up a sense of trust within the various parties — 'If Wendy says it's okay, then we'll go along with it,' was a sentiment commonly expressed. Yet a tiny minority of self-servers remained unconvinced.

Tricia Hecker marvelled at the way the Chamber of Commerce began to work as a coordinated organisation. The boss of K–T, David Osborne, saw for the first time the village groups working in harmony. Without doubt, the common denominator was Wendy O'Donohue. She brought in initiatives that worked — including a jazz festival in the summer which brought people into the village when it was normally deserted. She established a historical society, which may not seem much in itself yet it gave to this town of skiing nomads and itinerant drifters a feeling of stability and a sense of pride. People began to realise that this was not just a commercial enterprise built only three decades earlier. Thredbo was a lot more than just a place where well-heeled yuppies from Vaucluse or Toorak turned up once a year for seven days of skiing and seven nights of raging. It was a special and ancient place. At the dawn of time, the rock at the peak of Crackenback Mountain looked much the same as it does today — though five million years back it didn't have a restaurant on top. Thirty thousand years ago, dads from the Ngarigu people taught their sons the skills by which to snare bogongs and spear kangaroos. Ghosts of the swearing bullock drivers from last century haunt the region and they say the sound of stockwhips can still be heard, on the mountain wind. Just down the road, dozens had died in the Snowy Mountains Scheme — a wonder of modern engineering. And it is claimed (and quite possible) that, near the spot where the ecumenical church now stands by the Thredbo River, the Man from Snowy River stopped to boil his billy and to give his hardy mountain pony a drink. The people of Thredbo looked back at all this and realised that they had a past. Why not look forward, too, they thought. We can have a future. We can be a community!

Wendy began nudging the more difficult elements in Thredbo towards becoming a community. A large majority of the businesspeople of Thredbo trusted and loved her but she was continually let down by the small self-interest group and for the first time in her career she felt stressed and disillusioned with people. Then came a bombshell from home. Wendy's mother, Rosemary, was found to have a malignant melanoma and doctors had given her only a few months to live. Wendy made the decision to resign from her job, to return to Melbourne and to spend the short months that remained beside her beloved mother.

Before she left she met with David Osborne, the managing director of K–T. Osborne had marvelled at the work Wendy had managed and was amazed at the way she had pulled the threads together and united the often warring factions. Yet Osborne had also noted that Wendy seemed unhappy with her achievements and when they talked, over lunch, Wendy admitted that she felt she had failed. Osborne explained that he understood her feelings but believed they were much to do with her sadness regarding her mother. As far as the job was concerned, in the opinion of most people, she was a success. The job hadn't beaten her, said Osborne, Wendy was one of the most outstanding people he had ever met and she must be sure that neither the lesser people with whom she dealt, nor her own high standards should effect her self-confidence. Wendy took the advice on board and David Osborne made a mental note not to lose touch with this special woman with her wonderful smile and ability to make friends of people and people friends.

Wendy returned to Melbourne in March to live with Tom and Rosemary. It was the worst time of her life. To watch the person she loved above all others fading away was unbearably painful, although Rosemary faced her illness with such fortitude and gentle resignation that those around her were uplifted. Wendy valued the time to speak the words she wanted to speak and to say goodbye with love.

In this time of personal torment for Wendy her friends gathered round her, as always, and she needed them more than ever. Sally Keegan remembers some of the group going to a ball and Wendy insisting that, before they arrive, they all visit Rosemary to parade before her in their ball gowns. At this stage Rosemary was in hospital and had very little time left. Down the hospital ward waltzed half-a-dozen attractive young women to show their finery to a wonderful lady. Rosemary managed to prop herself up to inspect the 'models'. With a gaze of adoration she smiled and said, 'Oh, you all look so lovely. I'm so very proud of you. Now go out and have a wonderful time.'

Rosemary's death affected Wendy greatly. 'I thought I'd grow old with mum,' she told Tod Lewin. Afterwards, she would sometimes talk to her close friends on a deeper level and began to look into things in a spiritual way. The 'deeper' Wendy however did not inhibit the 'rage times' and now and then various tables in various establishments continued to be danced upon until well into the wee small hours. Once, after a week of skiing, Wendy attended a posh Saturday night party in an exclusive Melbourne suburb. Soon after she arrived, she unwrapped a parcel of thick foil paper, from which she took handfuls of snow which she proceeded to hurl at the well dressed guests.

Wendy had part-time work during her mother's illness, yet she still yearned for the snow. Soon after her mother's death she was offered, and accepted, the position of Chief Executive of the Victorian High Country Authority. She hardly had time to warm the chair when David Osborne came back into Wendy's life and offered her the position of Summer Business Manager for K–T Pty Ltd. Wendy accepted because she loved Thredbo, thrived on challenges and felt that she had some unfinished business in the little village.

From the time Lend Lease had started their operations in Thredbo, summer was the lazy time. Nothing much ever happened and those who couldn't be bothered to go elsewhere for six months mooched around the village and talked of 'pre-bookings for the season' and their hopes for heavy snowfalls, come winter. To be in Thredbo between October and March was like standing on a railway station during a train strike. Yet the countryside in summer is cool and beautiful, the views are magnificent, the restaurants and accommodation are first class and although in midwinter Thredbo transforms into an alpine wonderland, at the height of summer it is typically Australian.

David Osborne gave Wendy the brief to 'get summer moving' and she did. For the next three years Wendy used all her resources — particularly her wonderful people skills and her flair for doing something different. She started by organising special events for the summer which brought people into the village and these events became more popular and expanded as the summers went by.

The jazz festival which Wendy had initiated when she was working for the Chamber of Commerce soon became an important event for the musos, most of whom would have worked without pay just to appear with their peers in the swinging atmosphere and fun of Thredbo. Wendy also organised film festivals and art exhibitions, an alpine flower festival, a national running week, golf and tennis tournaments, carols by candlelight and a Thredbo Theatre in Residence which performed Shakespeare on the village green while ducks wandered on stage during dramatic soliloquies. Wendy's favourite event was the Thredbo Full Moon Party, a night on which organised groups took the cable car up to the top of the mountain and saw the Kosciusko National Park in a different light. Wendy would always accompany the group to the peak and she once described it as 'a mystical experience'. To be on the top of Crackenback Mountain with the moon at its height was Wendy's choice as her favourite place in all the world. She would stand at the summit, raise her arm and hold the moon in her hand. Mountaineers, marathon runners, musos and moon lovers, all came to Thredbo in the summer. Bands, blues singers, bike riders, buskers and others with a multitude of interests joined in. From a summer village that would have been even too slow for Rip van Winkle, Thredbo became a place that was alive and jumping. It was a different clientele from winter yet the people had just as much fun. As K–T executive Rachael Cleary described it, 'Thredbo changed unbelievably and now when I think of summer I think of Wendy. In Thredbo, Wendy was summer.'

To put the programs in place was not easy. Wendy achieved what she did by honest salesmanship and an ability to organise — yet there was more to it than that. Mainly she continued using the method she had started with the Chamber of Commerce — making people work in unison. The community came together, old antagonisms were forgotten for the good of the team, the runs were being put on the board ... and just about everyone was happy. Wendy was the thread that linked it all together.

Col Battersby is now one of the area's most successful businesspeople. Yet three years ago he was battling, though Col was never lacking in ideas. He suggested to Wendy that there could be a large summer market for the hiring of mountain-bikes. She agreed and said that she would support him if he was willing to take the chance. Early the following summer, Col turned up one afternoon with 10 mountain-bikes on the back of an old trailer. Wendy made sure that all the resources of K–T were available to Col and set about making the mountain-bikes an integral part of Thredbo's summer season. Not only did she promote the use of these bikes for family pleasure but she persuaded the Australian Mountain-bike Association to stage a Category One downhill race at Thredbo! She also organised, and arranged sponsorship for, a weekend of mountain-bike racing called the Quelch Dual Eliminator, a tremendous success.

Col Battersby now owns two profitable shops at Thredbo and another at Mt Buller. 'Wendy recognised potential in people and she followed her judgement all the way,' he says today. 'Wendy backed a lot of winners whom others thought were losers. The thing was, if Wendy was on your side you were never a loser. I turned out to be a winner but I would not have got to the starting gate if it wasn't for her. I owe everything to Wendy.'

Fully involved in her work, Wendy sometimes forgot about herself. Not so long ago she organised a large bike rally in which she participated. The riders met in the village mall and just before the event was about to start she walked into Col Battersby's shop pushing the mountain-bike she had bought from him 18 months before. 'Col, could you give my bike a quick check over before I leave,' she asked her friend.

Col looked at the apparition she was holding and declared, 'Wendy you can't ride that in a rally.'

Wendy was amazed, 'Why not?'

'Don't worry, give it to me and I'll fix it,' he said. Col and an assistant then set to work with the speed of a team of mechanics at the last pit stop in the Australian Grand Prix. They changed the tyres (both of which were flat), tightened the handlebars (which were facing east as the bike was heading north), adjusted the brakes (which would have been battling to stop the bike in the village mall, let alone when it was racing downhill on Crackenback Mountain) and they pointed the seat frontward. Then, without a word Col returned the bike to his 'customer'.

Wendy performed brilliantly in the rally and when she got home she remarked, 'I don't know why Col was so worried, the bike went beautifully'.

Thredbo created many challenges for Wendy yet in no way did these prevent her from continuing her habit of collecting friends. As always, the new friends met the old friends and then Wendy set about making sure that they all became close friends. Ian Foster, a Thredbo Lodge proprietor, and K–T employee Rachael Cleary, grew close to Wendy and they were soon embroiled in her adventures. Early in their friendship, a group of Wendy's Melbourne mates descended on Thredbo prepared to party the weekend away. Wendy insisted that Ian and Rachael join them in a midnight excursion out to an uninhabited old homestead called Currango, two hours drive from Thredbo. Ian had no intention of going but before he realised it, he and his wife had been bundled aboard a truck and were heading out into the night. At 3 am, the thought crossed Ian's mind, 'What the hell am I doing at this time of morning in the middle of nowhere, drinking red wine, lying on my back and gazing at the moon, laughing and swapping stories with people I've only just met'.

Then, a second thought, 'Oh well, that's the way Wendy wants it'.

Wendy used her friends to help in her work as well. Whenever she organised an important event, friends from all over the country would come and pitch in, partly as a confidence-booster for her and as a sort of rent-a-crowd as well. Rachael remembers a music evening when Wendy felt things were going a bit flat. 'Come on you guys,' called their leader, 'up on the tables with me.' And on to the tabletops Sally, Gab, Tod and the rest would hop and the dancing would begin. Once the place began to swing, Wendy would be down to see if the drinks were still flowing, to yarn to someone about next year's festival or just to 'work the room'.

'Wendy saw the big picture!' I heard those words many times. 'The big picture' is a hackneyed phrase, yet it was repeated by so many people remembering Wendy O'Donohue. And indeed, Wendy *did* see the big picture and then added some brush strokes of her own. Soon, the picture became clear to all. The 'picture' was certainly seen by those who count, for in 1995 Thredbo won the Major Tourist Attraction Award for Excellence. When the plaudits were heaped on Wendy, she could not understand the reason her peers were giving her so much of the credit. 'It was an award for *everyone* in Thredbo,' Wendy kept repeating, and she meant it. In 1996, Wendy was made Marketing Manager and promoted to the Board of K–T Pty Ltd. She was marked for very big things by those in high places.

HOLOCAUST

Included in Wendy's only moderately paid work package was accommodation at one of K–T's lodges, called *Bimbadeen* (where a number of other company employees also lived). Wendy didn't like *Bimbadeen* and her lodgings could best be described as an old-fashioned 'bed-sitter' with nothing much going for it apart from a great view of Crackenback Mountain. In the winter of 1997, Wendy was to receive income from the sale of a property owned by the O'Donohue Family Trust and had decided to purchase a small house in the village, where she would live — plus hold as a future investment.

On July 30, after spending the evening at a function at Thredbo's Sports Centre, Wendy arrived home at *Bimbadeen* sometime between 11 pm and

11.30 pm. She sent an e-mail to a friend telling of her recent doings and finishing, 'Life's great ... love Wendy'. At 11.34, there was a horrendous roar. Part of the Alpine Way suddenly gave way and slid down the incline. An avalanche from Hell had hit Thredbo.

There is a slope of about one in three dropping from this particular section of the Alpine Way down to the road that runs through the village. In the path of the avalanche that night were two lodges, *Carinya* and *Bimbadeen*. Down the hill rushed rock, soil and dammed-up water, with the force of a landing 747 jet. Six hundred tonnes of power tore *Carinya Lodge* from its foundations. The building materials which comprised the lodge were swept up in the slide and roared on with the rest of the debris towards *Bimbadeen*. Within seconds, *Bimbadeen* and all in it disappeared under a 20-metre high earthen tidal wave. A few seconds later, the landslide stopped — just short of two other lodges which stood near a lower road.

Just after 11.30 pm, Kim Clifford, the manager of K–T in Thredbo, returned home and turned on the tap to make a cup of tea. Suddenly the water cut off. A moment later the phone rang and he was told of the catastrophe.

Tricia Hecker was working at her restaurant, 'Bernties', when one of the villagers appeared at the door and yelled, 'There's been a landslide. *Bimbadeen's* gone.' Tricia immediately turned off the gas and raced outside to see what she could do.

Around midnight, David Osborne was fast asleep in Sydney when the phone jolted him awake. It was Kim Clifford at the other end. 'David, there's been a landslide. Part of the Alpine Way has collapsed and fallen on *Carinya* and *Bimbadeen*.'

David Osborne managed to stammer, 'My God, is anybody injured?'.

This was not the time to hedge. 'David, I believe they could all be dead,' Kim answered.

There were 13 employees of K–T (plus four of their partners) living in *Bimbadeen Lodge*. David knew them and respected them all, but still dazed, he asked, 'What about Wendy?'.

'David, at this moment we don't know anything.'

'I'll come straight away,' said Osborne and in three minutes he was on the road.

Tod Lewin heard the news in Sydney and not long afterwards threw some belongings in a bag and headed south.

Tom and Helen O'Donohue were in a small vessel, sailing around the coast of Turkey, when they heard news of the landslide on the BBC Overseas Service. Tom immediately rang home.

A few hours before the accident Gab Bennett was at Darwin Airport readying herself to board a plane for Indonesia, where she was going for a holiday. However, there was a mix up in arrangements and Gab missed the plane. Gab had always been a person who was well organised and on time and to this day she can't understand how the mistake happened. As she was standing at the airport cursing the gods of fate and her own incompetence, she looked up at the television screen and took in the news about the landslide at Thredbo. Immediately she changed plans and later booked a plane to Melbourne.

Rachael Cleary was contacted soon after the catastrophe and told to go to the lounge of the Thredbo Alpine Hotel, where all contactable members of the K–T company were to meet so that a strategy could be organised. In the turmoil of the moment, Rachael didn't ask for specific details. For over an hour, with the adrenalin pumping, she saw to the particular tasks to which she was assigned; she believes she worked effectively, though she remembers little of what she did. Yet even in the darkest of situations, there is often a small moment of humour. Rachael recalls a lady walking through the foyer of the hotel with her arm in a sling and one of the first-aid officers running up to her and saying, 'Sit down, madam, we'll attend to all your cuts and bruises. You're very fortunate to escape with only a bad arm.'

The lady looked at the man quizzically and said, 'What do you mean? I haven't got any cuts and bruises, I broke my arm while skiing last Tuesday. I just came in for a drink.'

Then somebody asked Rachael, 'Have they got anybody out of *Bimbadeen* yet?'.

'Not *Bimbadeen*,' cried Rachael, 'not *Bimbadeen*.'

Meanwhile, the BBC World Service and American broadcaster CNN seemed to know far more about what had happened than did Rachael and most of her fellow workers who were so close to the scene.

Soon after midnight, the phones ran hot on Wendy's 'friends' network. Family and friends began gathering at Martin and Judy's home in North Balwyn, though Martin had rushed away to be at the accident scene. Neighbours arrived with food and refreshments, the television sets were blaring as everyone listened to 'further updates' and the mood was one of disbelief. 'This can't be happening — not to Wendy!'

At Thredbo the mood was the same as the SES emergency crews poured in, with the media hot on their heels. In such situations there is no 'correct procedure'. At this early stage nobody knew if the road was going to slide further or whether the huge amount of built-up debris would remain where it was. If worse was to come and another slide occurred, hundreds of emergency workers and volunteers could also be victims. Conversely, those first on the scene believed they had heard the sound of human voices and wanted to jump in and start digging. Those in charge quickly forbade that natural but dangerous response. Overhead the winter sky was clear. The night bitterly cold. The scene was one of surrealistic carnage. Don't let anyone tell you that Hell is a hot place!

The SES crews worked in shifts as the days came and went. They were unflagging in their efforts and, for publication, talked of how they were still hoping to find people alive beneath the debris. Those closer to the scene like David Osborne and Kim Clifford knew differently however — for they had been told it would need little more than a miracle to save anyone from beneath the deluge of earth and rock. Two days after the landslide the first body was brought out. Still the prayers continued for a miracle and the digging continued.

At Martin and Judy O'Donohue's home in North Balwyn, the mood had changed from shock and disbelief to one of half hope. Friends and neighbours kept arriving with goodies and downstairs the house looked like a church in the British countryside at Harvest Festival. The bar had been opened — and remained open night and day. Tom and Helen, with the help of the Australian Embassy, were back home and everyone began to tell stories about Wendy ...

'Do you remember when she first went hang-gliding and finished up stuck on a wire fence by the seat of her pants?'

'I'll never forget Bridget's birthday party when she played Bozo the Clown.'

'How about the time she invented the game called 'strip tennis' and everyone had to remove a piece of clothing every time they played a bad shot.'

'Yes that's right, and that guy she knew from Brisbane finished up playing in his jock-strap.'

People react differently in times of tragedy; vast mood swings can occur. At one stage Judy O'Donohue moved out into the backyard and she found her sister-in-law, Peta Mary, standing quietly on her own. They were both silent for a moment and Judy said, 'In times like this, the one we need to help us is Wendy ... and Wendy isn't here'.

Peta Mary nodded and replied, 'If anything does happen to Wendy, who is going to talk to the people we don't like?' As in business, so it was in the family; Wendy was the peacemaker.

Then the miracle hoped for occurred. After 68 hours, a ski instructor, Stuart Diver, was brought out alive, a cause for great rejoicing through

Australia, even though Stuart's wife had perished beside him in the avalanche. As the week wore on, some of Wendy's friends and relations decided they had to do something rather than just wait in Melbourne for news. They packed bags and drove to Thredbo. On the evening of the fifth day as they dined at a Thredbo restaurant, they were filled with a new hope. 'Stuart is alive and although he is a very tough bloke, Wendy, in her own way, is just as tough.' They talked and reminisced; optimism ran rampant through the gathering. Someone said, 'I'll bet I know what she's lying there thinking at this moment — "How can I make this a plus for Thredbo?"'.

The next day the searchers found Wendy O'Donohue's body and brought her out into a world that was now different. The laughter had gone from the mountains, the tabletops would now be used only for dining, the thread had been broken. The peacemaker was at peace and the moon was lonely.

On 14 August, 1997, a requiem mass was held for the late Wendy Anne O'Donohue at St Bridget's Church, Greythorne. Sally Keegan, Pat Sutterby (Wendy's aunt) and David Osborne delivered magnificent eulogies with a huge crowd in attendance. On the front page of the Order of Service booklet was an appropriate verse from Banjo Paterson.

And down by Kosciusko where the pine-clad ridges raise
Their torn and rugged battlements on high,
Where the air is clear as crystal and the white stars fairly blaze
At midnight in the cold and frosty sky.

Wendy had been so much a part of those mountains. In November 1997 the New South Wales Department of Tourism announced that their 'Young Achiever Award for Tourism' would in future be known as 'The Wendy O'Donohue Award'.

By the definition of many churchgoing people, Wendy O'Donohue would not be seen as a 'Christian'. A good person, yes, but not a true believer in the terms of some who feel they have the right to judge. I'd argue forever on that. We all serve in different ways, yet it was the founder of the Christian religion who exhorted his followers to 'love your neighbour as yourself'. Wendy did that — and how — and what's more she made a habit of introducing one set of 'neighbours' to another set of 'neighbours' and making sure they all loved each other.

Whatever her own beliefs, she lived by the creed of goodness. I would be willing to bet that come Judgement Day, she will receive an eternal lease on a 600-metre ski slope and an executive position in Heaven's Marketing Department.

TOMORROW

As I write these final words, autumn is here and it will soon be winter again. The winter in Thredbo, that special time of the year — will be different this time. This winter and forever more the skiers, the merrymakers and the residents of this lovely alpine village will be joined by the spirits of *Bimbadeen*. Four years ago, I stood in a cemetery on a hillside in the small Welsh mining village of Aberfan, where 30 years ago a slagheap slipped and buried 126 schoolchildren from the local primary school. And I felt the spirit. I felt something that was neither spooky nor eerie, just something that was holy. So will it be with Thredbo. Time passes, but the past will not be forgotten.

YEAR: 2020 ... PLACE: CRACKENBACK MOUNTAIN

A group of skiers stands at the summit gazing down on the twinkling lights of Thredbo. The air is clear as crystal and the white stars fairly blaze at midnight in the cold and frosty sky. In the bitter air, the hands of the leading skier are throbbing from the cold but she is looking forward to the exhilarating run down the long slope, knowing that when all of them reach the valley below the good times will follow. They will drink schnapps and red wine, dance on the tables and party till dawn. 'Let's go,' calls Bridget O'Donohue as she pushes her stocks into the snow and starts off down towards the little village. Her friends see her flash away. As always, they follow her. And the moon shines down.

Also by Neil Marks

TALES FOR ALL SEASONS

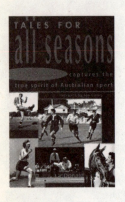

Tales for all Seasons is an often humorous and always inspiring collection of Australian sporting stories ranging through cricket, Australian football, rugby league, track and field, boxing and racing. Neil Marks, a renowned raconteur and writer, recalls some of our best-loved sporting legends, including Betty Cuthbert, Doug Walters and Phar Lap.

In an age where commercialism and the sponsor's dollar seem all powerful, it has become easy to forget the *true* value of Australian sport. In Tales for all Seasons, Neil Marks revives a spirit many thought lost. In doing so he has produced one of the most significant collections of sporting stories published in Australia.